Naturalism, Evolution, and Intentionality

edited by
Jillian Scott McIntosh

UNIVERSITY OF
CALGARY
PRESS

© 2001 Canadian Journal of Philosophy

University of Calgary Press
Calgary, Alberta, Canada

ISSN 0229-7051

ISBN 0-919491-27-8

University of Calgary Press
2500 University Drive NW
Calgary, Alberta
Canada T2N 1N4
www.uofcpress.com

National Library of Canada Cataloguing in Publication

Main entry under title:
Naturalism, evolution, and intentionality / Jillian Scott McIntosh,
editor.

(Canadian journal of philosophy. Supplementary volume, ISSN 0229-7051; 27)
Includes bibliographical references and index.
ISBN 0-919491-27-8

1. Philosophy of mind. 2. Naturalism. I. McIntosh, Jillian Scott,
1959- II. Series.
BD418.3 N37 2002   128'.2   C2002-911131-5

 We acknowledge the financial support of the Government of Canada
through the Book Publishing Industry Development Program (BPIDP) for
our publishing activities.

 The Canada Council for the Arts
Le Conseil des Arts du Canada

Printed and bound in Canada by AGMV Marquis.
∞This book is printed on acid-free paper.

Page, cover design, and typesetting by Kristina Schuring.
Cover art by Sylvia Verity.

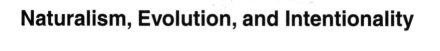

Naturalism, Evolution, and Intentionality

Table of Contents

CANADIAN JOURNAL OF PHILOSOPHY
Supplementary Volume 27

Introduction: Investigating the Mind

JILLIAN S. McINTOSH

> Holding as we do that, while knowledge of any kind is a thing to
> be honoured and prized, one kind of it may, either by reason of its
> greater exactness or of a higher dignity and greater wonderfulness
> in its objects, be more honourable and precious than another; on
> both accounts we should naturally be led to place in the front rank
> the study of the soul.

Aristotle, *De Anima*. 402ᵃ, 1–5

Setting aside what might seem to be an overly pious and self-congratulatory tone in the above quotation, we are left with Aristotle's expression of a sense of wonder and curiosity with regard to the human mind (i.e., the "soul"). Many things are worthy of investigation, but our own intellectual nature holds a special place, and this, urges Aristotle, is not simply narcissism. We *are* interesting. This volume seeks to celebrate and emulate Aristotle's enthusiasm and sense of reverence, while recognizing, perhaps to an even greater extent than did Aristotle, that we are a part of the natural world.

This brief introduction falls into three sections: 1) a characterization of two different approaches to investigating the mental; 2) an outline of the key concepts mentioned in the title; and 3) overviews of the layout of the remainder of the volume and of each of the papers. I end with some words of thanks.

§1: Two Ways of Proceeding

How do we go about investigating the mind? One strategy is the "intro-centric" one, most clearly exemplified by Descartes. He aimed to learn the fundamental nature of the mind purely through introspection and reason.[1] They, he thought, revealed the presence of indubitable, hence epistemologically basic, beliefs such as "I think," "God exists," and "a cause has at least as much reality as its effect." He believed that careful and scrupulous attention to one's own thoughts rationally led *a priori* to, among other things, the conclusion that mind is a completely different substance from matter, and, as such, is ontologically independent. This, notoriously, led to the vexing problem of how even to accommodate, let alone to explain, the causal interaction of mind and matter.

Although, given the phenomenology of conscious experience, the intro-centric strategy may have some intuitive appeal, adopting it would strike most current philosophers, and (I think it safe to say) all current psychologists, neurophysiologists, and cognitive ethologists as hopeless. A different "extro-centric" strategy is currently favoured and involves getting out of the armchair. The idea, of course, is not to leave one's mind behind, but rather to investigate the human mind much as one investigates other natural phenomena, especially those involving other animals. That is, the strategy includes taking the third-person perspective and accommodating data from a wide variety of sources. Psychological experiments, anthropological fieldwork, and bio-chemical/neurological investigation are ways to learn about our capacities, their limits, and their development. Knowledge of human evolutionary history and of animal ethology can help in the interpretation of data on current humans and in the forming of new hypotheses. While acknowledging that commonsense views about phenomenology and conscious experience must be explained (or, perhaps, explained away), this method is rigorously

---

1 These remarks are not intended to do justice to Descartes but only to suggest a rough caricature of Cartesian method with which to contrast the currently dominant approach.

empirical.[2] It uses all the tools available for scientific enquiry into the nature and causes of behaviour and experience, and, significantly, it assumes that we ought, at least *prima facie*, to treat our own mentality as significantly continuous with that of other creatures. Hence, we ought to expect some overlap in explanations, and some insight via comparative work.

Contrasting these two approaches is not meant to imply that Descartes was not concerned to get the empirical details right. He was. Famously, he postulated, on the basis of empirical investigation, that the pineal gland is the point of causal interaction between the mental and the physical.[3] And the lack of empirical evidence for the presence of linguistic capacities in non-human animals was part of what led Descartes to conclude that they had no minds, since the level of sophistication of his posited basic beliefs would seem to require linguistic capacities. Neither is the contrast meant to imply that the extro-centric approach ignores inner mental life.[4] Indeed, many experiments are designed to tease out what is going on from the subject's point of view, in order to incorporate that information into a wider explanatory framework.[5]

Nonetheless, the two approaches clearly are different. In the context of this discussion, there are at least three salient distinguishing features of the extro-centric strategy. First, although keeping global scepticism

---

2   Some current theorists are anxious to banish some (putative) mental phenomena from the realm of the scientifically acceptable. See, e.g., Dennett (1988) and Rorty (1979) on exorcising qualia (phenomenal aspects of experience), and Churchland (1986) and Stich (1983) on exorcising "folk psychological" states such as beliefs and desires. While none of the papers in this volume advocates radical eliminativism, all are sensitive to the possibility of the over- or mis-interpretation of data as a result of pre-theoretic, undefended commitments.

3   The pineal gland is one of few brain structures that is not paired, and it had no known function.

4   Some extro-centric theories (see footnote 2) have been accused of just this sort of neglect, but the approach itself is not essentially eliminativist.

5   E.g., Weiskrantz (1997), Wegner and Wheatley (1999).

at bay was a primary motivation for Descartes, the issue is largely bracketed by the extro-centric approach to the study of the mind. Second, introspection is not taken as incontrovertible. Since Freud, we have known that our access to our own mental states is partial and fallible. The mind is not fully transparent to itself, and a good theory of the mind will likely be the result of inference to the best explanation of all the evidence, positing states, events, processes, and structures not introspectively accessible. Third, we are to take seriously the fact that we are part of the natural world. This is not to say that Aristotle's enthusiasm for studying the mind was misplaced, but rather that we must take care not to assume too unique a position for ourselves. Humans share many attributes with many other animals, including an impressive ability to negotiate a changing and often hostile environment, and it would be surprising if some significant proportion of those abilities were not amenable to the same sorts of explanation.

§2: Some Key Concepts – Naturalism, Evolution, and Intentionality

Of the three concepts, naturalism, evolution, and intentionality, **naturalism** is perhaps the most difficult to define in any detailed way that would meet with broad agreement. This is because a great many people consider themselves "naturalists" while disagreeing about nearly everything else.[6] Nonetheless, I shall attempt a brief sketch, which should do for our purposes. Naturalism has two interacting components, one methodological or epistemological, and the other metaphysical or ontological. In its methodological vein, it is the view that our theories, at least those about non-abstract entities, must be informed by empirical data and must be compatible with our other well-confirmed empirical theories. In effect, it endorses the extro-centric strategy outlined above.

---

6 Consider the following otherwise quite heterogeneous crew: Chalmers (1996), Churchland and Churchland (1983), Davidson (1990), Dretske (1995), Fodor (1994), Millikan (1989), Papineau (1993), Quine (1969), Rorty (1979), and Tye (1992). Fodor considers himself a naturalist (1994), yet attacks "naturalism" (1980), without being inconsistent.

However, the methodological issue cannot be neatly separated from the ontological one since many take physics as the basic theory to which all others must be suitably related via some form of reduction.[7] The requirement of compatibility is thereby strengthened to more than that of superficial consistency. Many think that our current state of knowledge, when combined with methodological naturalism, entails an explicit commitment to ontological physicalism,[8] though others demur.[9] There is considerable debate over how to construe physicalism,[10] though a suitably circumspect characterization would find widespread assent. In any case, even if ontological neutrality were initially possible for the methodological naturalist, once one adopts the naturalistic approach, whatever ontological neutrality one might have had may need to be abandoned in light of what one discovers. What is and what is not natural is a matter of what is and what is not scientifically respectable. Perhaps it is safest to say that naturalists are happy to deny the existence of would-be phenomena for which science has no use.[11] Again, the ontological and methodological issues are intertwined.

Evolution, as a technical concept, seems to exhibit, in philosophical and scientific contexts, somewhat more uniformity of application than does naturalism. However, the term "evolution" is also common in everyday parlance, facility with which both helps one's understanding of the technical concept and hinders it. According to the OED, the root of "evolve," in Latin, means "to roll out," as in the manner of a manuscript. In our time, it denotes some sort of change, keeping its temporal aspect, and often connotes the idea of progress, of things unfurling as they should and for the better. Though there is a sense

---

7 See, e.g., Oppenheim and Putnam (1958) and Kim (1998).

8 E.g., Papineau (1993). and Kim (1998).

9 E.g., Chalmers (1996), who calls himself a naturalistic dualist, and Dennett, whose talk of stances (e.g., 1987) is often taken to be metaphysically or ontologically deflationary, and who explicitly eschews engaging in metaphysics or ontology (e.g., 1993).

10 See, e.g., Melnyk (1997), Poland (1994), and Crook and Gillett (2001).

11 But see Davidson (e.g., 1990) and, again, Chalmers (1996).

in which the idea of progress is appropriate, it is susceptible to an unfortunate interpretation – that evolution is somehow a guided process, that individual entities seek to transform themselves into members of a "better" species, that every aspect of change is a positive one.

Accommodating the idea of "progress" with respect to the technical concept of evolution crucially involves the notion of natural selection. Under certain conditions, organisms *are* generally better-suited to their environment than were their ancestors. An "improvement" in the attributes of a population of creatures over time is not explained by citing any intelligent outside improving force or any inner drive toward perfection, but rather by noting the "blind" action of natural selection. Simply put, what worked well was favoured, and what did not, was not. Given variability in the relevant attributes, heritability of those attributes, and sufficient stability in the environment, adaptive change over generations will follow. These conditions can be met without any intelligent intervention in natural processes, and they dictate that organisms in subsequent generations will tend to be better-suited to their environments. However, this is not because any individuals themselves became better-suited over their own lifetimes[12] and not because of any prescience or planning on the part of what some like to call, perhaps misleadingly, "Mother Nature."[13]

Intentionality is the property of being about, or being directed toward, something. The stock examples come from "folk psychology" and are mental states such as beliefs and desires.[14] Suppose I believe that Deception Pass is north of Redoubt Mountain. On the standard analysis, the content of this belief is the proposition that Deception Pass is north of Redoubt Mountain, and the belief is true if and only if its propositional content is true, i.e., if and only if Deception

---

12 This point serves to distinguish Lamarckianism from Darwinism. Lamarck thought that individual learning could be inherited, but, given advances in genetics, this seems more than a little unlikely.

13 See Sober's classic (1984), for more on evolutionary theory.

14 See footnote 2 for some dissenters.

Pass is north of Redoubt Mountain.[15] My belief is about those two geographical features and their relation, and it could be false.[16] Other items that exhibit intentionality include maps, natural language, and pictures, but their intentionality, most agree, is derivative, in that it is our use of them that makes them intentional, and this use presupposes intentional mental states.[17]

A great number of issues arise at this point; I will mention only three. First, we need to provide non-circular criteria for the individuation of intentional states in terms of both their attitude and their content. What, for example, makes a state a belief as opposed to a desire, and what makes it the belief that p as opposed to the belief that q? Second, we need to understand the rôle of intentional states in the production of behaviour. For example, is the specific content of the state relevant to its efficacy? If so, how? Third, we need to provide a story consonant with what we know about our own evolutionary history and about other animals. What constraints (or opportunities) does knowledge of our evolutionary history impose on (or afford) us? Other animals have quite efficient ways of negotiating their environments – what is the nature of their intentional states, and when, if ever, is their success to be explained by invoking beliefs and desires?[18]

---

15 The standard account of desires substitutes satisfaction conditions for truth conditions; my desire that Deception Pass be easy to climb is satisfied if and only if Deception Pass is easy to climb.

16 The situation is complicated by thoughts about non-existent referents, as famously noted by Brentano, who re-introduced the scholastic term "intentional" into philosophical discourse in the 1800s. Is somebody's belief that Ogopogo lives in Okanagan Lake false, if Ogopogo does not exist? What of someone's belief that Ogopogo does not live in Okanagan Lake? I set this aside here.

17 See, e.g., Fodor (1987), Searle (1983), and Sterelny (1990).

18 One of the interesting things about belief attributions is that they are intensional (not just intentional). The standard indication of intensionality is that the substitution of co-referring terms may change the truth value of the proposition in question. It might be true that I believe that Deception Pass is north of Redoubt Mountain, without it being true that I believe that the pass above Ptarmigan Lake is north of Redoubt Mountain, even though Deception Pass is the pass above Ptarmigan Lake. It is far from clear that intensionality is a feature of basic perceptual states, though intentionality surely is.

§3: Summaries

Part I, *Adaptation and Mental Capacities,* contains three papers that explore the broad issue of the explanatory relationship between the theory of adaptation by natural selection and our understanding of the mind. What does the fact that our minds are the products of evolution by natural selection tell us about their workings, and what methodological prescriptions does it entail? Although the theory of evolution by natural selection is well-entrenched, its philosophical and metaphysical relevance is a matter of some dispute.

Wayne Christensen and Cliff Hooker focus on self-directedness, arguing that insight into its evolution and nature will provide insight into that of intentionality, intelligence, and agency. Self-directedness is contrasted with mere reactive action processes and allows agents to anticipate interaction processes and to evaluate their own performance, thereby increasing their sensitivity to context. Christensen and Hooker's account requires that investigators look at biologically realistic problems from an agent-centred perspective. Information must come to the agent in a usable form, which, they maintain, suggests that "teleosemantic content" (see the summaries of Part II below) will not fit the bill. Ascertaining the "performance envelopes" (the set of capacities that could permit the performance of an open-ended set of tasks) and the "norm matrices" (the set of constraints governing viability) of the agent focuses on the agent as dynamic and situated in a changing environment. This leaves room for a rôle for affect and learning and for explanations of adaptive change. It also highlights the multi-dimensionality of intentional agency which, they argue, is poorly captured by traditional views that model intentionality on human language or offer a trait-by-trait selectionist account.

Phil Hanson looks at the views of two philosophers, Daniel Dennett and Jerry Fodor, who, as is well-known, occupy quite different niches in the logical space of positions in the philosophy of mind. Hanson distinguishes two different questions. To the first – what metaphysical consequences are there to the mind's being a product of natural selection? – he claims Dennett and Fodor agree that, under certain crucial but plausible assumptions, being a product of selection entails that intentionality is a natural trait. To the second – what specific insights into the nature of human intentional cognition can be gleaned by looking at the details of our natural selective history? – Hanson claims Dennett and Fodor also seem to agree, thinking that the details of selective history will tell us little about human intentionality's specific constitutive nature. But he then argues that this seeming agreement masks their more fundamental differences, which, when made explicit, show that Dennett and Fodor are both mistaken, for reasons *internal* to their respective viewpoints, in their answer to the second question. This is just as well, argues Hanson, since that answer is wrong.

Larry Shapiro argues that from the fact that minds are the products of evolution by natural selection, i.e., that they are adaptations, a number of substantive conclusions follow. One, minds are not epiphenomenal, since a trait that has no effects cannot be selected for benefits it bestows on its possessors. Two, it is overwhelmingly likely that non-human animals also have minds, given the time it would likely have taken for such a complex adaptation to evolve (i.e., the process would have started before *Homo sapiens* diverged), and the phenomenon of convergent evolution (good "solutions" tend to crop up in different lineages). Third, and most controversially, minds are not multiply realizable. This is so because adaptations are individuated in terms of both function *and* structure. Shapiro goes on to discuss some of the consequences of these conclusions for the study of the mind.

Part II, *Teleosemantics,* contains four papers concerning theories of the individuation of mental content that, partially in response to the so-called disjunction problem, appeal to natural selection history. Very roughly, if the content of a state is, say, that which causes or could cause it, its content is disjunctive and it can never be tokened in error. Appealing to selection history is an attempt to narrow the set of causes/situations relevant to the individuation of the content of the state by focussing on those that account for the proliferation of creatures that token it. The content of a state S is $<X>$, not $<X$ or $Y>$, even though S may sometimes be caused by Y, provided that S's having been tokened in the presence of X is what explains the survival and reproduction of the organism that tokens it.

Colin Allen notes that discussion of the disjunction problem (very briefly outlined above) seems to have proceeded under the assumption that, when we get the story right, the content of a state is identical to that of the English expression used to specify it. However, our choice between, say, <fly> and <fly or BB> in the case of frogs is not a real choice, if we are assuming identity. One reason is that the "or" in the disjunctive option plays no rôle in the cognitive economy of the frog. Allen argues that, hence, we can intend to use English to capture the content adequately at best, not exactly. He canvasses some approaches but concludes that there is no non-circular way of directly specifying our criteria for adequacy. Instead, we should look to the explanations in which content ascriptions occur – e.g., comparative psychology and cognitive ethology – and subject the implicit criteria there to a sort of "meta-empirical" test.

Paul Sheldon Davies argues that teleosemantics fails because the sorts of conditions involved in selective success are often quite broad; typically, those conditions will outnumber the relatively narrow range of objects relevant to mental content. Teleosemantics has no non-arbitrary way to preclude what should be background conditions from being part of the content of a state. He distinguishes object-specificity from description-specificity, such that, roughly, the former concerns what is represented (say, the bird at the window, not the retinal patterns it invokes) and the latter concerns how that thing is represented (as, say, a goldfinch, not a canary). Davies argues that object-specificity is theoretically more basic in the sense that ascertaining the specific description under which an agent represents a thing presupposes ascertaining just what object is being represented. This, Davies argues, teleosemantics cannot do.

Eric Saidel argues that teleosemantics renders the content of a mental state epiphenomenal. That is, the content of a mental state, if individuated teleosemantically, would have no bearing on its causal efficacy. This should be unacceptable to the naturalist, since there seems little reason to give a naturalistic account of something that has no effects, let alone any reason to countenance its existence. He canvasses the work of Dretske, Millikan, and Neander, arguing that they each fail to provide a theory compatible with the causal efficacy of content. Furthermore, Saidel argues, they fail for the same reason – it is central to these approaches that content be a matter of history. However, an item's history is an extrinsic property of it, and it is only intrinsic properties that can be causally efficacious.

Tim Schroeder argues that adopting teleosemantics entails accepting not only the possibility of what he calls "monsters," but their actuality.

Monsters are creatures that are behaviourally indistinguishable from, say, us, but that lack either an inner mental life (so-called "zombies") or propositional attitudes (so-called "swampfolk"). Teleosemanticists are willing to grant the physical (not just logical) possibility of monsters, but their widespread actuality would be troublesome. Schroeder sketches evidence of neural plasticity to show that the teleosemanticists' criteria for content attribution would render many that we would have thought non-monstrous, monstrous. This would leave a rather substantial percentage of the actual population not subsumable under intentional explanations. Schroeder suggests that it might be fruitful to look to some sort of non-historical teleosemantics, drawing on cybernetics, in which the norms are "control-based" rather than historical.

Part III, *Vision*, consists of two papers dealing with recent work on two central issues in the study of visual capacities: how vision aids in action, and the nature of colour and colour vision. Until recently, work in perception has largely been paradigmatic of intellectualist accounts of intentionality: the visual system functions to give us an accurate representation of the mind-independent world. Recent empirical work, combined with interest in evolutionary theory and skepticism about a Cartesian privileging of visual phenomenology, has led to new understanding.

Mel Goodale argues that "the" visual system is in fact a variety of different systems, each exhibiting a high degree of modularity. In particular, there is one system for perception and another for action. The former (the ventral stream in the brain) involves the formation of representations of objects and relations, which are then used in higher cognitive tasks, and the latter (the dorsal stream) directly guides the organism in manipulating and negotiating the environment. Goodale's evidence for the two systems comes from considerations of the evolution of vision; anatomical, behavioural, and neurophysiological studies in non-human animals; neuroimaging studies in humans; and clinical studies of brain-damaged patients who exhibit surprising patterns of deficits. Goodale also has some provocative results from experiments with intact subjects. Having shown that there are in fact two systems, Goodale takes the next task to be that of understanding how they work together.

Mohan Matthen seeks to provide an account of colour that respects subjectivist considerations (colour appearance is often dependent on contextual factors) and objectivist considerations (colour appearance is often constant across contexts), and the epistemology of colour vision (we seem to know what colour attributions mean). Matthen relies on a distinction between colour-"looks" and colours-properties; he suggests that colour-looks are "auto-calibrated signs" of colour-properties, i.e., signs calibrated by means of the epistemic task (for example, induction and re-identification) we perform with the aid of colour-looks. The properties that looks purport to tell us about are best understood pluralistically, argues Matthen, as equivalence classes defined over the many tasks for which we use colour vision, not as use-independent features of the world. This pluralism is meant to be a subjective counterpart of the "pluralistic realism" for which he has argued elsewhere. He elaborates his view by comparing colour and musical harmony.

§ 4: Acknowledgments

This volume began with the conference "Naturalism, Evolution, and Intentionality: An Interdisciplinary Conference in the Philosophy of Mind," held in April 1998 at the University of Western Ontario. Not all the presenters at that conference were able to contribute something to this volume, and other authors have been included; nonetheless, the conference was the volume's genesis.

For help with the conference, my sincere thanks to the Department of Philosophy at the University of Western Ontario, and particularly to the chair at the time, John Thorp, for giving me the opportunity to organize the conference and for providing encouragement and support, both financial and moral. I also gratefully acknowledge the financial support of a conference grant from the Social Sciences and Humanities Council of Canada, which made things go that much more smoothly, despite (or perhaps because of!) its arrival at the last minute. Thanks, too, to my co-organizers, Ausonio Marras, who was a constant source of good advice, and Kevin Delaplante, who was in charge of the graduate student component of the conference and who, along with other graduate students, helped with the quotidian tasks involved in running a conference.

For help with the volume, I thank Tom Hurka and the other members of the Editorial Board of the *Canadian Journal of Philosophy* for agreeing to publish it and for helpful advice. I also thank the University of Calgary Press, John King in particular, for their patience and willingness to answer my endless questions. Thanks, too, to John and to Julia Colterjohn for copy editing, and to Joan Eadie for indexing.

Finally, a special thanks to the contributors for their hard work and for dealing with the vagaries of the publishing process with aplomb; many are to be particularly commended for their exemplary patient perseverance in the face of editorial and philosophical persnicketiness. I will not claim to speak for them, but I know I had fun and learned a lot.

I hope the reader finds much of interest and much to dispute in these pages.

References

Chalmers, David J. 1996. *The Conscious Mind: In Search of a Fundamental Theory*. Oxford: Oxford University Press.

Churchland, Patricia Smith. 1986. *Neurophilosophy: Toward a Unified Science of the Mind-Brain*. Cambridge: MIT Press.

Churchland, Paul M., and Patricia Smith Churchland. 1983. "Stalking the Wild Epistemic Engine," *Noûs* **17**, 5–18.

Crook, Seth, and Carl Gillett. 2001. "Why Physics Alone Cannot Define the 'Physical': Materialism, Metaphysics, and the Formulation of Physicalism," *Canadian Journal of Philosophy* **31.3**, 333–59.

Davidson, Donald. 1990. "Representation and Interpretation." In *Modeling the Mind*, K. A. Mohyeldin Said, W. H. Newton-Smith, and K. V. Wilkes, eds. Oxford: Clarendon Press, pp. 13–26.

Dennett, Daniel. 1987. *The Intentional Stance*. Cambridge, MA: MIT Press.

Dennett, Daniel. 1988. "Quining Qualia." In *Consciousness in Modern Science*, A. Marcel and E. Bisiach, eds. Oxford: Oxford University Press, reprinted in *Mind and Cognition: A Reader*, William Lycan, ed., Oxford: Basil Blackwell, pp. 519–47.

Dennett, Daniel. 1993. "Back from the Drawing Board." In *Dennett and his Critics*, Bo Dahlbom, ed. Cambridge: Blackwell, pp. 203–35.

Dretske, Fred. 1995. *Naturalizing the Mind*. Cambridge, MA: MIT Press.

Fodor, Jerry. 1980. "Methodological Solipsism Considered as a Research Strategy in Cognitive Psychology," In *RePresentations: Philosophical Essays on the Foundations of Cognitive Science*. (1981) Cambridge: MIT Press, pp. 225–53.

———. 1987. *PsychosemanticsL The Problem of Meaning in the Philosophy of Mind*. Cambridge, MA: MIT Press.

———. 1994. *The Elm and the Expert: Mentalese and its Semantics*. Cambridge, MA: MIT Press.

Kim, Jaegwon. 1998. *Mind in a Physical World*. Cambridge, MA: MIT Press.

Melnyk, Andrew. 1997. "How to Keep the 'Physical' in Physicalism," *Journal of Philosophy* **94**, 622–37.

Millikan, Ruth Garrett. 1989. "In Defense of Proper Functions," *Philosophy of Science* **56**, 288–302.

Oppenheim, Paul, and Hilary Putnam. 1958. "The Unity of Science as a Working Hypothesis." In *Minnesota Studies in the Philosophy of Science*, vol. 2, Herbert Feigl, Michael Scriven, and Grover Maxwell, eds., pp. 3–36.

Poland, Jeffrey. 1994. *Physicalism*. Oxford: Clarendon Press.

Quine, W.V.O. 1969. "Epistemology Naturalized," In his *Ontological Relativity and Other Essays*. New York: Columbia University Press, pp. 69–90.

Rorty, Richard. 1979. *Philosophy and the Mirror of Nature*. Princeton: Princeton University Press.

Searle, John. 1983. *Intentionality*. Cambridge: Cambridge University Press.

———. 1992. *The Rediscovery of the Mind*. Cambridge, MA: MIT Press.

Sober, Elliott. 1984. *The Nature of Selection*. Cambridge, MA: MIT Press.

Sterelny, Kim. 1990. *The Representational Theory of Mind*. Oxford: Basil Blackwell.

Stich, Steven. 1983. *From Folk Psychology to Cognitive Science: The Case Against Belief*. Cambridge, MA: MIT Press.

Tye, Michael. 1992. "Naturalism and the Mental," *Mind* **101**, 421–41.

Wegner, Daniel M., and Thalia P. Wheatley. 1999. "Apparent Mental Causation: Sources of the Illusion of Conscious Will," presented at ASSC3 (the third annual conference of the Association for the Scientific Study of Consciousness), June, London, Ontario.

Weiskrantz, Lawrence. 1997. *Consciousness Lost and Found: A Neuropsychological Exploration*. Oxford: Oxford University Press.

I. Adaptation and the Mental

CANADIAN JOURNAL OF PHILOSOPHY
Supplementary Volume 27

Self-directed Agents[1]

W. D. CHRISTENSEN AND C. A. HOOKER

1. Introduction

In this paper, we outline a theory of the nature of self-directed agents. What is distinctive about self-directed agents is their ability to anticipate interaction processes and to evaluate their performance, and thus their sensitivity to context. They can improve performance relative to goals, and can, in certain instances, construct new goals. We contrast self-directedness with reactive action processes that are not modifiable by the agent, though they may be modified by supra-agent processes such as populational adaptation or external design.

Self-directedness lies at the nexus of issues concerning the evolution and nature of intentionality, intelligence, and agency. It provides some insight into the evolution of intelligence because it helps explain how organisms are able to manage variable interaction processes, e.g., a hunting strategy that varies with prey type, ground condition, and hunger level. Simple self-directed organisms like bumblebees manage variability in one or a few dimensions. They are able to track changes in the types of flowers that are yielding nectar by evaluating the outcome of flower visits using a gustatory reward signal, and learn

---

1 We would like to thank Mark Bickhard, John Collier, and Bill Herfel for constructive discussions. Jill McIntosh made numerous editorial suggestions which have greatly improved the clarity of the paper and some of the content. CAH thanks the Philosophy Department, Durham University, UK, for generous hospitality during part of the preparation of this paper.

to anticipate which flower types have reliable nectar yields. In more complex forms of self-directedness, the variability may be in many dimensions, and effective management can require a form of learning we term *open problem solving*. Open problems occur where the agent initially lacks the ability to identify or act upon the key factors for producing a solution and must discover the relevant factors and the actions that influence them through extended interactive learning. Skill formation is a form of open problem solving, and skilled activities such as hunting count as relatively sophisticated forms of self-directedness. At the high end of the spectrum are highly sophisticated and open-ended human cognitive abilities such as commanding a warship, starting a business, or conducting scientific research.

This account has widespread implications for understanding the nature of intentionality. First, it carries a general commitment to pursuing a dynamically situated agent-oriented approach, grounded in biologically realistic problems. Self-directedness is an 'information hungry' form of adaptiveness, in roughly the sense of Clark (1997, chap. 10). Self-directed agents acquire information from the environment as part of the process of forming anticipations.[2] Understanding this process bears on understanding information content, because information must come in a form that the agent can use to modify action and integrate with other information. We will discuss these issues and suggest that the currently popular teleosemantic theory of content does not satisfy the requirements on the nature of information posed by the kinds of processes with which we are concerned. Teleosemantic content is defined in terms of selection history and therefore cannot be used by the agent because typical biological agents do not have information about their selection history. As an

---

2 Forming anticipations sounds cognitively sophisticated but, as in the case of bee foraging we discuss below, it can occur through quite simple processes like operant conditioning. The ability to form anticipations is most likely to have arisen in animal evolution through the specialization of more general capacities of neural systems for experience-based modification. Even the simplest neural systems, such as the two-neuron tentacle withdrawal reflex in coelenterates, are capable of habituation, so basic anticipative abilities like event expectancy and action priming are not too difficult to achieve. For a discussion of neural mechanisms for anticipative learning, see Montague and Sejnowski (1994).

alternative, we will propose an interactivist-constructivist account of intentionality that relates information content to action.[3] This allows us to understand how agents can use and process information.

Second, this approach introduces a rich conception of the higher order cognitive processes involved in intelligence and agency. Affect processes, like hunger and thirst inducement and satiation, supply the norms required for evaluating interaction and are thereby key factors in shaping the goals and learning processes of the agent. Agents may learn relationships among their basic affect conditions and also construct new, derived activity norms from them, leading to the development of a complex normative array for evaluating and guiding action (see §2). Self-directedness also involves the integration of information from multiple sources to focus action into coordinated activities. This can include resolving action conflict when there are several possible actions that are mutually exclusive or have antagonistic effects, learning about the relations between actions and outcomes, and planning ahead to achieve particular outcomes. Understanding these processes can also provide some insight into how diverse sources of information can be combined to form an overall situational awareness.

Third, it is plausible that the learning processes that are involved in strong forms of self-directedness play a central role in the formation of cognitive representations and concepts. Self-directed agents need to learn what affects success and failure. Part of this involves differentiating specific states-of-affairs, objects and object types. With experience, the concepts of an agent gain increasing definition and richness as the agent discovers more of the interaction characteristics

---

3 Christensen and Hooker (2000a,b) develops an account of interactivist-constructivism (I–C) as an approach to understanding intelligence. See also Bickhard and Ritchie (1983), Bickhard and Terveen (1995), Christensen (2000, chap. 1). I–C is Piagetian in spirit, though not in detail. It emphasizes the embodiment of intelligence and has philosophical connections with pragmatism and aspects of phenomenology. Perhaps more importantly, though, I–C is designed to articulate a perspective on cognitive science and philosophy of mind that reflects contemporary research focussed on dynamical interaction and development. See, e.g., Brooks (1991), Edelman (1987), Glenberg (1997), Hutchins (1995), Karmiloff-Smith (1992), Lakoff (1987), Pfeifer and Sheier (1999), Quartz and Sejnowski (1997), Thelen and Smith (1994).

of these entities. Moreover, the agent's ability to use concepts becomes increasingly flexible and open-ended as the agent gains greater interaction skills and is thus able to appropriately utilize concepts in a range of contexts.

All this adds up to a graded multi-dimensional conception of intentional agency that contrasts with the currently common one-dimensional conception of intentionality as a capacity for reference modelled on human language use. The more complex conception based on self-directedness provides a richer framework for understanding the evolution and development of intentionality and intelligence.

2. The envelope and the matrix: Some general dynamical issues for understanding adaptive agents

2.1 *How not to study the evolution of mind: Matching cognitive and evolutionary modules*

One of the key challenges for evolution of mind research is developing an adequate approach to grappling with the overlap of the biological and cognitive domains. The problem is that biology, cognitive science, and philosophy employ very different methods, theories, and concepts. In certain respects, the most obvious strategy for solving this problem is to find a direct association between entities postulated by theories in one domain and entities postulated by theories in another. And the simplest way to do this is by demonstrating that the functional modules in one domain turn out to be functional modules in another. Thus, evolutionary psychology compartmentalizes the mind into a suite of 'domain specific computational modules,' such as for mate selection and detection of social cheating, that are assumed to be heritable traits, and then speculates about the circumstances under which these putative traits might have been favoured by evolution. Similarly, though at a more general level, teleosemantics attempts to characterize representation as a kind of evolutionary function. However, the theoretical assumptions upon which such a unification strategy rests are controversial. Both evolutionary psychology and teleosemantics hinge on linking adaptationist neo-Darwinism with representationalist cognitive science.[4] These theories make the job seem easy because they employ strong modularity assumptions, encouraging the idea that there may be a straightforward cross-theory mapping. Unfortunately, adaptationism and representationalism have each come under strong criticism, not least because of their functional modularity assumptions.

In particular, it has been argued that the modularities assumed by adaptationism and representationalism characteristically tend to neglect interaction and development. In biology, the localization of heredity to genes has been challenged by developmental approaches, which stress that heredity depends on the organizationally distributed dynamical processes of development.[5] Likewise, the assumption in cognitive science that adaptive behaviour is mediated by representations, forming a categorically distinct set of entities uniquely associated with intelligence, has been challenged by developmental, dynamical systems and behaviour-based robotics approaches which stress that adaptive behaviour is generated by organizationally distributed interaction processes.[6] The similarity of these critiques is striking, especially given that the disciplinary contexts are quite different.

If, as evidence suggests, distributed dynamical processes play a fundamental and widespread role in adaptiveness and cognition, and orthodox approaches neglect this, two things follow. First, theories and concepts for understanding both biological and cognitive phenomena must explicitly recognize holistically structured dynamical relations. Second, where functional localization is attributed, it must be given detailed context-specific justification.

It is here that the problems with drawing a general link between adaptationism and representationalism really bite. Neither adaptationism nor representationalism respect these two conditions. They can

---

4 See Stotz and Griffiths (2001) for a critical analysis of evolutionary psychology that makes this case.

5 E.g., Griffiths and Gray (1994), Jablonka and Lamb (1995), Oyama (1985).

6 E.g., Beer (1995; 2000), Brooks (1991), Hendriks-Jansen (1996), Thelen and Smith (1994), van Gelder (1995; 1998).

make little sense of holistically structured dynamical relations because the entire thrust of both theories is to localize functionality to particular structures: adaptations in the first case and representations in the second. Moreover, they both assume functional modularity as an *a priori* given, or at most as justified on very general grounds. But such generality is only achieved by neglecting the biological mechanisms involved, and unfortunately the nature of those mechanisms can make a large difference to the kinds of functional organization that actually occur.[7]

Many people leap to the assumption that, since mind has evolved, it must be composed of adapted functional units. Hence, the search for a basic cognitive 'toolkit,' as some evolutionary psychologists refer to it. However, the inference from evolution to functional units is faulty. Cognition doesn't have to be composed of discrete functional units in order to evolve; selection may instead adjust the parameters of an integrated neuro-hormonal developmental process (cf. Kauffman 1993). Exactly how much modularity actually occurs in cognition is an

---

7　For example, proponents of evolutionary psychology argue that cognition will be highly modularized because specialized cognitive modules will tend to out-compete generalist cognitive modules. In a similarly general way, Millikan argues that traits whose function is to represent will be produced by evolution because other traits need to correlate their activity with the environment in order to function properly. Both of these arguments are seriously weakened by the fact that they make no reference to the underlying biological mechanisms involved. Modularity has the strengths and weaknesses characteristic of any specialization. Without information about system possibilities and costs in relation to required tasks, it is impossible to specify what the possibilities and trade-offs are with respect to various modularizing schemes. (Cherniak 1986 provides an illuminating general discussion of these tradeoffs for human memory: too little compartmentalization and it takes too long to search a compartment, too much compartmentalization and it takes too long searching for the relevant compartment.) The problem for evolutionary psychology is that without more information about neural architectural possibilities, niche characteristics and developmental processes, it is simply impossible to specify what the possibilities and trade-offs are with respect to cognitive modularization. The problem for Millikan is that, without a more detailed account of how the interaction processes are organized, it is impossible to specify in any detail how system-environment correlations are generated and whether they are mediated by structures appropriately thought of as representations. We will discuss this further in the next section.

empirical question, but we suggest that the evidence for distributed processes in interaction and development is strong enough to justify a very different project for understanding the evolution of mind. As Karmiloff-Smith (1992) argues, the issue for this kind of project is understanding how evolutionary biases and environmental interaction act in concert to shape the development of cognition.[8] From this perspective, understanding the evolution of mind is not a matter of finding a mapping between evolutionary and cognitive units; it is a matter of understanding the various factors and complex interactions that shape the developmental processes of cognitive agents.

2.2 *Integrated adaptive agency*

Our strategy is not to find cognitive units that are also adaptations – it is to piece together some of the factors that are likely to have played a role in shaping the phylogeny of intelligent organisms. Our account of self-directed agents is designed to serve as a synthetic model for relating the diverse conceptual and empirical issues that bear on intelligence. Moreover, the place to start is not with functional units but with whole systems and processes. Our account of self-directedness begins with the concepts of **performance envelopes** and **norm matrices**. These concepts provide a basis for understanding organisms as dynamically integrated systems and help illuminate some of the adaptive issues that underlie the evolution of intelligent agents.

The concept of performance envelopes is useful for understanding the dynamical way that organisms survive and reproduce as complete integrated systems. Organisms clearly have functionally specialized components; however, it doesn't follow that the overall adaptiveness of the organism should be thought of as a sum of discretely adaptive individual traits. In fact, overall adaptiveness is a complex nonlinear product of the interactions of many factors. These factors include at least the following general kinds:

---

8 For similar arguments, see Griffiths (1997), Stotz and Griffiths (2001).

(i) Gross performance parameters of ecological interaction (e.g., running speed, sensory acuity).

(ii) Fundamental systemic processes of the organism (e.g., cellular metabolism, development).

(iii) Specialized component structures and sub-systems (e.g., heart, lungs, muscles).

(iv) Factors that differentially affect development (e.g., DNA-protein synthesis, developmental molecular-cellular interactions, environmental resources).

The relations amongst these kinds of factors are many–many: a given gross performance parameter such as running speed will be influenced by many systemic processes, many structures and subsystems, and many developmental factors; a given systemic process, such as cellular metabolism, will play a role in many performance parameters, involve many components, and be affected by many developmental factors; and so on.

Thus, it is important to understand how adaptive systems perform as integrated systems under a potentially open-ended range of conditions. Performance envelopes provide a way of describing this: a performance envelope is determined by the interrelationships of a number of key system parameters. For example, we can characterize the performance envelope of human hand–eye coordination with respect to object manipulation. Given the broad parameters of upper-body strength, humans can lift objects within a certain weight range. This range affects what a human can do with an object. A human can hurl a small object a considerable distance, but as weight goes up, the distance the object can be thrown decreases, until a point is reached where the object can barely be lifted. With stereoscopic vision and fine motor control, humans can perform finely structured actions with objects, but the degree of control decreases as object size, temperature, slipperiness, or weight, increases. Thus, the interrelations amongst the parameters of human hand–eye coordination establish a performance envelope for object manipulation that determines the kinds of object manipulation tasks that humans can perform.

Note, however, that a performance envelope is *not* the same kind of thing as a task specification. The human performance envelope for object manipulation encompasses an open-ended range of tasks, ranging from peeling fruit to throwing rocks at wild dogs, making stone tools, playing musical instruments, painting, writing, and driving cars. In contrast, a task specification measures the performance of a system against a specific kind of task, such as stone tool making. This difference is important because in certain situations performance envelopes are more adaptively important than task specifications, particularly for understanding adaptive change. In this respect, it is worth observing that the etiological theory of functions is a theory of task specification: proper function is performance of the task that led to selection for the trait.

2.3 *Performance norms for integrated agents*

The performance envelope that is of most fundamental significance for adaptive systems is the one that corresponds to the integrity of the system itself. This is the system's **viability envelope**. We call this condition **autonomy** and have analyzed it at some length elsewhere.[9] Here, we focus on using it to understand adaptive agents as integrated systems. Autonomous systems are self-regenerating (or 'self-governed') in the sense that they interactively contribute to the conditions required for their own existence. They engage in interaction processes that acquire resources from the environment and transform these resources into the energy and infrastructure of the system itself, regenerating the whole, including the interactive capacities themselves. In this respect, autonomous systems are distinct from entities such as rocks, which are merely passively internally stable (if a rock is damaged it won't perform work to reform itself), and from gases which are wholly externally stabilized by their environment. Autonomous systems include living cells, multicellular organisms, species and cities.

The key feature of autonomous systems is that they are composed of networks of interdependent processes whose integrated activity

---

9 See Christensen and Hooker (2000a; in press), Christensen and Bickhard (2002). A reasonably comprehensive discussion of autonomy is Christensen, Collier and Hooker, 'Autonomy,' which forms chapter 2 of Christensen's PhD thesis and is available at: http://www.kli.ac.at/personal/christensen/homepage.html

is self-generating. Thus, the **viability envelope** of the system is the range of conditions under which the process network constitutive of the system is self-generating. This process interdependence provides a way of understanding adaptive norms, because, for the whole system to be self-generating, its process activity must meet coordination requirements, and these coordination requirements act as the constraints, or norms, that determine success and failure for the system. For instance, a fundamental process involved in the viability of a cheetah is cellular metabolism, which imposes many requirements that must be satisfied by other processes in the cheetah, such as a supply of oxygen generated by breathing and a supply of nutrients generated by hunting and feeding. Thus, a primary normative standard that determines success or failure for a cheetah's autonomic activity is adequate oxygen supply, and a primary normative standard for its hunting activity is the adequate supply of nutrients coordinated with the locations, quantities and timing of metabolic requirements.

This account of norms has some significant advantages over the standard etiological account. In particular, because it takes into account the overall organization of the system and isn't tied to task specifications derived from previous behaviour, it allows us to understand adaptive change. In other words, we can understand how a change in an adaptive system's activities that has no precedent might still be considered normatively good or bad. This is important with respect to understanding evolutionary processes in general, but it is especially crucial for understanding intelligent agents because it allows us to characterize the norms that apply to choice. In particular, the norms that matter to an agent faced with a choice situation are those that concern its possibilities for action in the present circumstances and their likely outcomes, not what it or its ancestors did in the past.

We can illustrate this intuitively in terms of managing a business. Gerry's Cleaner Crisper Laundromat business has expanded slightly since Gerry hired Sandra to assist with dry cleaning and pressing clothes whilst he deals with customers, monitors the washing machines, performs minor tailoring, and does the accounting. However, after Gerry hires Sandra, the government introduces a new tax system that requires small businesses to submit very complicated forms at frequent intervals. Gerry can't fulfil his current tasks as well as fill out the forms, so he needs Sandra to take over some of his jobs. She could either do the tailoring or deal with the customers, but since Gerry often feels awkward with customers he would prefer to delegate this to Sandra, even though it isn't what he originally hired her for. Sandra prefers the tailoring and is better at it than customer relations but can do the latter well enough and accepts the new task.

The issue here is that in order to be viable Gerry's business must satisfy a complex set of constraints, including doing the jobs that bring in paying customers and satisfying the obligations imposed by the taxation authorities. Under a particular set of conditions, the business can settle into a specific functional task distribution that satisfies those constraints. This occurred during the process in which Gerry hired Sandra and they adjusted the functioning of the business based on her original job description. However, an unexpected perturbation can change the viability constraints on the business and make the old task distribution unworkable. What matters at this point is whether the business can redistribute the functional load in a way that satisfies the new constraints. Gerry no longer wants Sandra simply to fulfil her original job description, he wants her to take on new tasks. There may actually be several kinds of redistribution that will work, with perhaps only minor differences in relative advantage between them. The most important thing is that any functional redistribution that occurs must maintain the viability of the business. This is the basic norm applying to Gerry's management problem. For this reason, *the norms of the business shouldn't be uniquely associated with a specific set of tasks.*

This holistic structure is a general feature of the norms that apply to intelligent agents. Agents need to remain viable through a coherent pattern of activities, or lifestyle (broadly construed). When a problem arises, the agent must identify the problem and attempt to determine its ramifications for the agent's overall activities. The agent then needs to perform compensatory action that re-establishes coherency in the activity complex. This might involve a minor change in activity that 'tweaks' an existing lifestyle, or it might involve a major shift in the lifestyle itself. Gerry's brother Frank was forced to give up his plans to become a dentist when he discovered that he found looking into people's mouths revolting. He became an accountant instead.

Thus, performance envelopes determine norms for an agent, and it is an important characteristic of norms that there are typically many of them and they act in concert. For this reason, we describe the norms that apply to adaptive agents in terms of a norm matrix rather than in terms of individual goals. This makes an important difference, because when faced with multiple norms an agent must find the best balance between them. For cognitive agents in realistic contexts, this is the central, not the derivative, decision-making situation.

There is a further distinction that is important for understanding norms and agency, namely the distinction between **implicit** and **explicit** norms. We can illustrate this difference in terms of what Gerry does and does not know about his management problems. There are many features of the operation of Gerry's business that he doesn't understand and consequently is unable to fix if they go wrong. For instance, Gerry doesn't realize that his personality grates on Sandra and that as a result she is working much less hard than she could. Gerry fails to detect this problem both because he isn't very good at reading Sandra's state of mind and also because he doesn't have any previous experience with hired staff on which to base expectations of productivity. On the other hand, there are other kinds of problems that Gerry can detect: Gerry can tell when the books don't balance, he knows when jobs aren't completed on time and when customers complain, and he knows that if he fouls up his tax forms he'll be audited. Consequently, in analyzing the viability of Gerry's business and the nature of his management problems, we can make a distinction between norms that Gerry can identify and those he can't. We shall refer to the norms that Gerry can identify as his **explicit norm matrix**.

The explicit norm matrix is of enormous significance because it provides the steering information for Gerry's management decisions. Gerry's ability to keep his business viable depends on whether his explicit norms (balancing the books, completing jobs on time, etc.) guide his actions well enough that they sustain the overall viability conditions of the business. If problems develop that Gerry can't recognize or take action to correct, then the business may cease to be viable.

The distinction between implicit and explicit norms also applies in non-human contexts. Affective processes (aversion and reward) provide one of the fundamental steering mechanisms for organisms, and we shall refer to the array of affective processes that an organism possesses as its explicit norm matrix. Thus, hunger indicates that the animal's feeding requirements are not currently being met, while satiation indicates that at the moment they *have* been met. In this respect, affect processes are explicit, not necessarily because they are conscious, but because they provide a direct informational pathway for evaluating action. They do this by forming a direct part of the neuro-anatomical control of motor action. On the other hand, the underlying systemic conditions to which they correspond, e.g., inadequate cellular nutrition in the case of the hunger signal, are typically not explicit for organisms; it takes a science of nutrition to uncover the details of the nutritional requirements that underlie hunger.

By providing explicit norms, affective processes have wide-ranging effects on adaptive interaction capacity. They permit behavioural flexibility by specifying goals for action rather than specifying action directly (cf. Rolls 2000). They also serve as a mechanism for integrating multiple factors in action production because many affective norms can apply to a given action, and properties such as relative intensities allow comparison and trade-off amongst affective signals. For example, an animal might use relative intensity of thirst and hunger signals to determine whether it seeks water or food in a particular context.[10] Furthermore, affective norms allow organisms to learn about their implicit norms through processes such as **stimulus reinforcement association** (Rolls 2000) and **predictive reward learning** (Montague and Sejnowski 1994). Essentially, these learning processes work by allowing an organism to associate aspects of interaction with reward information, which is a fundamental requirement for skill construction. Thus, norms play a fundamental role in interaction ability and the processes of cognitive development.

---

10 Christensen and Hooker (2000a), Raubenheimer and Bernays (1993), Rolls (2000).

3 At the threshold of self-directedness

3.1 *Of mosquitoes, bumblebees and cheetahs*

The concept of self-directedness is designed to capture the distinction between reactive and anticipative forms of adaptiveness. Self-directedness involves the ability to acquire information from interaction and to use it to modify performance so as to satisfy the agent's norms. To convey a clearer sense of what we mean by self-directedness, we first contrast mosquito blood-host search behaviour, which by our account is not self-directed, with cheetah hunting, which is relatively strongly self-directed. We then turn to examining bumblebee foraging, which lies right at the threshold of self-directedness.

Mosquitoes are morphologically relatively simple and depend on a comparatively simple set of niche relations to complete their life-cycle. One of the most important requirements of this life-cycle is that females acquire blood in order to produce eggs. Females locate blood hosts by locating chemicals, including carbon dioxide, produced by blood hosts. The simple chemotaxic process of flying in the direction of increasing carbon dioxide concentration brings a mosquito into proximity with a blood host, whereupon feeding behaviour is initiated (Klowden 1995).

Cheetahs, on the other hand, are morphologically more complex and in particular have much greater nutritional requirements and much more complex sensorimotor systems than mosquitoes. The niche relations they exploit are correspondingly more complicated and most significantly involve a number of variables to which mosquitoes are insensitive. For a mosquito, blood hosts are common and indistinguishable; any blood host will do. In contrast, cheetahs must be highly sensitive to both prey type and context. Large and dangerous animals can injure them, they can expend too much energy trying to catch fast healthy animals, and different species and different individuals have different flight/fight strategies, etc. For these kinds of reasons, there are no simple reliable signals that indicate suitable prey, comparable to the role carbon dioxide plays for mosquitoes. Cheetahs must learn to recognize appropriate prey using complex, context-sensitive discrimination honed by experience. Moreover, simply travelling in the direction of the prey is unlikely to result in catching it. Cheetahs must tailor their actions to the behaviour of the prey by stalking it and responding to its movements during the chase (Eaton 1974).

With respect to understanding self-directedness, there are several noteworthy features of this contrast. Most obviously, although both species are adapted – mosquitoes more widely so than cheetahs – cheetahs have a greatly elaborated ability to shape their actions to the environmental context. Furthermore, achieving this context-sensitivity crucially involves the ability to coordinate many factors, simultaneously and over time. Whereas mosquito behaviour has a highly modularized organization in which each type of action, such as carbon dioxide tracking, is governed by at most a few signals, cheetah behaviour is highly integrative; many kinds of signals are used to shape action at any given time, and the response to particular types of stimuli is context sensitive. For instance, when it is extremely hungry, a cheetah may attempt to catch types of prey that it would ignore if it were less hungry. These processes of integration play a key role in the context-sensitivity of cheetah behaviour, both because they can allow a given action to be shaped by many sources of information, and because they permit the propagation of information to many relevant activities. Learning is an important part of this. The sheer number of interrelated factors involved in successful hunting, such as available cover, stalking distance, prey speed and agility, means that cheetahs must learn many of the relevant relationships through experience. For instance, learning to stalk to a sufficiently close distance depends on discovering the relative speed and agility of the prey, and its characteristic sensory acuity.

Mosquitoes are not self-directed on our account because they don't anticipate interaction processes, and hence cannot modify their responses context sensitively. Instead, they react to local stimuli with fixed behaviours. On the teleosemantic theory of intentionality, mosquitoes *do* anticipate, since the meaning of the CO_2 concentration signal is interpreted as something like 'a blood host in this direction' (cf. Millikan 1989; 1993). This interpretation gives the impression that mosquitoes anticipate that by flying up a CO_2 gradient they will arrive at a blood host. Now, there is a certain respect in which this interpretation makes sense. Because CO_2 gradients often enough culminate in a blood host, following them is an adaptively successful behaviour for mosquitoes. However, there are other important respects in which it is highly misleading to interpret mosquitoes as anticipating that a CO_2 stream will culminate in a blood host.

One important problem is that there is no informational pathway active in the control of flight behaviour that associates CO_2 concentration with arriving at blood hosts. The blood search process is organized in terms of serial action modules: CO_2 governs a particular parameter of the operation of a particular behaviour module, namely the spatial orientation of flight. Proximity to a blood host engages a separate feeding behaviour module. There is no process in the flight module that connects these relationships. The connection is made through the environment, which scaffolds the overall organization of the interaction process, not by motor control processes internal to the mosquito. In other words, there is nothing in the architecture of the CO_2-tracking module that primes it for culmination in proximity to a blood host as a specific event amongst a variety of kinds of outcome that can occur. In this respect, no recognition of the outcome is involved in the control of the action, and there is no learning about outcomes. Thus, on the not-unreasonable proposal that anticipation involves some form of expectancy derived from experience, mosquitoes do not anticipate arriving at blood hosts. To be sure, it is an implicit normative requirement (in the sense we characterized in §2.3) of the overall process organization of the mosquito life cycle that CO_2-tracking results in proximity to blood hosts. Nevertheless, the relationship between action and outcome is not explicitly differentiated by mosquitoes in the control of action.

One way to pose this distinction is by looking at the processes by which the relations between flight control and blood host location can be modified; specifically, either by mutation and preferential selection or by external intervention in design. The key point is that the *mosquito itself* cannot modify the relation.

Bumblebee flower foraging provides a biological example of how on-board modification of action-outcome relations can occur. It is an example of a behavioural process that has a level of complexity close to that of mosquito blood-host search but with the important difference that anticipations about the outcome of action do play a role in motor control, making bumblebees minimally self-directed. Mosquitoes don't need to explicitly anticipate the outcome of CO_2-

guided flight behaviour because the adaptively significant relationship between CO_2 and blood hosts is stable. Populational adaptation has been sufficient to find and sustain a simple correlation that is sufficiently adaptive. For bumblebees, however, the relationships between the availability of flower types, flower colour, and nectar yields are both variable (over species, times, and locations) and adaptively significant. In this case, populational adaptation would be unable to find the appropriate correlations rapidly enough for adaptive success because the relations are spatially and temporally variable relative to the life cycle of bumblebees. Differentiation of the correlations must be performed by a process that is more rapid than the rate of change of the correlation and is complex enough to carry out the cross-correlational signal processing required to extract the relevant adaptive relationships. Bumblebees solve the problem by learning when foraging. They sample the flower types within their range, then preferentially visit those with an adequate nectar reward (Real 1991).

In so doing, bumblebees illustrate a simple ability to interactively differentiate an adaptively relevant relationship and use it to modify behaviour. It is worth identifying some of the capacities that underlie this ability (see Montague et al. 1995). Bumblebees possess:

- An ability to differentiate environmental stimuli (colour of flowers, amount of nectar).
- An ability to differentiate the affective value of interactive relations (a preference for greater nectar quantities, an ability to associate nectar quantity with flower colour).
- An ability to modify behaviour (modify the type of flower visited).

What makes bee foraging behaviour self-directed is the connection between the affective evaluation of the outcome of flower visits and the modification of subsequent flower visitations. The bees are capable of a very simple form of learning, specifically, a very simple form of anticipation, constituted by the bias to fly towards flowers of a particular colour. Thus, after learning, there is a significant sense in which *the bee itself* anticipates that visiting a flower of a particular colour will result in reward.

3.2 Some implications for intentionality

Self-directedness depends on utilizing and cross-correlating information. It therefore presupposes *some* form of intentional content. However, self-directedness also imposes some constraints on the nature of intentional content. In particular, such content must be interpretable by the system; the system must be able to evaluate the information and relate it to other information, including by cross-correlation. This is a constraint that the teleosemantic theory of intentional content doesn't satisfy, because teleosemantic content is specified in terms of the organism's selection history, and organisms typically have no access to information about their selection history. So organisms have no way of evaluating or cross-correlating teleosemantic content.

In this respect, it is significant to note that the form of anticipation characterized above satisfies the criterion for misrepresentation that preoccupies teleosemantics. A bee's anticipations can be wrong, since the particular flower visited may not have nectar, or not enough nectar. Moreover, not only can they be wrong, the bumblebee can detect the error in the form of a reduced gustatory reward from the flower. So the anticipation is a form of information which the organism itself can evaluate.[11]

It would take us beyond our current focus to develop a detailed theory of intentional semantics; however, several features relevant to such an account suggest themselves. The fundamental adaptive problem that signal utilization solves is the control of the nature and timing of actions an organism performs. From this perspective, the most natural way to interpret the information a signal provides for an organism is in terms of the difference the signal makes to the actions the organism performs. In the basic case, then, the norm that applies to information utilization is, 'is the action performed successful?', rather than, 'does the signal correspond to the appropriate object or external state of affairs?' There are general adaptive reasons for preferring this interpretation since the success of action is more significant

---

11 See Bickhard (1993) for a theory of representation based on indication and system-detectable error.

than accurately representing objects or states of affairs. Moreover, an action's success is something that organisms can and do evaluate readily, whereas evaluating correspondence between representation and represented is a task that is, at best, complex and resource intensive, frequently impractical and, especially among simpler agents, often impossible.[12] The success and failure of action is therefore likely to play a more basic role in learning and cognition than is reference. Relating the fundamental form of information to action gives information, partly via affect, a common currency that the system can use as a means for relating multiple sources of information. This makes it information 'from the system's perspective,' and thereby likely to be the basic form of information relevant to cognitive processes.

To place the issue of cognitive relevance in perspective, it is worth contrasting the standards for attributing intentional content employed by teleosemantics with standards used in developmental psychology. As articulated by Millikan, the raison d'être of teleosemantics is explaining misrepresentation.[13] For example, in the case of the frog tongue-flicking behaviour, the content of the perceptual small-dark-moving-object stimulus is supposed to be 'bug here now.' The fact that frogs will also flick their tongues at BB pellets can thereby be explained as a misrepresentation, since in this case the stimulus doesn't correspond to the type of object that made the behaviour adaptive and resulted in its selection. But compare this attribution with a situation in which a psychologist is attempting to determine the conceptual knowledge of a young child. The psychologist shows the child a picture of a horse and a truck, and says, 'which one is the horse?' Even if the child points to the horse, there is not yet enough evidence to justify assuming that a picture of a horse means 'horse' to the child. The psychologist next shows the child a picture of a horse, a cow, a pig, and a dog, and again asks to be shown the horse. This

---

12 Insofar as the represented is taken to be the source of the signal, it is physically impossible, since the source is in the past. It is usually assumed that the represented is a temporally persistent object, but this will often not be the case, especially amongst simpler organisms. We thank Mark Bickhard for pointing this out.

13 See especially Millikan (1993, Introduction).

time, though, the child is uncertain. When the question is repeated, the child points at the dog. Now the evidence points in the other direction, suggesting that the child doesn't properly understand the concept of 'horse.' To ensure that this isn't a one-off error, the psychologist repeats the experiment a number of times, each time using different pictures of the same animal types to control for the possibility that some feature of the pictures is confusing the child. If the child tends to get it right most of the time, then the psychologist is likely to interpret this as meaning that the child does in fact understand the concept of horse but makes occasional errors. On the other hand, if the child makes persistent errors, then the psychologist will take this as evidence that the child doesn't understand what 'horse' means. The child can differentiate four-legged animals from vehicles and associate the word 'horse' with the animals, but she can't be more specific than this.

Based on this kind of experimental methodology, a psychologist would not attribute the representation 'bug here now' to a frog. Even though the frog gets it right on one kind of discrimination task, the fact that the frog persistently gets it wrong on another similar task would be sufficient for the psychologist to decide that the frog doesn't really understand the concept of 'bug.' We believe that the psychologist's interpretation is preferable to the teleosemantic one because it makes assumptions about the nature of intentional content that are more stringent and better attuned to cognitive relevance. Specifically, the psychologist's experimental methodology assumes the following:

- Intentional content should be attributed based on the actual discriminatory abilities of the subject. If the representation is supposed to be of an object type, the subject should be able to robustly identify the object type under a range of conditions, including against a range of relevant contrasts.[14]

---

14 Deciding what counts as a relevant contrast is clearly crucial, but there is no *a priori* answer. Which alternatives are relevant depends on the concept and the context of use. Clearly, concept possession cannot be required to rule out all logically possible contrasts, but equally clearly it should rule out some contrasts in practice.

- Consequently, it is important not to attribute more features to a concept held by the subject than the subject can reliably differentiate. For example, it might be argued that the child has a relatively undifferentiated concept of 'animal' with which she associates the word 'horse,' but not a concept of 'horse' *per se*.
- Occasional error may be the result of misrepresentation[15]; however, persistent error is evidence that the subject doesn't have representational competency.

The problem with the teleosemantic interpretation of content is that it is unduly generous. In the frog case, teleosemantics attributes representation of an object type without requiring that the subject be able to differentiate distinctive attributes of the object type or differentiate the object type from contrasting object types. In this respect, it is interesting to note that, using the looking time methodology, Xu and Carey (1996) find that infants do not track the identity of objects by type until after ten months of age.[16]

With respect to self-directedness, the most important fundamental issue concerns error. If intentional content is to be in a form that is interpretable by the agent, then the agent must be able to detect when the content is wrong. As we noted, the teleosemantic account cannot satisfy this criterion, and its major claim to fame is that it solves the problem of the possibility of misrepresentation! To appreciate the implications of this issue, it is helpful to draw a comparison with the internalist/externalist debate in epistemology.[17] Externalists claim that the justification for belief is concerned with the nature of the process connecting the belief to its referent (which need not be understood by the believer), whilst internalists require that the believer should understand or have access to the warrant for belief. Although internalism is regarded by some of its adherents as involving a stand

---

15 Or carelessness, or a misunderstanding of the question, etc.; what is important, however, is that they all tend to be occasional, rather than consistent over time.

16 This and related experiments are discussed in Hauser and Carey (1998).

17 We thank Jill McIntosh for drawing this to our attention.

against naturalist epistemology,[18] Kitcher (1992) points out that naturalist approaches need to characterize real-world knowledge processes as self-correcting in order to retain normative ambitions. But this means that epistemic norms must be accessible to epistemic agents – at least in part – otherwise there could be no *self*-correction. The same reasoning applies to naturalist theories of representation: the ability to learn about representational content is an essential postulate for an adequate naturalist theory of representation, and the ability to detect misrepresentation is required in order to learn about content. Teleosemantics can provide no role for misrepresentation in cognition, and this is a serious problem. It should be noted that the detectability-of-error criterion for content that we are proposing does not imply that agents cannot misrepresent; it implies that if they do misrepresent then they should be able to discover the fact. This is why persistent error is evidence, not of misrepresentation, but of failure to represent.

4 Improving self-directedness

In this section, we will look at how self-directedness improves, and some of the implications this has for intentionality and high-order cognition. In essence, self-directedness increases in strength as the processes for targeting action become more sophisticated in the way they coordinate the interaction process. As organisms become increasingly self-directed, they are better able to manage complex variable interaction processes and begin to exhibit distinctively cognitive processes such as choice and planning. This primarily occurs through increases in the ability to anticipate and evaluate. Bees are only weakly self-directed because their capacity to form anticipations is fairly limited. Stronger forms of self-directedness require more powerful learning processes for forming anticipations.

Some kinds of interaction processes show nonlinear sensitivities, in that variation in any of a number of factors may produce highly divergent interaction pathways, many of which have effects that are not adaptive for the system. For example, a small mistake when

---

18   E.g., Fumerton (1988).

a cheetah is stalking a gazelle can alert the gazelle and allow it to escape. Tasks of this nature impose particularly strong demands on an organism's capacity for anticipation since the organism must initiate and be responsive to extended temporal patterns in interaction that involve many interdependent factors.

Improvements in anticipation capacity allow the system to shape its actions over longer timescales and with respect to more detailed, in some cases modal, information concerning the interaction process.[19] As we saw in the bee example, evaluation plays an important role in the process. Evaluative signals function to cross-correlate the control of action with the success of its outcome.

A powerful interactive learning process called **Self-Directed Anticipative Learning** (SDAL) can be generated by the coupling of anticipative and evaluative processes. SDAL is effective for solving open problems, in which the nature of the task to be performed is not known in advance. SDAL uses interaction to acquire information about the nature of the task and thereby improves performance. The system learns from experience and modifies its behaviour, continually tracking the success of subsequent modifications. As the system interacts, it generates information that allows it to construct anticipative models of the interaction process; in turn, these anticipations modify interaction, which allows the system to perform more focussed activity and generates further feedback to the system. This feedback serves to evaluate the success of the anticipations, whilst the anticipations themselves help the system improve its recognition of relevant information and evaluate its performance more precisely. If the anticipations prove unsuccessful, the system will hunt fruitlessly, but if they are even partially successful the system can progressively improve its ability, bootstrapping its way to a solution.

An example of SDAL is the process by which cheetahs learn to hunt. Gaining the skills required for successful hunting requires extensive learning, in which cheetahs evaluate their own performance and use information from interaction to improve performance. As cubs,

---

19   See further Christensen and Hooker (2000a). For some of the neural mechanisms involved, see Montague and Sejnowski (1994). See also Glenberg (1997) for an interactivist interpretation of the role of memory.

cheetahs spend a great deal of time learning hunting skills by playing with siblings, chasing lizards, and so forth. The mother facilitates this process by bringing small live prey, such as a hare, back to the cubs, allowing them to practice chasing and killing techniques. As the cubs begin to mature, they accompany the mother on hunts and observe the real process first-hand. Even so, actual hunting experience is required before proficiency is achieved; many juveniles, for instance, make the mistake of initiating the chase from too great a distance. The hunting capacity of a mature cheetah is thus a complex product of an extended history of mutual shaping between internally generated action and the success and failure of the ensuing interaction processes.

Hunting is an integration problem: prey is caught only when a complex array of factors are brought into coordination. Achieving this coordination requires detailed knowledge. To hunt successfully, cheetahs must differentiate many specific objects (such as the prey and obstacles) and relations (such as distance to the prey and to flight/fight opportunities). Part of this differentiation process involves recognizing sources of error, such as startling the prey too early or tackling an animal that is too large. These differentiations are not simply given to a cheetah perceptually, they are acquired through an extended interactive learning process, and they concern interactive characteristics (alertness, speed, agility, aggressiveness, etc., relative to the cheetah's behaviour).

On our approach to intentionality, cognitive reference arises through these interactive differentiation processes. Specifically, as part of the problem of coordinating complex interaction processes, self-directed agents learn to differentiate specific states-of-affairs, objects, and object types. Our hypothesis is that they do this by learning the effects these things have on interaction processes. In this context, it is worth briefly discussing a standard argument against associating content with action, which is that representations might be used to indicate an open-ended range of actions, depending on the circumstances. For example, representation of the presence of a chair might lead an agent to sit on it, stand on it to change a light bulb, use it to block the door, belt an intruder over the head with it, break it up for firewood, and so on.[20] This

---

20 Cf. Millikan (1989, 289–90).

observation is supposed to justify an in-principle separation of action and content, the idea being that, because representations need not be associated with any specific actions, their content isn't connected to action at all. But the argument hardly justifies this conclusion. At most, it shows that some representations are relatively open with respect to action possibilities. But this does not mean that they are disconnected from action. Cognitive agents learn to represent *through* interaction, and even sophisticated representations are grounded in interaction relations.

The capacity to represent multiple action possibilities can be understood from an interactivist standpoint by examining the nature of the developmental learning processes that give rise to representation and concept formation. These learning processes involve, in part, the agent partitioning interaction processes into increasingly finely differentiated categories by learning to recognize important sources of influence on the nature of the interaction. A fundamental distinction to be made concerns effects that arise from the agent versus effects that arise from elsewhere. It is to be expected that evolution will impose biases on the developmental processes of cognitive agents that facilitate differentiating objects and important object and event types, but this is should not be interpreted as evolution imbuing innate knowledge of those things (see Karmiloff-Smith 1992, who argues for this type of interpretation of cognitive development). Nor will cognitive agents suddenly come to acquire concepts of event and object types as they are encountered, or at some specific later point. For instance, a child's concept of apples is acquired progressively as the child learns what an apple looks like, feels like, tastes like, etc. A child does this by interacting with apples, and as the range of interactive experiences increases, the child's concept of an apple gains increasing richness. Even after the stage when a child is able to use the concept of apple appropriately in many circumstances, such as in normal conversation and at lunchtime, the child may still be learning about the nature of apples. It comes as a pleasant surprise to many children that apples explode nicely when hurled at brick walls.

A key feature of this learning process is a progressive shift from crude to increasingly fine differentiation of interaction characteristics, linked to the child's improving sensorimotor skills. As learning progresses, the child will gain enough information about the interaction characteristics of apples to spontaneously associate apples with novel actions within a particular range of action types, such as being able to know without specific experience that one can juggle apples. Consequently, the concept becomes less tied to specific action contexts.

However, this doesn't mean that the child's representation of apples is fundamentally separated from action, it just means that the child knows enough about the interaction characteristics of apples to relate apples to a particular range of sensorimotor skills. In other words, once the child knows what an apple feels like to grasp and throw, the child can generalize by using apples in new actions within the child's range of grasping and throwing abilities. Nonetheless, the action range within which a child can use a concept will show a high level of experience-dependency, notwithstanding the fact that the child is able to generalize to novel actions *within* the range. Thus, although a young boy may, with no prompting or prior experience, throw an apple at a window in order to break it, that same boy is extremely unlikely to know how to prepare a pork and apple pie.[21]

Thus, the argument for divorcing content from action has the situation on its head. It is a very important feature of representations that they can sometimes be used to indicate open-ended action possibilities. But this doesn't justify a fundamental, in-principle separation of action and content. Our way of representing the world is experience-dependent. And concept boundaries – the ways in which an agent decides that something *doesn't* belong to a category – are also strongly related to action. If a person sees a chair and attempts to sit on it, but falls through thin air onto the floor, the person is likely to decide

---

21 To put this in the terms we introduced earlier, concepts are closely associated with the performance envelopes and norm matrices of the agent that apply in the interaction context. Young boys have good performance envelopes for throwing, and consequently their concept of apple can include a rich understanding of throwing potential. In contrast, they generally have poor cooking performance envelopes, and so little understanding of apples in relation to cooking potential. Moreover, since they have a very limited ability to tell good cooking from bad, their ability to learn about the cooking potential of apples is similarly restricted. Even though they might memorize recipes involving apples, they won't be able to exercise judgment or improvise in the way that a skilled chef can.

that what they see isn't really a chair. It might be a hallucination, or a hologram. Similarly, if a child tries to bite into an apple and gets a mouth full of wax, the child will probably decide that the object isn't really an apple.

There are important reasons for preferring an interactivist account of reference of this type to standard teleosemantic ones. We discussed one of the most fundamental earlier; interpreting information in terms of action acknowledges and incorporates the fact that agents interpret information and utilize it flexibly. Also, there is extensive empirical evidence that human concepts have a highly interaction-oriented character. According to prototype theory, categories are grounded in interaction properties as experienced from the perspective of the cognitive agent.[22] Furthermore, the interactivist account fits well with evidence in developmental psychology concerning the dynamical nature of cognitive development and the importance of interaction[23], and with evidence in neuroscience concerning massive levels of activity-dependency in neuronal organization, and consequently very high levels of experience-dependency in neuronal functional organization.[24]

For all the emphasis placed on representation and categorization by most approaches, the integrative aspects of intentionality are no less important. It is a mistake to assume that cognitive integration processes occur as operations on atomistic representations; for the

---

22 These include prototype effects themselves, namely the fact that often some members of categories are treated as more typical than others, where what determines typicality is some aspect of the agent's physical makeup or interaction experience, such as treating primary colours as more typical than non-primary colours, or treating robins as more typical examples of birds than penguins (Lakoff 1987; Rosch 1973). They also include the phenomenon of basic level categories, which, roughly, are categories most commonly used, have the simplest names, are the first to be learned, and are distinguished by commonly experienced interactive attributes (Lakoff 1987, 46–47). Examples of basic level categories include *dog, chair, book*, and *car*.

23 E.g., Glenberg (1997), Karmiloff-Smith (1992), Thelen and Smith (1994), Thelen (1995).

24 E.g., Christensen and Hooker (2000a), Florence et al. (1998), Jones and Pons (1998), Quartz and Sejnowski (1997).

reasons discussed in §2.3 and §3, integration is a more basic process than representation and in fact takes priority in interaction and learning. Moreover, integration is a feature of high-level cognition as exemplified in the phenomenon of holistic situational awareness in highly skilled activities.[25] Playing professional tennis, for example, is a highly cognitively demanding task that requires considerable strategic skills and acute situational awareness. A player with clear physical advantages, such as more powerful groundstrokes, can be outplayed by a player who is able to shape the game so that those strengths are negated. One of the most cognitively demanding aspects of professional tennis is that it requires highly developed anticipations concerning the performance interrelationships of the game. Some of the kinds of things professional tennis players must be able to anticipate include the differing characteristics of a baseline player as opposed to a serve-volleyer, and the effects that playing on a grass or a rebound-ace or a clay surface has on each style of play. The only way to acquire these anticipations, at least to a level sufficient for being competitive, is through a long learning process involving experience of actual game conditions.

The role of these anticipations is to focus action appropriately for the variety of conditions the player will experience, and to facilitate the rapid localization of success and error needed to adapt effectively within a match. Note that, although a novice player may have a conscious goal to win a game, this goal has little anticipative content since the novice has no understanding of the kinds of performance relations it involves. As a result, the novice flounders in a morass of unfamiliar relations that must be somehow coordinated to play well. The unfamiliarity of the situation means that the novice has little ability to recognize sources of error or to take well-directed corrective measures, i.e., she cannot differentiate the adaptively relevant relations for the context. In contrast, the professional player's performance anticipations, built up through years of coaching and match play, allow her to learn quickly about the opponent's characteristics and match her performance to their strengths and weaknesses. This may

---

25 Cf. Merleau-Ponty's (1962) account of intentionality. See also Dreyfus (1996) and Brown (1988).

be as detailed as being able to anticipate the likely direction of the serve at set point when the score is 30–40, or anticipating that the opponent's service game will be likely to crack under the pressure of a tie-break. The professional's anticipations help localize success and error by making salient important game relations. For instance, if the opponent is attempting to disrupt the player's baseline strategy by frequently coming to the net, the player may counter by attempting some dramatic low percentage passing shots which, if successful, may reduce the other player's confidence and create doubt about when to go the net.

5 Conclusion

This account of self-directed agents develops a perspective for drawing together diverse issues involved in the evolution of cognitive agency, including intentionality. Here is a summary of the main points of our account:

- **Autonomy**: Adaptive systems are composed of networks of processes that are interdependent and collectively self-sustaining and self-repairing. The theory of autonomy is an analysis of the identity conditions for such systems. The concept of performance envelopes provides a way of understanding the adaptive behaviour of autonomous systems from an open-ended dynamical perspective rather than in terms of fixed task specifications.
- **Norm matrices**: This in turn provides us with a radically different conception of norms to etiological theory. The concept of a norm matrix identifies norms with conditions of viability and provides a way of characterizing the fact that in realistic biological conditions many norms are operative simultaneously. Adaptive interaction requires the continuous satisfaction of many norms. An explicit norm matrix is the array of normative conditions that an agent can explicitly recognize. In biological organisms, affect processes provide the basic explicit norm matrix.
- **Anticipation and evaluation**: Explicit norm matrices provide steering information for behaviour and in particular provide a basis for 'on-board' processes that modify action-outcome rela-

tions. Evaluation allows an agent to assign an affective value to features of interaction to modify performance accordingly and to anticipate future outcomes.

- **Interactive differentiation**: Organisms use signals to control the nature and timing of the actions they perform. More complex intentional content arises from the information processing involved in learning to recognize the various contributing factors to interaction, tracking sources of success and error.
- **Self-directedness:** Anticipation and evaluation combine to generate the capacity for self-directedness. Self-directedness involves the ability to acquire information from interaction and use it to modify performance so as to satisfy the agent's norms. As agents become increasingly self-directed, they are better able to manage complex variable interaction processes and begin to exhibit distinctively cognitive processes such as choice and planning.
- **Self-directed anticipative learning**: In certain circumstances, anticipation and evaluation can be mutually amplifying as more focussed action and improved interactive differentiation further improve anticipation and evaluation. We hypothesize that these powerful learning processes play a central role in cognitive development. We further think it is likely that reference and concept formation occurs through these processes as agents come to differentiate object and event types in interaction.

Rather than attempting a simplistic unification of representationalist cognitive science and adaptationist evolution theory, our account focuses on important adaptive issues that are likely to have played a role in shaping the phylogeny of intelligence. It develops an account of intentional agency that is grounded in biologically realistic adaptive problems and which coheres well with a number of strands of research in contemporary cognitive science, including autonomous agent robotics, developmental psychology, cognitive psychology, and cognitive neuroscience.

References

Beer, R. D. 1995. "Computational and Dynamical Languages for Autonomous Agents." In *Mind as Motion: Explorations in the Dynamics of Cognition*, R. F. Port and T. van Gelder, eds. Cambridge, MA: MIT Press.

———. 2000. "Dynamical Approaches to Cognitive Science," *Trends in Cognitive Sciences* 4, 91–99.

Bickhard, M. H. 1993. "Representational Content in Humans and Machines," *Experimental and Theoretical Artificial Intelligence* 5, 285–333.

Bickhard, M. H., and D. M. Ritchie. 1983. On *the Nature of Representation: A Case Study of James J. Gibson's Theory of Perception*. New York: Praeger.

Brooks, R. A. 1991. "Intelligence without Representation," *Artificial Intelligence*. 47, 139–59.

Brown, H. I. 1988. *Rationality*. London: Routledge.

Cherniak, C. 1986. *Minimal Rationality*. Cambridge, MA: Bradford/MIT Press.

Christensen, W. D. 2000. An Interactivist Approach to Adaptive Intelligence and Agency. Ph.D. thesis, University of Newcastle, Australia.

Christensen, W. D., and M. H. Bickhard. 2002. "The Process Dynamics of Normative Function," *Monist* 85, 3-28.

Christensen, W. D., and C. A. Hooker. 2000a. "An Interactivist-Constructivist Approach to Intelligence: Self-Directed Anticipative Learning," *Philosophical Psychology* 13.1, 5–45.

———. 2000b. "Autonomy and the Emergence of Intelligence: Organised Interactive Construction," *Communication and Cognition – Artificial Intelligence* 17.3–4, 133–57.

———. In press. "Representation and the Meaning of Life." In *Representation in Mind: New Approaches to Mental Representation*, H. Clapin, P. Slezak, and P. Staines, eds. Westport: Praeger.

Clark, A. 1997. *Being There: Putting Brain, Body, and World Together Again*. Boston: Bradford/MIT Press.

Dreyfus, H. 1996. "The Current Relevance of Merleau-Ponty's Phenomenology of Embodiment." In *Perspectives on Embodiment*, H. Haber and G. Weiss, eds. London: Routledge.

Eaton, R. L. 1974. *The Cheetah; the Biology, Ecology, and Behavior of an Endangered Species*. New York: Van Nostrand Reinhold Co.

Edelman, G.M. 1987. *Neural Darwinism: The Theory of Neuronal Group Selection*. New York: Basic Books.

Florence, S., H. Taub, and J. Kaas. 1998. "Large Scale Sprouting of Cortical Connections after Peripheral Injury in Adult Macacque Monkeys," *Science* **282**, 1117–21.

Fumerton, R. 1988. "The Internalism/Externalism Controversy," *Philosophical Perspectives* **2**, 443–59.

Glenberg, A. M. 1997. "What Memory Is For," *Behavioral and Brain Sciences* **20**, 1–55.

Griffiths, P. 1997. *What Emotions Really Are*. Chicago: University of Chicago Press.

Griffiths, P., and R. Gray. 1994. "Developmental Systems and Evolutionary Explanation," *Journal of Philosophy* **91**, 277–304.

Hauser, M., and S. Carey. 1998. "Building a Cognitive Creature from a Set of Primitives: Evolutionary and Developmental Insights." In *The Evolution of* **Mind**, D. Cummins and C. Allen, eds. New York: Oxford University Press.

Hendriks-Jansen, H. 1996. *Catching Ourselves in the Act: Situated Activity, Interactive Emergence, Evolution and Human Thought*. Cambridge, MA: MIT Press.

Hutchins, E. 1995. *Cognition in the Wild*. Cambridge, MA: MIT Press.

Jablonka, E., and M. J. Lamb. 1995. *Epigenetic Inheritance and Evolution: The Lamarkian Dimension*. Oxford: Oxford University Press.

Jones, E., and T. Pons. 1998. "Thalamic and Brainstem Contributions to Large-Scale Plasticity of Primate Somatosensory Cortex," *Science* **282**, 1121–25.

Karmiloff-Smith, A. 1992. *Beyond Modularity: A Developmental Perspective on Cognitive Science*. Cambridge, MA: MIT Press.

Kauffman, S. A. 1993. *The Origins of Order: Self-Organization and Selection in Evolution*. New York: Oxford University Press.

Kitcher, P. 1992. "The Naturalists Return," *Philosophical Review* **101**, 53–114.

Klowden, M. J. 1995. "Blood, Sex, and the Mosquito: Control Mechanisms of Mosquito Blood-Feeding Behavior," *BioScience* **45**, 326–31.

Lakoff, G. 1987. *Women, Fire and Dangerous Things: What Categories Reveal about the Mind*. Chicago: University of Chicago Press.

Merleau-Ponty, M. 1962. *Phenomenology of Perception*. Trans. C. Smith. London: Routledge & Kegan-Paul.

Millikan, R. G. 1989. "Biosemantics," *Journal of Philosophy* **86**, 281–97.

———. 1993. *White Queen Psychology and Other Essays for Alice*. Cambridge, MA.: MIT Press.

Montague, P. R., and T. J. Sejnowski. 1994. "The Predictive Brain: Temporal Coincidence and Temporal Order in Synaptic Learning Mechanisms," *Learning & Memory* **1**, 1–33.

Montague, P. R., P. Dayan, C. Person, and T. J. Sejnowski. 1995. "Bee Foraging in Uncertain Environments Using Predictive Hebbian Learning," *Nature* **377**, 725–28.

Oyama, S. 1985. *The Ontogeny of Information*. Cambridge: Cambridge University Press.

Pfeifer, R., and C. Scheier. 1999. *Understanding Intelligence*. Cambridge, MA: MIT Press.

Quartz, S. R., and T. J. Sejnowski. 1997. "The Neural Basis of Cognitive Development: A Constructivist Manifesto," *Behavioural and Brain Sciences* **20.4**, 537–96.

Raubenheimer, D., and E. A. Bernays. 1993. "Patterns of Feeding in the Polyphagous Grasshopper *Taeniopoda eques: A* Field Study," *Animal Behavior* **45**, 153–67.

Real, L. A. 1991. "Animal Choice Behavior and the Evolution of Cognitive Architecture," *Science* **253**, 980–86.

Rolls, E. T. 2000. "Precis of 'The Brain and Emotion'," *Behavioral and Brain Sciences* **23**, 177–233.

Rosch, E. 1973. "Natural Categories," *Cognitive Psychology* 4, 328–50.

Stotz, K., and P. Griffiths. 2001. "Dancing in the Dark: Evolutionary Psychology and the Argument from Design." In *Evolutionary Psychology: Alternative Approaches*, S. Scher and M. Rauscher, eds. Dordrecht: Kluwer.

Thelen, E. 1995. "Time-Scale Dynamics and the Development of an Embodied Cognition." In *Mind as Motion: Explorations in the Dynamics of Cognition*, R. F. Port and T. van Gelder, eds. Cambridge, MA: MIT Press.

Thelen, E., and Smith, L. B. 1994. A *Dynamic Systems Approach to the Development of Cognition and Action*. Cambridge, MA/London: MIT Press, Bradford Books.

van Gelder, T. 1995. "What Might Cognition Be, If Not Computation?" *Journal of Philosophy* **92.7**, 345–81.

———. 1998. "The Dynamical Hypothesis in Cognitive Science," *Behavioral and Brain Sciences* **21.5**, 615–27.

Xu, F., and S. Carey. 1996. "Infants' Metaphysics: The Case of Numerical Identity," *Cognitive Psychology* **30**, 111–53.

CANADIAN JOURNAL OF PHILOSOPHY
Supplementary Volume 27

Darwin's Algorithm, Natural Selective History, and Intentionality Naturalized

PHILIP HANSON

I. Introduction

Dan Dennett and Jerry Fodor have recently offered diametrically opposed estimations of the relevance of the theory of natural selection to an adequate theory of intentionality. In this paper, I show, *first*, how this opposition can be traced largely to differences both in their respective understandings of what the theory of natural selection includes, and in their respective 'pre-theoretic' takes on the *datum* to be explained by a theory of intentionality. These differences, in turn, have been 'pre-selected' by contrasting outlooks on the general nature of the explanatory enterprise. While no final adjudication of these large issues is attempted, I argue, *second*, that it is important to distinguish two rather different questions about the relevance of natural selection to the nature of intentionality, and that, having done so, one can see that, from standpoints purely *internal* to their respective projects, Dennett and Fodor each in his own way misconstrues the relevance of natural selection.

First Question: What constraints, if any, are imposed on our account of the nature of human intentional cognition – cognition involving representational mental states, states with semantic content – by the bare supposition that our capacity for it is an adaptive trait; that, roughly, it became prevalent amongst our ancestors through natural selection? I will argue that nothing of any metaphysical significance about the inherent, 'constitutive' nature of human intentionality follows from this supposition. However, when taken together with the further assumption that natural selection produced human intentionality from naturalistically circumspect initial conditions, what follows is simply that our capacity for intentional cognition is, itself, naturalistically circumspect. It is a trait whose occurrence accords with a certain 'baseline naturalism,' to be elaborated. Thus, being an adaptation, given the aforementioned assumption, implies something about the *general* nature of our capacity, without implying anything about its specific constitutive nature, or about what inherently distinguishes it from other adaptations.

The following is a sufficient diachronic condition for such naturalism.

> Any type of phenomenon whose instances occur as the terminus of an 'algorithmic' type of temporal process (1) whose initial conditions were natural, (2) whose controlling mechanisms were natural, and (3) which ran its course without external interference, is itself natural. (**Diachronic Baseline Naturalism**, or 'DBN')

The requirement that the process be 'algorithmic' will be elaborated in due course. Because this condition is recursive, its satisfaction establishes that a phenomenon is natural only provided the initial conditions and controlling mechanisms have already independently been established as natural. This will normally be an empirical matter of establishing that said conditions and mechanisms are constituted in ways that are agreed to be paradigmatically or uncontroversially natural. Diachronic Baseline Naturalism has a 'synchronic' counterpart.

> Any type of phenomenon (1) whose simplest functional units are natural, (2) whose mechanisms of functional composition and cohesion are naturally realized, and (3) whose instances result solely from the operation of these mechanisms on its functional units, is itself natural. (**Synchronic Baseline Naturalism** or 'SBN')[1]

---

1 'Synchronic' is not intended to be interpreted strictly, as referring to strict simultaneity. The contrast is with the evolutionary time scale of DBN. The synchronicity can be at least as temporally 'thick' as the time span of a given stage of structural development of a given type of organism. A type of organism, at a given developmental stage, is a certain complexly organized functional/causal system. SBN expresses a sufficient condition for naturalism with respect to this functional/causal organization. The term 'structural' could be used in place of 'synchronic.'

Diachronic and Synchronic Baseline Naturalism need not be taken to express *necessary* conditions. For instance, not all natural processes need be algorithmic, and some natural phenomena may be structurally simple, structurally complex in ways that do not yield to functional characterization. But these sufficient conditions are 'baseline' in the following sense. Where applicable, they determine that a phenomenon is natural using the least amount of information about its nature, in a way that does not prejudge its specific nature, in a way that is, in fact, *a priori*, relative to the prior determination of the truth of their respective antecedent conditions.

Of course, the specific natures of the phenomena thereby established as natural may nevertheless be of pressing interest to us. There might also be interesting stronger (narrower) sufficient conditions – whether diachronic or synchronic – that some baseline natural phenomena *also* satisfy. Recognizing that these stronger conditions are also satisfied may contribute importantly to our understanding of specific natures, without interfering in any way with what DBN or SBN has already secured about their general natures; a point that will be illustrated in what follows.

Second Question: What insights, if any, into the specific constitutive nature of human intentional cognition may be afforded by particular details of our (relatively recent) *natural selective history*, details about the processes of genotypic variation and phenotypic selection that culminated in our intentional capacity? I will argue that, to the extent that we can plausibly reconstruct those details, we stand significantly to advance our understanding of the specific constitutive nature of our capacity; e.g., what dedicated neural structures may contribute to it and in what ways, and its relation to other capacities such as our linguistic capacity and our capacity for conscious reflective thought. A plausible strategy for getting an empirical fix on these mechanisms is to correlate the behavioural manifestations of our distinct kinds of intentional, referential capabilities with features of our brain structure and function not present in the brains of our primate evolutionary forebears and cousins; then, using the genetic 'fossil record' and other data sources, to construct a plausible natural selective history that would explain the transition from their brain structures and functions to ours. This approach is well exemplified by Terrence Deacon's recent theory of the co-evolution of language and brain.

I will elaborate and defend my answers to these questions in the context of moderating Jerry Fodor's and Dan Dennett's boisterous debate about the relevance of natural selection to the nature of intentionality. To the casual onlooker (not us, of course, but bear with me), it may appear that Fodor denies that there is any relevance at all, while Dennett takes natural selection as providing the answers to all outstanding questions. Fodor has allowed that the very credentials of selectionist explanations of anything are still an open empirical issue with him, and that in particular the selectionist theory of speciation is, so far, still "'optional'" (Fodor 1996, 247; cf. also 247–51). If selectionism is false, then of course, trivially, it should place no constraints on, nor contribute to, our account of human intentionality. But more interesting to someone who, unlike Fodor but like Dennett, readily accepts the explanatory credentials of selectionist theory, is Fodor's further insistence that even if it is true that our ancestors' intentionality was selected for its 'cleverness,' "... intentionality does not consist in its having been [so] selected."[2] That is, the *origin* of our capacity sheds no light on its specific inherent *nature*. Dennett, by contrast, has called for a 'reductive explanation' of intentionality, or of the predictive utility of ascriptions of intentionality, *via* an adaptationist account of biological function (cf. Dennett 1996, 263; 1995, 73–84). The specific nature of our capacity for intentionality, then, admits of explanation in terms of its evolutionary origins. All this might be thought by our casual onlooker to place Dennett and Fodor at polar extremes when it came to the question of the explanatory relevance of natural selection.

But a closer and more charitable inspection (that's us) suggests that both Fodor and Dennett *agree* with my proposed answer to our First Question. That is, both think that intentionality's being selected for, under the assumption of naturalistically circumspect initial conditions, would imply that it is a natural trait. In the previous quotation, Fodor is charitably interpreted not as denying that intentionality's being selected for would place any constraints *at all* on its *general* nature, but rather as denying that it would, in itself, determine its *specific, constitutive* nature. And Dennett is charitably interpreted not as claiming that the specific constitutive nature of intentionality admits of

---

2 (Fodor 1996, 261). Here and in other quotations, square bracket inserts are mine.

explanatory reduction to its having been selected for, but rather merely that its *general* status as a natural trait is thereby secured.

Interestingly enough, Fodor and Dennett also at least implicitly appear to give the same answer to our Second Question, and this time it differs from mine. They appear united in wanting to deny that insight into the specific constitutive nature of intentionality may be afforded by specifics of our recent natural selective history. I will argue that in that case they are both wrong. But at this point one might well ask how two philosophers thus revealed as agreeing on so much can still manage, as they do, to give the impression of diametric opposition on the relevance of natural selection. Is it the disagreement or the agreement that is really illusory here?

The answer to this question is not straightforward. It turns out that they have *radically disparate reasons* for their shared estimations of relevance and irrelevance, largely traceable to differences, both in their respective 'pre-theoretic' takes on the datum to be explained – i.e., human intentional cognition – and in their respective understandings of what is included in the theory of natural selection. Though both nominally agree with the answer I proposed to our First Question, they in fact tend to mean different things by the key terms 'intentionality,' and 'selected for' (and even 'natural'), and exhibit the deep differences of outlook on the *general nature of the explanatory enterprise* alluded to in our opening paragraph. Fodor's robust realism[3] opposes Dennett's deflationary 'interpretationism,' and imposes a correspondingly stronger constraint on what will pass for an acceptable 'naturalistic' account of intentionality.[4]

This last point, about their differing general outlooks, will hardly be news to the initiated, and hardly a matter to be adjudicated here.[5] My limited aim will be, first, to show how their shared views about the irrelevance of natural selective history arise, respectively, from

---

3 Dennett (1989, 71) calls it 'Realist with a capital *R*.'

4 Dennett (1989, 15, 24, 37) insists that his 'interpretationism' about intentionality is a subtle, nuanced form of realism.

5 I confess to being among those whose visceral reactions, at least, favour robust Realism!

their disparate takes on intentionality and natural selection. Second, I will argue that even from standpoints *internal* to their respective projects, each in his own revealing way misconstrues the relevance of the theory of natural selection. Fodor *under*estimates the potential relevance of selection-historical considerations to his claim that our internal mental syntax tracks our external-relational mental semantics. Since *The Elm and the Expert*, Fodor has sought an explanation of what he calls the 'nomological concomitance of mental syntax and mental semantics,' of how this concomitance is implemented. He sees no help from Darwin. But I will argue that distinguishing our Second from our First Question does help one to see how the right implementational story need not be arbitrary relative to selective origins; indeed, the insights into the specific constitutive nature of our intentional capacity to be gleaned from our selective history are liable to be not at all negligible. Dennett, by contrast, happily embraces the idea that our cognitive capacities are an adaptation, a product of natural selection, and in *Darwin's Dangerous Idea* takes this as lending support to an ontologically deflationary construal of attributions of intentionality. If minds have been generated from non-minds in a purely mindless way, then the nature of our mental capacities must be qualitatively continuous with the non-mental, he supposes. I argue that this is a *non sequitur*, that the nature of natural selection *per se* cannot by itself rule out the possibility of qualitative discontinuities emerging from a natural selective process. Dennett has many reasons to resist any *a priori* stipulation of the specific nature of our intentional capacity, such as 'analytic functionalism,' the view, roughly, that mental types as a matter of meaning are simply functional types. Therefore, he should not underestimate but remain open to the possible empirical corrective of whatever the contingencies of our recent natural selective history may reveal.

Finally, I will argue that, though the baseline naturalness of our capacity for intentional cognition follows from its having been selected for, this eventuality by itself leaves unanswered questions that matter to us, about the specific constitutive nature of our capacity. The mere fact that our capacity has been selected cannot help us with these questions. In particular, it cannot help us decide between Fodor's and Dennett's accounts, each of which appears to satisfy baseline naturalistic constraints. On the other hand, pertinent *details* of our natural selective history may provide an illuminating fix on answers to our questions about the specific nature of intentionality, and in the process help us choose between such competing accounts.

II. Dennett

Let us proceed, then, with a closer look, first at Dennett's and then at Fodor's views. Darwin's dangerous idea, as graphically encapsulated by Dennett, is that what "...best accounts for the speed of the antelope, the wings of the eagle, the shape of the orchid, the diversity of species, and all other occasions for wonder in the world of nature" (Dennett 1995, 59) is the historical process of natural selection. The most important thing about this process for Dennett is that it can be seen to be 'algorithmic,' and that, seen as such, it is seen *a priori* to exhibit a kind of conditional necessity, expressible as follows (Dennett 1995, 40–41).

> Any population of reproducing entities (1) exhibiting significant variability in their traits, (2) competing for limited resources in a relatively stable environment, and (3) tending to pass these traits on to their offspring, would be guaranteed to have future generations that tended, respectively, to exhibit traits increasingly adaptive to that environment. (**Darwin's Algorithm**)

So the presence of presumptively adaptive traits that we find in living populations today is in principle explainable by a selection process of this sort, provided, of course, their ancestry goes back enough generations, and provided it continuously satisfied conditions (1)–(3).

A process is algorithmic, according to Dennett, provided it has the characteristics of 'substrate neutrality,' 'guaranteeing results,' and 'mindlessness.' Natural selection has all three, as follows. First, to be substrate neutral an algorithmic process must figure in explanations "... due to its logical structure, not the causal powers of the materials [/entities] used [/involved] in the instantiation, just so long as those causal powers permit the prescribed steps to be followed exactly" (Dennett 1995, 51; parenthetical inserts mine). But this is true of natural selection. Thus, it is not essential that the selection be in populations of *living* organisms. It would take place in any population of reproducing entities, living or not, that managed to satisfy conditions (1)–(3).

Second, to guarantee results, an algorithm must be a 'foolproof recipe' when 'executed without misstep' (Dennett 1995, 53). This way of talking is most natural in connection with rule-governed, step-wise *procedures* that we endeavour to carry out. But *the carrying out* of such a procedure is a process, and Dennett wants to regard processes as algorithmic if they lend themselves to being characterized *as if* they resulted from such a step-wise procedure having been carried out. Natural selection was already characterized as guaranteeing a particular *tendency* in future generations of a population. This guarantee lacks a certain excitement, since clearly the specific natures of adaptive traits are not thereby predicted. But what interests Dennett in this context is the *general* character of adaptive traits as *natural*. This is all he wants to 'predict' by appeal to their algorithmic selective history.[6]

The third feature of algorithmic processes Dennett slyly dubs 'mindlessness.' Mindlessness actually seems to be a combination of two distinguishable features, one having to do with the nature of the 'steps' *per se*, the other having to do with the nature of the sort of mechanism that could carry out these steps. First, the individual steps must be simple, incremental, determinate, and in principle specifiable. Second, and *a fortiori*, they must be the sort of steps that are readily seen by us as capable of being carried out by a "straightforward mechanical" (read 'non-mental') device.[7] Natural selection seems to

---

6 Evolution is not usually taken to be a deterministic process, yet algorithmic processes usually are. It might well seem that if algorithmic processes need not be deterministic, then trivially all natural processes are algorithmic. As I construe Dennett here, he takes both their tendency to be adaptive and the naturalness of the traits that result from evolution to be deterministically guaranteed. His explicit stand here is that, indeed, *any* natural process *may be considered as* algorithmic at some level of abstraction, although by no means all natural processes are theoretically illuminated when so considered (cf. Dennett 1995, 57–59).

7 (Dennett 1995, 51). Dennett's other comparison here, to a chef following a recipe, is somewhat unhelpful, if the physical basis of the chef's 'intentional uptake' when reading the recipe is at all part of the datum to be explained. And surely it is.

have both of these features, at least if viewed at the right level of abstraction. Thus, it consists of incremental, mechanically realizable steps such as pre-reproductive death of a particular member of a population, or the appearance of a new phenotype because of the particular crossover of two nucleotides.

Given that natural selection is algorithmic in this sense, the natural character of its products is guaranteed via DBN, provided only that the mechanisms of natural selection *not only could be* but *are* natural (more on this important distinction later), that the initial conditions from which the process commences are also uncontroversially natural, and that there has been no external interference with the process. All of this having been established, all that remains, to show that in particular our capacity for intentional cognition is natural, is to show that it is an adaptive trait.

Now it is here that Dennett is at his most elusive. The problem may be that at *some* level he thinks (if only wistfully) that there is *something* deeply right about behaviourism. But if so, our would-be capacity for intentional cognition cannot *straightforwardly* be an adaptive trait, though our capacity to *attribute* intentional cognitive states can be. Dennett has in fact recommended that we see attributions of intentional states as attributions of 'abstracta' from a certain interpretive perspective that we have been perhaps innately prefigured to find natural to adopt. Abstracta aren't selected for, surely; nor are external interpretations. Dennett therefore allows that something's being interpretable as an intentional system has its 'objective basis' in phenotypical patterns of behaviour it can be observed to exhibit.

> These patterns are objective – they are *there* to be detected – but from our point of view they are not *out there* independent of us, since they are patterns composed partly of our 'subjective' reactions to what is out there, they are the patterns made to order for our narcissistic concerns (Dennett 1989, 39; cf. also Dennett 1995).

We find that human behaviour can be pretty reliably predicted by supposing humans to be agents acting rationally, in accordance with attributed beliefs and desires, where the contents of these beliefs tend to be what they *ought* to be, given presumed human perceptual capacities, epistemic needs, and history, and where the contents of human desires also tend to be what *they* ought to be, given presumed human biological needs and the most practicable means of satisfying them (a close paraphrase of Dennett 1989, 49). So, to be characterized as an intentional system is to be characterized as satisfying certain *normative, optimizing* conditions, and thereby as being *successful,* or *well-adapted* in a particular way, all this from the point of view of the ascriber. The beliefs and desires are not being posited as *underlying causal structures,* to be sought out empirically at a 'sub-personal' level of characterization (cf. Dennett 1989, 52–57). Intentional attribution, being normative and narcissistic, does not admit of such micro-reductive legitimation. It is legitimized simply by its predictive utility. Being an intentional system, then, is simply being a system reliably so characterizable. What is ascribed in belief and desire ascriptions is thus *fully given* by an elaboration of something not far from the spirit of our folk-psychological functional characterizations of the would-be roles of these beliefs and desires in a rational agent's cognitive economy.

Not that this is a matter of anything so heavy-handed as linguistic convention or stipulation, as so-called 'analytic functionalists' claim. First, Dennett has never shown any enthusiasm for analyticity, while showing considerable sympathy for Quinian indeterminacy of interpretation. In any case, second, he parts company with the analytic functionalist's goal of justifying our intentional ascriptions by finding underlying mechanisms that are the realizers of these would-be analytically stipulated functional roles. Instead of explanation by micro-reduction, Dennett offers (what we might think of as) explanation *by elaboration.* One can explain a functionally characterized system or process in terms of a more detailed but still functional characterization. What such elaborations reveal is not details of the underlying constitutive nature of our suitability for intentional characterization. Rather, they reveal merely that notwithstanding the narcissistic and normative character of our own intentional ascriptions, characterizing human cognitive processes as intentional reveals *their* algorithmic nature, too.

Clearly, intentional characterizations, if functional, are substrate neutral. Just as clearly they guarantee results: behaviour of a certain sort is guaranteed to be made likely by the appropriateness of a certain intentional characterization together with salient external factors. Third, human cognitive processes are 'mindless.' To the incredulous stare, prompted by bewilderment as to how such intentional cognitive processes could fail to be mental, mindful processes, Dennett responds as follows. First, a gross functional characterization of an intentional system can be progressively refined so as to reveal simpler constituent functional sub-units, and these in turn decompose into still simpler units, until we arrive at the characterization of a series of determinate, functionally basic units. William Lycan (1981) has dubbed this view 'homuncular functionalism,' but of course the idea is that the decompositionally most basic functional constituents are such that there is no temptation to think that they are realized by anything mental. Second, provided an intentional system is ultimately realized by non-mental uncontroversially natural simple constituents that are also functionally organized in a purely natural way, this establishes the general naturalistic credentials of our capacity for intentionality in accordance with Synchronic Baseline Naturalism. Rather than revealing the specific constitutive nature of intentionality, elaboration merely provides a finer-grained functional characterization. To think that something has been left out in such an accounting – the mental – would be to have truck with mysterious ghostly mentality, or intrinsic mental essence, which is precisely what it is the point of this account to exorcise.

Matters of functionally specific and functionally general nature thus settled independently of natural selection, what remains for natural selection to settle? Actually, nothing, Dennett thinks. So he agrees with my deflationary answer to our First Question. But he sees his algorithmic view of natural selection as *deeply reinforcing* his (independently arrived at) algorithmic view of mind. Darwin's Algorithm, mechanically, blindly, and continuously over eons of time, and without the aid of any interventions, took the chaotic primal soup of primitive life and eventually produced us, in all our genotypic and phenotypic and intentionally interpretable glory. Minds – what we interpret as intentional systems, semantic engines, true believers – were selectively produced from non-minds in a purely mindless way.

> There are [thus] two paths to intentionality. The Darwinian path is diachronic, or historical, and concerns the gradual accretion, over billions of years, of the sorts of Design – of functionality and purposiveness – that can support an intentional interpretation of the

activities of organisms.... Before intentionality can be fully *fledged* it must go through its awkward ugly period of featherless pseudo-intentionality. The synchronic path is the path of Artificial Intelligence; in an organism with genuine intentionality – such as yourself – there are, right now, many parts and some of these exhibit a sort of semi-intentionality or mere *as if* intentionality, or pseudo-intentionality – call it what you like – and your own genuine, fully fledged intentionality is in fact the product (with no further miracle ingredients) of the activities of all the semi-minded and mindless bits that make you up... There is a deep affinity between the synchronic and diachronic paths to intentionality.... Not only are you descended from macros; you are composed of them. (Dennett 1995, 205–6)

To summarize, then, an intentional system is simply one that usefully satisfies an intentional characterization. The naturalistic credentials of such a system can be established either diachronically or synchroni-cally. Diachronically, they may be established by showing how the system arose as a result of Darwin's algorithm operating in a natural way on populations of naturally realized 'macros.' Synchronically, something's being appropriately characterizable as a natural intentional system is a capacity resulting from being composed in a natural way of naturally realized 'macros.' And that is as much explanation as intentionality so conceived could want, or admit. We are also curious about the specific natures of the underlying synchronic structures that make intentional ascriptions viable. But whatever they may be falls outside the scope of the theory of intentionality proper. The *specific* nature of human intentionality *per se* is exhausted in terms of its (sufficiently elaborated) abstract functional normative narcissistic characterization. And that something's capacity to be so interpreted is of a generally naturalistically acceptable nature is guaranteed independently of such details.

While Dennett agrees with my answer to our First Question, what he *means*, though, is that, being a product of Darwin's Algorithm under conditions that accord with DBN, the baseline naturalistic status of our capacity for functional, algorithmic, intentionality is guaranteed. And clearly he also thereby *dis*agrees with my answer to our Second Question. Details of our natural selective history are irrelevant to understanding the specific nature of our capacity, for the reason that that specific nature is simply to be reliably characterizable in that intentional way, independently both of how our specific physical or biologically selected traits may contribute to this, and of how this came about.

III. Fodor

Fodor takes it that our pre-theoretical, functional characterizations of intentional states are meant neither as exhaustively stipulative of their essence nor simply as the precursors of more detailed functional elaboration. Rather they are meant simply to identify and individuate them in a provisionally useful way. Their essence is, at least in part, initially, hidden from us, and is a matter for empirical discovery. What must be discovered are the underlying neuropsychological and psycho-social-environmental causal structures and processes that implement and make true our intentional characterizations. It is in ascertaining these that the general as well as the specific ontological nature of intentionality will be clarified. This 'implementation-inclusive' functionalism, as we might call it, is held by Fodor in conjunction with what we might also call his 'source-law inclusive' construal of natural selection (explained below). It will readily be seen why Fodor thinks that source-law-inclusive natural selection has so little to offer our understanding of the nature of implementation-inclusive functional intentionality.

The most important thing we know about minds, according to Fodor (1994, 121n11), is that often their states are conscious, including their intentional states. This underlines their status as *concreta*: as part of, indeed causally contributing to, the spatio-temporal causal manifold. But although the fact of consciousness is the most important thing we know, for Fodor, it is also the aspect of mind about which he has the least to say. He once quipped that you shouldn't try to eff the ineffable (Fodor 1981, 18). He has lots to say, however, about what he takes to be the second most important thing we know about minds, namely that thought processes involving intentional states tend to be truth preserving, a feature that contributes in an essential way, e.g., to the over-all reliability of our beliefs – their tendency to be true (Fodor 1994, 8–9).

Cognitive psychology, the empirical theory that attempts systematically to explain the (objective) patterns discernible in human behaviour,
is taken by Fodor to be ineliminably committed to explanations that
appeal to intentional laws. A folksy example of an intentional law is: if
S strongly wants to do *A*, and believes that she can best do *A* by doing
B, and is able to do *B*, then, *ceteris paribus*, *S* will do *B*. For instance, if
Sheila strongly wants to support the Liberal Party and believes that
she can best do so by donating money to it, then, *ceteris paribus*,
she will donate money to it. Sheila's donation can be explained *via*
this law, in part by appeal to her belief, whose content is attributed
to be: that her supporting the Liberal Party is best done by her
donating money.

But to be properly scientific, intentional explanations must include
an account of the specific constitutive nature of intentional contents.
It won't do simply to note that behavioural predictions based on such
laws have a good track record. Maybe their luck is about to run out.
Nor will it do to appeal to our interpretive proclivities. That's just too
Leibnizian, and besides in this context it is circular. It is as though Fodor
sees the disanalogy between Dennett interpreting what he observes to
be an intentional system – a 'true believer,' and Leibniz interpreting
what he observes to be a physical object – a 'real phenomenon.'
Leibniz, a sophisticated idealist, thought that what we observe in
the world is both 'real' – when it results from aggregations of real
monads – and a 'phenomenon,' because both the way the monads
were aggregated and their resulting appearance is contributed by
the mind of the observer.[8] This was all very well for Leibniz, an
unabashed idealist who took minds – willing, perceiving substances –
as ontologically fundamental. Leibniz also had a way of explaining the
fidelity or reliability of such perceptions, in terms of the optimization
required in any world that God would create. But Dennett is an
Unabashed Basher of appeals to Unmoved Movers, Unmeant Meaners,
and Undesigned Designers. So questions internal to his position
arise here, which Fodor can press, first, about what sanctions *his*
appeal to apparently mental acts of interpretation, in his account of

---

8 Cf., e.g., Leibniz's letter to Arnauld of 1687, letter to de Volder of 1704, and letter
to Des Bosses of 1716, collected in Leibniz (1989, 80, 82, 179–181, 202–5).

intentionality; and second, what it is about such interpretive acts that could explain their reliability.

One can imagine the following response: natural selection is what explains *both* the emergence of organisms interpretable as intentional systems *and* the emergence of organisms capable of making such interpretations. We interpreters are among the systems appropriately interpreted as intentional. Among the very synchronic mechanisms that make our being thus interpreted appropriate, are the mechanisms that underpin our own interpretive abilities.

But is this coherent? Surely our capacity to ascribe intentional *abstracta* to other systems cannot *itself* be a mere *abstractum*. And surely our capacity to ascribe intentional states to ourselves picks out states whose intentionality is 'original,' not derived in the sense of owing their content to some *other* intentional agent's interpretive overlay. The point isn't that one's belief, or even one's capacity for belief, has no etiology. Most everything does, and in *that* sense is 'derived.' The point is rather that what *needs* causal explanation is *that we really do have such beliefs.*[9] The would-be intentional states of a desktop computer, by contrast, *are* derivative, that is, dependent for their very existence *qua* intentional states on some programmer's or user's interpretive overlay, and on the computer itself having been designed by us to accommodate such interpretation. So far as one takes seriously an explanation of intentionality from natural selection, it *is* an explanation of original intentionality. After all, a mindless algorithm is said to have generated from mindless macros what fully deserves to be characterized as an intentional system. Since there were no mind-like interventions, therefore, in the relevant sense, the intentionality generated is original.

Dennett is waiting with the retort that it is derived after all, because Mother Nature designed and interpreted it. Fodor inveighs strongly against this appeal (Fodor 1996, 257–61). That is: we do not, nor is it appropriate to adopt, an intentional stance towards the process of natural selection, and that for Dennett to do so at *this* juncture, he suspects, is deeply circular. No amount of Darwinian bootstrapping

---

9 And we really do have them, even if their contents are, as Dennett thinks, subject to Quinian indeterminacy.

could justify or even make coherent the line that our intentionality is essentially interpretive (i.e., derivative) because it is a product of natural selection, itself a derivatively interpretive process, by the lights of our *interpretive* stance towards it! The derivative intentionality of the desktop computer is *genuinely* explained by our *original* intentionality. If our intentionality is derivative, then it is *not* explained by an appeal to the derivative intentionality of natural selection/Mother Nature, derivative on our interpretive stance towards it.

What empirical science aspires to provide, then, according to Fodor – certainly for any non-basic science like psychology – is an understanding of why that predictive track record is and will continue to be good, in terms of underlying structures and mechanisms. Such an explanation will be synchronic and, at least token-wise, micro-reductive. If intentional laws are not to be relegated to the status of mere pragmatic conveniences, then the intentional contents to which they appeal must in turn be legitimated by identifying the implementing mechanisms that 'fix' and sustain them.

> An implementing mechanism is one in virtue of whose operation the satisfaction of a [universal conditional] law's antecedent reliably brings about the satisfaction of its consequent (Fodor 1994, 8).

Characterizing these implementing mechanisms has been Fodor's chief concern. What he currently proposes is as follows. The content of a thought (typically) depends on external informational relations to its (typically) extra-mental subject matter. The reliability of thought processes depends on their being computational. Computational processes have regard only for syntax: they are syntactically driven manipulations of syntactically structured objects. Since content is external-relational, the implementing mechanisms of content will be partly external and partly internal (i.e., 'between the ears,' not necessarily 'subjective'). The internal component will include all the symbol crunching.

A vexing question is whether that is *all* that it includes. Fodor has always been predisposed to think that it isn't (cf., e.g., Fodor 1991). After all, consciousness is presumably internal, and some intentional states are conscious in a way that includes consciousness of their (apparent) content. Nevertheless, of late, Fodor has been actively exploring the possibility that the internal component is all and only the syntax, that the rest is all external-relational.

For computational states to have content and computational operations to be semantically reliable, they must track the informational relations that constitute their intentional contents. There must be an harmonious lawful concomitance between our mental syntax and our mental semantics. Our world and those nomologically nearby must not allow for too much systematic syntactic indiscriminability between semantic differences, or too much systematic semantic indiscriminability of syntactic differences (Fodor 1994, chap. 2). Fodor does not want Leibniz's theology any more than Dennett does, of course, but he *does* want Leibniz's mental/physical harmony, which he postulates as a brute harmony, as a brute metaphysical contingency and nomological necessity. It is just lucky for us, given that we are 'intrinsically' mere syntactic engines, that we find ourselves in such a co-operative world (cf. Fodor 1994, esp. 52–54).

This is problematic, though. It amounts to the claim that the laws by which mental syntax tracks mental semantics have something like the same metaphysically basic status as the laws of physics. Yet surely we think that once all of the microphysical facts of our world have been established – the quantities, types and spatio-temporal distributions of all the basic forces and particles – pretty much everything else is thereby established, too. It couldn't be that all these microphysical facts and all the facts of mental syntax were fixed, but the facts of mental semantics were not.[10] But then surely the tracking of mental semantics by mental syntax is not brute, but derivative, and so there must be some account of it.[11]

Can evolutionary considerations help us here? Consider the following passage from Elliott Sober's classic, *The Nature of Selection*.

---

10 This is so whether or not the facts of mental semantics are taken to include 'etiological' ones. Cf., e.g., Dretske (1988).

11 This argument is a particular application of a more general version sketched by Michael Tye (1994, 133).

> Evolutionary theory aims not only to describe the patterns that may be found in the history of life on Earth but also to characterize the processes that produced them. Its strategy for identifying the actual causes that have shaped the tree of life is the usual scientific one: scientists try to characterize a range of possible causes of evolution, and then to determine which of these possibilities actually obtained....... Natural selection is one kind of cause.... Evolutionary theory describes selection, not just in terms of its consequences, but in terms of the ecological conditions that can produce it. (Sober 1985, 13–15)

Following Sober, an account of natural selection embodies two sorts of laws. *Consequence laws* identify what consequences follow from the presence or absence of certain conditions. Darwin's Algorithm is a consequence law: it explains the environmental adaptiveness of an organism's phenotypic characteristics as a biasing effect of their having been inherited and selectively advantageous to the organism's ancestors, relative to phenotypic variants that were present in the population at the time. Besides consequence laws there will also be *source laws* that characterize the implementing mechanisms of phenotypic variance and heritability.

> *Whenever a model describes phenotypic characteristics in terms of their relative advantageousness, and then reaches a conclusion about the evolution of those characteristics, there is a genetic presupposition that is needed to underwrite the inference.* (Sober 1985, 42, emphasis his)

Sober notes that we are so confident of this now that we just characterize evolution in genetic terms: a population has evolved just in case its gene frequencies have changed (Sober 1985, 36).

If evolution is characterized in terms of changes of gene frequencies in a population, but Darwinian fitness is a function of morphological, behavioural, and other phenotypic characteristics of members of the population, what ensures that these two types of characteristics properly track each other? More Leibnizian harmony, more brute metaphysical contingency and nomological necessity? Selection theorists propose to go Leibniz one better, by appealing to causal laws and implementing mechanisms linking the two: laws of developmental genetics, linking genotypes to phenotypes, and what we might call 'laws of the jungle,' linking phenotypic variation to relative reproductive success in an environment, and thus to genotypic heritability, and so on (cf. Sober 1985, 36ff.). Note the obvious parallel with Fodor's theory of intentionality (see below).

Now Fodor would surely allow that *if* the mechanisms that implement our capacity for intentional cognition are an adaptation by the lights of *source-law-inclusive natural selection*, then our capacity is baseline natural. After all, the source laws are not needed to establish DBN, nor implied to exist by it. But Fodor is interested in whether or not our capacity can be established as natural in a way that takes proper account of the status of intentional psychology as a special science, and of the presumptive need for non-basic special science laws to be implemented by structurally 'lower level' mechanisms, ultimately by micro-physical mechanisms (cf. esp. Fodor 1995, 294).

Michael Tye has argued for the naturalism, in this sense, of intentional states roughly as follows. Intentional mental states are natural phenomena, because intentional aspects of such states figure in causal transactions that fall under special science laws. But special science laws project properties that are ultimately realized by microphysical properties. So, for any such special-science-projected property, P, there are 'upward directed bridge laws,' the antecedents of which respectively specify some microphysical property and the consequent of which projects the property P. For the reasons previously articulated, such bridge laws must, like the laws of the special science, be regarded as derivative, as implemented by microphysical mechanisms (Tye 1994, 132–36). This suggests the following *sufficient* condition, which we will dub 'Supervenience Naturalism.'

> Any phenomenon is natural, provided it is explainable by the laws of a special science, given that special science laws project only properties that are ultimately realized microphysically, and realized in a way that is itself microphysically determined. (**Supervenience Naturalism, 'SN'**)

We dub it thus because the notion of microphysical determination is naturally interpreted as involving what Jaegwon Kim has called 'strong supervenience,' roughly that given the microphysical structures and processes, the realized phenomenon in question had to occur (cf. Kim 1990).

What are the relations between Supervenience Naturalism, on the one hand, and Synchronic and Diachronic Baseline Naturalism, on the other? First, the latter do not imply the former. There are no *a priori* guarantees that a phenomenon that is natural according to either SBN or DBN will also be natural according to SN. What these latter doctrines leave undecided, by not insisting upon it, is microphysical determination. What about the converse; i.e., do SBN or DBN imply SN? There are two cases to consider. If a phenomenon is *synchronically microphysically realized, à la* SN, in a way that is itself microphysically determined, then, provided only that we can agree that the microphysical facts are natural, our phenomenon is bound to be a structurally complex one, whose simplest functional units are natural, whose mechanisms of functional cohesion are natural, and which results solely from the operation of these mechanisms on its functional units. That is, if a phenomenon is synchronically Superveniently Natural, then it is also Synchronically Baseline Natural.

But what if the special science in question has a *diachronic* subject matter, dealing not with issues of synchronic microphysical realization, but with issues of how a phenomenon diachronically came about? In particular, what if the special science concerns the origin of species here on Earth? If selectionist explanations of adaptive traits were shown to be Superveniently Naturalistic, then for reasons analogous to those just given for the synchronic case, it would follow that they were also Diachronically Baseline Natural. Any *diachronic properties* projected by selectionist theory – e.g., the property of a trait's having been selected for – would have to be at the same time microphysically realized by correspondingly diachronic implementation mechanisms of selection.

So Fodor wants to establish that intentional states are Superveniently Natural, and no doubt realizes that this does not follow from either DBN or SBN taken singly or in conjunction. How, then, would Fodor answer our Second Question? Given the rather disparate sorts of implementation mechanisms postulated by the theory of intentionality on the one hand and the theory of natural selection on the other, he would see *no prospect at all* for any kind of account (reductive or otherwise) of the *specific, constitutive* nature of the former in terms of the latter. On the one hand, the implementing mechanisms of natural selection are diachronic mechanisms that produce genotypic, and hence phenotypic, variability in a population, mechanisms that sustain heritability of traits, and that regulate selection of traits by an environment in a population. On the other hand, the implementing mechanisms of human intentionality are synchronic mechanisms that sustain the human brain as a cohesive syntactic engine, that enable its syntactic states and processes to reliably track informational relations they bear to the environment. They are synchronic mechanisms of cohesion, persistence, and representational fidelity. What could be more different? Fodor presses the point:

> No doubt, if there is something in situ that coordinates the intentional properties of mental states with their computational properties, then some Darwinian process must have selected it, and its having been selected explains why there is now so much of it around. But the question before us is *what the mechanism that effects this correlation is,* and evolutionary explanations *aren't of the right form* to answer that kind of question. Evolution maybe explains why there are more things around that work than there are things around that don't. But it doesn't explain *how* things work, and it is decisively a 'how' question that we're faced with. (Fodor 1994, 20)

The fact that intentionality came into existence historically because of a natural selective process that is Superveniently Naturalistic goes no way towards showing that intentionality *per se* supervenes synchronically on a natural substrate. But it is the latter that Fodor thinks needs to be established and identified by an adequate naturalistic theory of intentionality.[12] Perhaps evolutionary theory shows how it is possible that the connection between mental syntax and mental semantics came about. What it could not show is that given roughly

---

12 This is related to a more general point made by Sober (1999). Sober gives probabilistic formulations of the doctrine of the supervenience of the mental on the physical and of the causal completeness of physics, from which it is readily seen that the latter even in conjunction with causal determinism does not entail the former. Sober is rather less sanguine, less committal, than Fodor about the supervenience thesis.

the way we are internally, and the way the environment is and the laws governing it, it follows as a matter of law projecting upwards from physical, chemical, and neurophysiological realizations, that the semantic relations between elements of our mental syntax and elements of the environment are fixed. To Fodor, the past seems irrelevant for showing this.

So, like Dennett, Fodor disagrees with my answer to our Second Question, but for a different reason. Dennett's reason, recall, was that intentionality is simply (being usefully interpretable as having) a certain kind of algorithmic functionality. Fodor's reason, in the above quotation, is apparently that evolutionary explanations simply appeal in a general way to Darwin's Algorithm and its implementing mechanisms; they do not, for instance, include special explanatory reconstructions of actual sequential bits of our natural selective history that might yield insights into the specific constitutive nature of our intentional capacities. *But why shouldn't they?*

IV. Conclusions: What Matters

A. The Relevance of Natural Selection.... Fodor's dismissal of natural selection as largely irrelevant to his project is just perplexingly hard to fathom. After all, he ought to be very much in the market for mechanisms to sustain his harmonious concomitance of mental syntax and mental semantics, mechanisms that will at least defer the need to appeal to brute necessities or contingencies. Consider this remarkable summaric statement.

> The picture I'm painting is sort of Leibnizian: Qua P-believers, we are all monads (only with our windows open) mirroring the fact that P. 'Mirroring the fact that P' is something like: being in states that are caused by, and hence bear information about, the fact that P. These information-bearing states are syntactically structured, and their syntax drives our behavior, just as Turing said. It's a fact about the world that the causal properties of our minds are pretty similar, and that the causal chains that connect our minds to the fact that P aren't *arbitrarily* various. In consequence, the syntax of the mental representations which have the fact that P in their causal histories tends to overlap in

ways that support robust behavioral similarities among *P*-believers. The world thus sustains a harmony between the (extrinsic/historical) properties in virtue of which a Mentalese sentence is a mode of presentation of the *proposition* that *P* and the (intrinsic/syntactic) properties in virtue of which a Mentalese sentence is reliably a cause of the sorts of behavioral proclivities that the laws of psychology say that *P*-believers share. ... computational-syntactic processes can implement broad-intentional ones because the world, and all other worlds that are nomologically nearby, arranges things so that *the syntactic structure of a mode of presentation reliably carries information about its causal history.* Just as the cops so arrange things that dollar-lookingness reliably carries information about dollarhood. (Fodor 1994, 53–54)

So, the 'Long Arm of the Law' makes sure that mental syntax behaves the way it ought to.

But this *isn't* just a fact about the world order. The world got to be that way, whereas before, it wasn't. Our natural selective history explains how. And we want to know how, how it got to be that way, and how it is sustained. We do not want to settle for the bare necessity of nomological concomitance. What matters to us are the specific contingencies that ground those nomological necessities.[13] Now surely these mechanisms will include those that implement our capacity for symbolic reference. As intimated at the outset, a plausible strategy for getting an empirical fix on these mechanisms is to try to correlate the behavioural manifestations of our distinctive kinds of referential

---

13 So it would be a mistake to try to interpret the dispute between Dennett and Fodor simply as their failure to recognize a distinction between 'proximate' and 'ultimate' explanation. This is a distinction recognized in biology, roughly corresponding to the distinction between the concerns of the 'functional' biologist and those of the 'evolutionary' biologist. It is not simply that Dennett seeks an ultimate explanation of intentionality and Fodor a proximate one in this sense. Rather, Fodor thinks that evolutionary explanations have little to offer the theory of intentionality, while Dennett thinks that, although there are both types of explanation, the proximal ones are merely functional and do not concern constitutive natures. However, Ernst Mayr, a biologist who has emphasized the distinction, gives as his example of proximate causes of bird migration the *physiological condition* of the bird interacting with photoperiodicity and a drop in temperature (Mayr 1961, 1503).

capabilities with special features of our brain structure and function not present in the brains of our primate evolutionary precursors, and then to look for a plausible natural selective story to explain the transition from their brain structures and functions to ours. Even if intentional content is 'wide' or external-relational, and even if there is nothing narrow – between the ears – that deserves to be called 'narrow content,' there may nevertheless be naturally selected, narrow, dedicated brain structures that subserve the well-behaved tracking of wide intentional, symbolic, referential content by narrow mental syntax. Terrence Deacon's recent theory of the co-evolution of language and brain, and the rich and plausible story he tells about symbolic reference, at least suggestively illustrate the principle.[14]

Deacon weaves an elaborate, empirically well-anchored 'just so' story about how our brain structures could have been selected for their ability to engage in and take advantage of symbolic reference, where this is sharply distinguished from mere 'indexical' or 'iconic' referential uses of words. The symbolic referential use of words involves their being embedded in particular ways in combinatorial systems of language. Symbolic reference is indirect reference mediated by these word–word relations. While developmentally we may begin by learning direct symbol-to-object correlations, these associations, once learned, are treated by us as mere clues to the more crucial word–word associations involved in the linguistic systematicity of symbolic reference.[15] This learning problem should not be seen as one that can be addressed in some gradual or incremental way, but as involving a discontinuous 'restructuring,' or 'recoding,' or 'a radical change in cognitive strategy' (Deacon 1997, 67). Previously learned associations are suddenly seen in a new light as part of an implicit 'higher order' pattern. Now something about human brains makes this easier for humans than for chimps. From a natural selection perspective we need to see how the usual "mnemonic and intentional threshold that tends to prevent sets of rote

---

14 Deacon (1997). For a good general introduction to the method of phylogenetic comparison and its application to our understanding of the evolution of language, see Hauser (1996). For an instructive application of this method to primate brain size see Milton (1993).

15 This is a close paraphrase of Deacon, 83.

indexical associations from becoming recoded into symbolic systems of association" (Deacon 1997, 334–35) could have been overcome. Deacon details how this bias could have come about.[16]

Why wouldn't Fodor wish to avail himself of this avenue of inquiry? There is one glaringly bad *a priori* argument that he has floated more than once as revealing of the explanatory limits of natural selection. Whereas we, as intentional agents, can discriminate nomologically equivalent properties, because, roughly, we give them different representations, natural selection cannot. For instance, Jerry has argued that:

> ... if '*F* iff *G*' is a law, then for every explanation according to which trait *T* is selected for because it causes *F*, there will be a corresponding, equally complete, equally warranted, explanation according to which *T* is selected for because it causes *G*. (Fodor 1996, 255)

This is related to what Frances Egan has called 'the conjunction problem.' The occurrences of internal tokens of a given symbolic type, if correlated with the presence of instances of some type of external object that they are taken to represent, are, at the same time, bound to be correlated with instances of every (nomologically, or whatever) necessarily coextensive type, and thus with their conjunction. So how can any natural relation underpinning such representation pick out the intended referent from among these?[17]

---

16 Cf. Deacon (1997, esp. chaps. 3, 11–14). The idea of 'Baldwinian' selection figures prominently in Deacon's just so story. Baldwinian selection is a Darwinian process named after the American psychologist, James Baldwin, who first articulated it a century ago. An organism with sufficient capacity for learning and behavioural flexibility, by adjusting its behaviours or physiological responses to novel conditions, can produce irreversible changes in the adaptive context of future generations. (The preceding sentence is a close paraphrase of Deacon 1997, 322–23.) Deacon's proposal is very roughly that the pre-frontalization of the hominoid brain co-evolved with language, that, e.g., critical and strategic survival functions associated with an evolving learned *and passed on* repertoire of signals (alarm calls, mating calls, calls to members of one's foraging group, etc.) created a Baldwinian selection pressure that biased the pre-frontalization. For details and further references, see Deacon.

17 Egan (unpubl. ms., 24). Dennett (1996, 265 ff.) is also rightly suspicious of this argument.

Dennett's interpretationism avoids the problem, of course.[18] Suppose a theorist is interested in explaining the behaviour of subjects in relation to medium-sized objects *per se*, not their temporal stages or undetached parts. Whereas neither causation nor asymmetrical dependence nor natural selection selects among such necessarily co-instantiated natural properties, a theorist's interpretive interests can, precisely because those explanatory interests are intensional. The trouble with interpretationism, though, as was argued above, is that its baseline naturalistic status is moot.

Take the nomologically necessarily coextensive properties of generating an electric field and generating a magnetic field (at right angles). Or take even the metaphysically necessarily coextensive properties of triangularity and trilaterality for closed plane figures. We can certainly process the members of each of these pairs differently. Electric and magnetic fields, besides being discriminable because of their differing spatial orientations, will have different effects, and discriminatory capacities can be keyed to these different effects. In the geometric case, if tokens of an internal symbol are regularly occasioned by the presence of a triangle *via* a 'side detector,' and a counter registering '3,' while tokens of another internal symbol are regularly occasioned by the presence of a triangle *via* an 'angle detector' and a counter registering '3,' that *prima facie* suggests that the first symbol represents the property of trilaterality, the second triangularity (cf. Sober 1982). Note that for each pair, the difference between causal relations connecting each respective symbol to its referent *includes a difference in their internal, narrow segments.*

So, while Fodor might be right to doubt the idea of a source-theoretic natural selective explanation of the specific nature of implementation-theoretic human intentionality, he needs to take more seriously the possibility of exploiting the explanatory framework of natural selection to locate the explanatory mechanisms his theory needs. The right implementational story about the nomological concomitance of mental syntax and semantics will not be arbitrary relative to natural selective origins. The constraints of natural selection on the specific nature of intentionality as construed by Fodor are therefore liable not to be negligible.

---

18 I didn't always think so, but Wm. Seager kindly set me straight.

B. ... and its Irrelevance. My favourite Turing Machine is one described by Boolos and Jeffrey, in which the tape is a railroad track, the ties mark the boundaries of the squares and work crews are stationed at both ends to add more line as needed. The symbols are written between the ties. On the line is a very short boxcar, about one tape square in length, and capable of moving along the track in either direction. Installed in the black box car is a man who cannot be seen from the outside, who does all of the scanning and writing and erasing. The boxcar has no bottom: the poor mug just walks along between the ties, pulling the car with him. The man (who is said to resemble John Searle) has a list of instructions written down on a piece of paper. He is in machine state qi when he is carrying out instruction number i, and so on (Boolos and Jeffrey 1974, 20–22). Note, this is not a literally mindless automaton – though it just might as well be, for all it's doing – for the explanation of how this particular 'black box' car works will need to invoke the mechanisms of mind. Algorithms, *per se*, are substrate neutral, and their being 'mindless' in Dennett's technical sense just means that they *could* be carried out by a purely physical, mechanical machine, not that they in fact *are* being so carried out (cf. note 7, above).

Dennett, recall, thinks that the capacities that make humans appropriately characterizable as algorithmic intentional systems have themselves been algorithmically and thus mindlessly generated, by incremental steps, from primitive mindless macros. If we add, then, to the assumption that our cognitive capacities are algorithmic just that they were also algorithmically generated, does that constrain their specific nature any further? Obviously not, given what has just been said. But, in order to drive the point home, and because it is fun, consider Dennett's own example of tempered steel. The presence of that trait can be explained by the steel's having undergone a process of annealing. But this process, he tells us, is 'algorithmic,' and so can and should be described in substrate neutral language. Thus, "we should expect optimization of a certain sort [e.g., strength] to occur in any 'material' [e.g., steel] that has components [e.g., molecules] that get put together by a sort of building process [e.g., crystallization] that can be disassembled in a sequenced way by changing a single global parameter [e.g., heat]" (Dennett 1995, 58; parenthetical inserts mine). As Dennett notes, the explanation of the presence of the strength is in this way lifted clear of the physical details. Indeed, the details do not need to be physical. For all the algorithm says, the heating of the steel induces little massless homunculi in the vicinity of the disassembled atoms, previously asleep, to wake up and simulate the molecular bonding of the non-disassembled molecules with their mighty (though massless) suction-cupped appendages.

This latter fairy tale points to *a reason*, unacknowledged by Dennett, why we in fact do *not* rest content just with determining the algorithmic character of the process of annealing but want to know the physical details of the process, the specific field-theoretic characteristics of the disassembly and rebinding that is induced: what matters to us is not simply how things generally *could* be, but also how they specifically *are*.

Back to the main line. Suppose we are *also* given that the realizing mechanisms of the producing algorithms are natural *and* that the algorithm starts out acting on a domain of uncontroversially natural entities. Then DBN tells us that our capacity is natural. It doesn't follow from this that we are literally mindless, nor does anything specific about our capacity, anything useful that would help us decide between Dennett's ontologically deflationary proclivities and Fodor's robust realism.

The crux here is that there appears to be a variety of relationships that macrostates and their associated features may have to the underlying microconditions that generate and sustain them, and these relationships are not on a par ontologically. The remarkable causal powers and robustness of specific sorts of macrofeatures may originate in and be explained by the particular sort of relation they bear to their microconditions. Interesting macrophenomena may 'average over' microphenomena in a way that 'compresses' microphenomenal information. Or they may have their source in a kind of nonlinear, chaotic dynamic at the microlevel (cf. Bedau 1997, esp. 375–79). Or, they may result not simply from mereological aggregation or functional structure but from causal interactions (binding exchanges of energy) among microelements (cf. Searle 1992, 111–12). Given that there are macrophysical threshold effects, such as changes of phase state and superconductivity, the possibility of specifically psychological threshold effects cannot be ruled out *a priori*.

Dennett does not like ontological surprises, even mild ones. He doesn't want discontinuities to appear in the natural selective process. But no mere appeal to Darwin's Algorithm and its naturalistic implementing mechanisms can rule out the possible empirical relevance of chaotic factors, causal emergence, and threshold effects, controversial though these may be, to our understanding of intentionality and other mental phenomena.[19] The naturalism that Dennett embraces, as well as the other naturalisms we have considered, do not rule these out.[20] Dennett believes that the 'essence' of intentionality – its specific nature – is exhaustively functional, algorithmic. But he cannot want this to be true by analytic stipulation. And if not, then he must stay open to the possible empirical corrective of whatever the contingencies of our recent natural selective history may reveal. In these respects, then, I submit that Dennett has overestimated the relevance of Darwin's Algorithm to his specific conception of intentionality, and underestimated the potential relevance of our natural selective history to its empirical evaluation.[21]

---

19 Indeed the case has been argued that chaotic factors are integral to natural selection itself, but that is another story. Cf., e.g., Kaufmann (1993).

20 Nor are these possibilities plausibly construed as 'skyhooks' – Dennett's word for question-begging mind-dependent explanatory assumptions like Cartesian dualism or the Judeo-Christian God.

21 I am very grateful to the following people for their penetrating and helpful comments on earlier drafts of this paper: David Braddon-Mitchell, William Seager, and Elliott Sober, and especially Jill McIntosh. Their comments led to a number of clarifications and corrections, only a few of which have been explicitly identified and acknowledged. Alas, they may still find fault.

References

Bedau, Mark A. 1997. "Weak Emergence," *Philosophical Perspectives* **11**, 375–99.

Boolos, George, and Richard Jeffrey. 1974. *Computability and Logic*. New York: Cambridge University Press.

Deacon, Terrence W. 1997. *The Symbolic Species*. New York: W.W. Norton & Co.

Dennett, Daniel C. 1989. *The Intentional Stance*. Cambridge, MA: Bradford Books/MIT Press.

———. 1991. "Real Patterns," *Journal of Philosophy* **88**, 27–51.

———. 1995. *Darwin's Dangerous Idea*. New York: Touchstone/Simon and Schuster.

———. 1996. "Granny versus Mother Nature – No Contest," *Mind and Language* **11**, 263–69.

Dretske, Fred. 1988. *Explaining Behavior*. Cambridge, MA: Bradford Books/MIT Press.

Egan, Frances (unpubl. ms.). "A Pragmatic Theory of Content."

Fodor, Jerry. 1981. "Something on the State of the Art," Introduction to *Representations*. Cambridge, MA: MIT Press.

———. 1991. "A Modal Argument for Narrow Content," *Journal of Philosophy* **88**, 5–27.

———. 1994. *The Elm and the Expert*. Cambridge, MA: Bradford Books/MIT Press.

———. 1995. "Fodor, Jerry A." In *A Companion to the Philosophy of Mind*, Samuel Guttenplan, ed. Oxford: Blackwell, pp. 292–300.

———. 1996. "Deconstructing Dennett's Darwin," *Mind and Language* **11**, 246–62.

Hauser, Marc D. *The Evolution of Communication*. Cambridge, MA: Bradford Books/MIT Press.

Kim, Jaegwon. 1990. "Supervenience as a Philosophical Concept," *Metaphilosophy* **21**, 1–27.

Kaufmann, Stuart. 1993. *The Origins of Order: Self-Organization and Selection in Evolution*. New York: Oxford University Press.

Leibniz, G. W. 1989. *Philosophical Essays*. trans. R. Ariew and D. Garber Indianapolis: Hackett.

Lycan, Wm. 1981. "Form, Function and Feel," *Journal of Philosophy* **88**, 24–49.

Mayr, Ernst. 1961. "Cause and Effect in Biology," *Science* **134** Oct.-Dec.

Milton, Katharine. 1993. "Diet and Primate Evolution," *Scientific American* August, 86–93.

Searle, John. 1992. *The Rediscovery of the Mind.* Cambridge, MA: Bradford Books / MIT Press.

Sober, Elliott. 1982. "Why Logically Equivalent Predicates May Pick out Different Properties," *American Philosophical Quarterly* **19**, April.

———. 1985. *The Nature of Selection.* Cambridge, MA: Bradford Books / MIT Press.

———. 1999. "Physicalism from a Probabilistic Point of View," *Philosophical Studies* **95**, 135–74.

Tye, Michael. 1994. "Naturalism and the Problem of Intentionality," *Midwest Studies in Philosophy* **19**, 122–42.

CANADIAN JOURNAL OF PHILOSOPHY
Supplementary Volume 27

Adapted Minds

LARRY SHAPIRO

Introduction

Minds are obscure things. This is especially obvious and especially onerous to those interested in understanding the mind. One way to begin an investigation of mind, given its abstruseness, is to explore the implications of something we believe must be true of minds. This is the approach I take in this paper. Whatever uncertainties we have about the mind, it's a safe bet that the mind is an adaptation. So, I begin with this truth about minds: minds are the product of evolution by natural selection. In what follows, I trace some of the consequences of this fact. Doing so will take us some distance toward answering a variety of questions about the mind.

In exploring the consequences of the mind's origin I will speak of the mind generally. While I grant that this adds an element of vagueness to the project at hand, it does not in any way cast doubt on the conclusions I draw. This is so because the inferences I make about minds follow not from any assumptions about the nature of mind but are derived purely from the nature of adaptation. Indeed, this paper is as much an examination of adaptation as it is of mind. Insofar as my goal is to wring implications from the fact of something's being an adaptation, my conclusions about minds generalize to all adaptations. Thus, if one cannot stomach my talk of minds in general, one can replace the term 'mind' with some list of more specific mental capacities like memory, attention, consciousness, perception, etc. As long as one allows that these mental capacities are adaptations, what I say about minds in general will be true for them as well.

Moreover, though to conceive of the mind as an adaptation is to take an evolutionary perspective on the mind, the current exercise differs significantly from the pursuits of evolutionary psychologists. Whereas an evolutionary psychologist begins her study of a particular mental trait with the assumption that it is an adaptation, there's often nothing in the investigations to follow that looks to consequences of this fact other than that the trait has some function. I do not offer this observation as a criticism of evolutionary psychology. For the purposes of evolutionary psychology, a focus on the functional aspect of adaptations may be all that is appropriate. But, there is more to being an adaptation than having a function. My goal in this paper is to use what we know about adaptations in general to justify inferences about mind in particular.

One last note before beginning. Because my conclusions about minds draw their inspiration from what we know about other adaptations, arguments from analogy will play an important role in some of what follows. The main analogy on which I will depend is that of the evolution of eyes. Eyes have long been a focus of evolutionary theory. Early on, biologists including Darwin fretted that the theory of natural selection may lack the power to explain traits as patently complex as the eye. Ironically, biologists today, e.g., Dawkins (1982), invoke the eye's complexity as the best evidence of natural selection's operation. The near certainty that eyes are adaptations justifies the analogy I will occasionally rely on between eyes and minds.

With that said, it is now time to turn to several questions one might raise about minds that have their answers in the fact that the mind is an adaptation. The questions are ordered in roughly an ascending degree of difficulty.

Question One: Are Minds Epiphenomenal?

Assuming that minds are adaptations, this question is very easy to answer. If minds are adaptations, they have been selected for their effects. Minds must do something that has benefited their possessors. According to epiphenomenalism, minds are effects of brain processes but do not themselves cause anything. Obviously, if minds have no effects then they cannot have been selected for their beneficial effects.

Hence, if minds are adaptations then epiphenomenalism about the mind must be false. Moreover, any view of mind that denies to them the power to produce effects conflicts with the hypothesis that the mind is an adaptation. Thus, in addition to giving us reason to reject epiphenomenalism, the assumption that minds are adaptations allows us to reject occasionalism and parallelism. Because both these views of mind deny any real interaction between mind and body and thus any interaction between mind and environment, they cannot be true if minds are adaptations.

Question Two: Do Nonhuman Animals Have Minds?

Granting that human beings have minds, what does the fact that minds are adaptations tell us about the likelihood that nonhuman animals have minds? Consider the two competing hypotheses:

O: Minds belong only to *Homo sapiens*.
C: Minds are common to *Homo sapiens* and other taxa.

Hypothesis O would be true if the mind were an autapomorphic character, i.e., a trait derived after the speciation event that separated us from our sister groups. Certainly human beings do exhibit autapomorphic traits. Distinguishing us from the other members of the superfamily *Hominoidea* are our cranial capacity, our sparse body hair, our upright posture, etc. Each of these traits derived in the time since the separation of our lineage from gorillas, chimpanzees, orangutans, and gibbons. Humans diverged from chimpanzees, our nearest sister group, about five million years ago (Futuyma 1998). If the mind is an autapomorphic character, i.e., one that arose after humans diverged from their sister groups, it must have evolved in this period of time. Whether this is possible depends on how quickly evolution occurs. If it is credible that the transition from non-mind to mind is a short step – that the brain structures of the ancestral hominoid from which humans are descended were, so to speak, *poised* to think – then O might seem reasonable.

On the other hand, if the evolution of minds required more than five million years, then we should expect mind to be a pleisomorphic character, i.e., one belonging to an ancestral species from which at least some non-human members of the *Hominoidea* superfamily evolved (e.g., perhaps the ancestor from which gorillas, chimps, and humans descended, but not gibbons). Hypothesis *C* then becomes more likely, for now *O* could be true only if our sister groups lost their minds. Such an occurrence requires at least one but possibly many more evolutionary reversals. Parsimony then favours hypothesis *C*.

But how can we evaluate whether five million years is sufficient time to derive a mind? Perhaps the suggestion that the mind is an autapomorphic character is not so incredible as it may first appear. After all, human beings clearly have evolved a language far more complex than any language primatologists have identified in nonhuman apes. Perhaps some rudiments of language are sympleisomorphic, i.e., ancestral and so common to some or all members of *Hominoidea*, but there's no denying that the great sophistication of human language has largely been derived since *Homo* diverged from *Pan*. Moreover, though the complexity of the eye leads us to expect that its evolution must have required great spans of time, Nilsson and Pelger (1994), using very conservative assumptions about selection pressure, heritability, and variability, estimate that a very good fish eye could evolve from a flat layer of photocells in 364,000 generations. Given that the sort of organisms their model assumes has a generation span of about a year, the evolution of a fish eye from a layer of photocells might occur with surprising rapidity (Nilsson and Pelger 1994). Similarly, perhaps the apparent complexity of the mind does not rule out the possibility of its speedy evolution.

But, if the complexity of minds does not preclude its rapid evolution, and if minds are good things to have, the scale tips once again in the direction of hypothesis C. If minds are a good solution to a common selection problem, as are eyes, and take not too long to evolve, then we might expect to find minds in all sorts of taxa. By one estimate, simple eye spots have evolved independently forty to sixty-five times (Salvini-Plawen and Ernst Mayr 1977). Moreover, the advanced eyes that are most familiar to us are present in only six of the thirty-three metazoan phyla, but these six phyla account for ninety-six per cent of known species (Land 1991). This fact suggests that eyes clearly provide their possessors with some competitive advantage, and if the same is true of minds perhaps natural selection has endowed most animals with minds of some sort. Hypothesis *C* would now be more likely than *O* because minds may have vast numbers of homologues or analogues.

In sum, conceiving of the mind as an adaptation provides one with, if not an answer, at least a framework with which to decide whether nonhuman species have minds. It's certainly true that complex adaptations tend not to be autapomorphic – they do not usually arise *de novo*. They usually have homologues in other taxa. It's also true that convergent evolution is common. Good solutions to selection problems often have analogous solutions in other taxa. Hence, I tend toward hypothesis *C*. If minds are adaptations then it is unlikely that minds belong only to *Homo sapiens*.

Question Three: Are Minds Multiply Realizable?

If minds are adaptations then they are not multiply realizable. The argument for this claim requires a study of how adaptations are individuated. Surprisingly, neither biologists nor philosophers have had much to say about how to classify adaptations into kinds. This is startling because biologists often appeal to episodes of convergent evolution in order to illustrate the power of natural selection. The potency of natural selection is no more evident than when it begins with distinct traits and shapes them into a single kind of adaptation. Analogously, while the shape of the rough slab of marble sets the project for the novice sculptor, it places far fewer constraints on the vision of the expert. The phenomenon of convergent evolution shows natural selection to be an expert sculptor, albeit one without foresight. From starting points as distinct as *Chondrichthyes* and *Mammalia*, natural selection has produced taxa with the same streamlined shape: sharks and dolphins. But, of course, judgments of convergence, if they are to serve as an illustration of the power of selection, require a means by which to say of two adaptations that they are the same or not; and it is for this reason that principles of individuation for adaptations become valuable.

But convergence is not the only evidence of the power of natural selection. Sometimes a biologist cites the divergent evolutionary paths an ancestral species takes in order to illustrate the pervasiveness of selection. Indeed, Darwin's observation of the adaptive radiation in finch species on the Galapagos Islands was instrumental in the development of his theory of natural selection. As with claims of convergence, claims of divergence also rest on a scheme for classifying adaptations as same and different. Without such a scheme, Darwin could not justify his assertion that the beaks of finches on different islands were different adaptations. In sum, both convergence and divergence are notions central to evolutionary theory and both presuppose a classification of adaptations. Below I defend a particular characterization of adaptations, and I argue that on this characterization adaptations cannot be vastly multiply realizable. This, we shall see, has obvious but distressing consequences for biologically inclined functionalist theories of mind.

On my view, the individuation of adaptations depends on both their structural properties and what these properties do. Recommending this analysis of adaptation is the fact that natural selection selects *for* properties because of *what* these properties do. Accordingly, an adaptation is a property of an organism that has been selected because of what it does. More specifically, a kind of adaptation A is a structural property P that has been selected because of its effects E. Granting this analysis of adaptation, one cannot identify a kind of adaptation without consideration of both the structural property that has been selected for and the effects this property has caused that explain why the property was selected, i.e., the function of the property.

The significance of both structure and function in the classification of adaptations is apparent in classic examples of homoplasies.[1] The torpedo shape of the shark and dolphin is a single kind of adaptation because it is a shared structural property that, in each case, has been selected for its capacity to decrease resistance through water. Likewise, fossil evidence shows that the eponymous sabre-tooth character of a Pleistocene cat evolved independently in a mammal-like reptile and

---

1 Within evolutionary biology the word 'homoplasy' seems sometimes to refer to any trait that is similar to another for reasons other than common ancestry. I shall use the word to refer to any *adaptation* similar to another as a result of convergent evolution. Thus, on the analysis of adaptation I shall adopt, homoplastic traits are those that are structurally and functionally similar despite having evolved independently of each other.

a marsupial (Futuyma 1998, 111). Again, justifying the claim that the sabre-teeth of these distinct species are a kind of adaptation is the fact that sabre-teeth are similar both structurally and functionally.[2] Finally, another common example of convergent evolution is the eye of vertebrates and cephalopods, which, except for the inverted retina in the vertebrate eye, share many structural and functional features. Being an eye that uses a lens to focus light on a retina has been selected in both vertebrates and cephalopods because such a structural configuration provides information about the distal environment.

However, because classification of adaptations involves consideration of both property *P* and its effects *E*, it is conceivable that two structurally identical traits may be distinct kinds of adaptations. That structural factors alone are not sufficient for the classification of adaptations is apparent when we reflect on the phenomenon of mimicry. In some cases of mimicry, a mimic will evolve the coloration of an indigestible model (a structure), so that predators that have previously encountered the model will avoid the mimic (a function). Mimicry like this is common among species of butterflies. If we suppose the model's coloration was originally selected for because it

---

2 One might object that my claims of structural similarity are arbitrary. What justifies my claim that the shark and dolphin have the same shape? In fact, the flanges on a dolphin's tail are horizontal and so the dolphin moves its tail up and down while a shark's tail is oriented vertically and so is moved side to side. Does this not drive us to distinguish the shapes of dolphins and sharks? I have two responses to this sort of objection. First, all systems of classification rely on judgments of similarity. While the differences in the shapes of dolphins and sharks might lead us to deny that they are exactly the same kind of structure, they are certainly closer in structural kind to each other than they are to many other body shapes, e.g., our own. This suffices for the work I intend to make of structural similarity judgments. Second, doubts about judgments of structural similarity come at great cost. As I've already noted, biologists rely on concepts like convergence and divergence in order to justify claims about the power of selection. Insofar as these notions depend on judgments of structural similarity, such judgments appear entrenched in biological practice. Moreover, given that this practice seems not to have suffered from any arbitrariness that may infect structural similarity judgments, I see no reason to think that this alleged arbitrariness will prove vicious in the present context. I shall have more to say below about the sorts of considerations that help to ground judgments of structural similarity.

provided the capacity for conspecific identification, the structurally similar coloration of the mimic will be a different kind of adaptation. Similarly, there exist instances of aggressive mimicry, where a predatory mimic comes to resemble a non-aggressive model. The sabre-toothed blenny manages to approach and nibble portions of other fish because it has evolved the shape, coloration, and behaviour of the parasite-removing cleaner wrasse (Futuyma 1998, 82). Perhaps these structural properties of the cleaner wrasse are adaptations for camouflage or locomotion or sexual attraction, or perhaps they are not adaptations at all. Nevertheless, these same structural properties in the blenny are adaptations for obtaining food. Finally, we may imagine populations of rattlesnakes, some of which developed their rattles as a means for attracting mates and others of which evolved identical rattles for the purpose of scaring off predators. Again, though the rattles in the two groups of snakes are structurally identical, they are distinct kinds of adaptations because the effects for which they were selected differ.

Furthermore, just as the analysis of adaptation leaves open the possibility that identical structures may be different adaptations, it also allows that traits with the same functions may nonetheless be distinct kinds of adaptation. In the cases above, the property P was held fixed while the functions of P – the effects P caused that explain the selection for P – varied. But it is equally plausible that various kinds of properties might cause the same kinds of effects. When Ps vary but E remains constant, we again have reason to distinguish between kinds of adaptation. Accordingly, distinct kinds of adaptations can have the same kind of function, or, equivalently, the same kind of function can be realized in a variety of kinds of adaptations. Intuitively, this seems plausible. Firefly lights and cricket songs share many of the same functions, e.g., attracting a mate and reproduction. Yet, the reason they are not treated as instances of the same trait is because their structural properties differ. Likewise, a primary function of the vertebrate eye is very similar to that of bat sonar: both vision and echolocation are senses that have been selected for their capacity to provide information about shapes and surfaces in the environment. Nonetheless, bat sonar and vertebrate eyes are not the same kind of adaptation because the properties by which each extracts information about the environment differ. Even within species, there are examples of properties that evolved in response to the same selection pressure but that nevertheless constitute distinct adaptations. Frederick Cohan (1984, 495) notes that "different populations of the spider mite *Tetranychus urticae* have responded to selection for organophosphate (OP) resistance by alternative mechanisms: a New York population has responded by detoxifying the poison, while a European population has altered its neural sensitivity to OP's." In this example, different populations of the spider mite have evolved different means to the same effect. They evolve different adaptations for the same function.

So far, I have argued that because adaptations are a combination of a structural property and its function (those effects it produces that explain why it has been selected) we should distinguish between kinds of adaptations when they differ in either their structural properties or their functions. But it is now time to put this argument to work. What can we say about the nature of minds given that they are adaptations? As before, let's work up to claims about minds by way of the eye. For purposes of the point I wish eventually to make, let's simplify the details about eyes. In particular, let's suppose there are only two basic kinds of eyes – camera eyes and compound eyes – and that these eyes have the same function, i.e., the detection of surfaces and shapes in the environment. Are these eyes the same kind of adaptation? If they *are* homoplastic, it is only because they are similar in structure and function. However, though granting their similarity in function, there seems little reason to accept that they are similar in structure. Because of their structural differences they have entirely distinct optical properties. The optical laws that describe how one kind of eye performs its function differ from the laws that describe the other (Land 1991).

In contrast, consider that the same laws apply in describing how the torpedo shapes of the dolphin and shark aid in their locomotion, or that the same laws describe why the sabre-tooth of the mammalian tiger and that of the marsupial tiger are efficient meat-tearers. Moreover, the reason to accept that cephalopod and vertebrate eyes are homoplastic is that they perform their functions in the same way – by use of the same properties. Naturally, judgments about structural similarity will sometimes run into gray areas, but appeal to how a given structure performs its function – with what properties it causes beneficial effects – will often enough vouchsafe decisions about whether two functionally similar traits are also structurally similar and, thus, homoplastic. The conclusion to which the above analysis of adaptation drives us is that camera eyes and compound eyes, because they differ enormously in their structural properties, are not the same kind of adaptation. The word 'eye' does not name a single kind of adaptation.

This claim will trouble advocates of functionalism. A core tenet in the functionalist program is the idea that functional kinds are multiply realizable. Mouse traps, watches, carburetors – functionalists have offered all these as examples of kinds that, because of their functional natures, can be realized in all manner of bizarre ways. I do not care here to contest the functionalist's claim that artifacts can sustain a variety of multiple realizations. However, if functionalists wish to extend the idea of multiple realizability into the life sciences, and this is surely their primary aim, then they must address the above observations about adaptations. For, if it is the case that the kinds the life sciences recognize are kinds in virtue of being adaptations, then the functionalist is wrong that these kinds can be multiply realized. Different realizations, if they differ in the properties by which they produce the effects for which they have been selected, cannot be realizations of the same adaptation. Various realizations *may* have the same function – as the firefly's light and the cricket's song do – but realizing the same function is a far cry from realizing the same adaptation. But, if functionalism is wrong about eyes then it is wrong about minds as well. If minds are adaptations then they are not multiply realizable. Shortly I will fill in the details of this claim. First, however, it is time to consider a functionalist response to my argument.

The functionalist can respond to this argument against multiple realization with the claim that individuation in the life sciences trades on functional considerations alone, and hence facts about the individuation of adaptations are beside the point. On this view, the kind *eye* includes whatever provides information about surfaces in the world, the kind *tooth* includes whatever mashes or tears food, and the kind *organophosphate resistor* includes whatever decreases vulnerability to organophosphates. Because function alone determines membership in a kind, the functionalist may insist, the only constraint on what sort of structures realize the above kinds is that they be selected because they produce the relevant effects.

Now, I do not wish to raise any in-principle objection to individuation of kinds on functional grounds alone. If the life sciences have a need for such a classification of kinds then they should help themselves to it. However, there are two arguments that militate against individuating kinds by function alone. If these arguments are persuasive, then the complaint against functionalism as a framework from which to approach the study of the mind grows more serious. The first argument is this. Function attribution is at best difficult and at worst hopelessly indeterminate.[3] Consider, for instance, the notorious mechanism in the frog that responds to moving black dots. Should one describe the function of this mechanism as a black dot detector, a fly detector, a food detector, an energy provider, or, most basically, a fitness enhancer? All of these effects are synchronic: it does one at the same time it does all the others. However, depending on which assignment one chooses, the frog's mechanism will be of a kind with, respectively, a lizard's black dot detector (assuming they have them), a fly's mate detector (assuming they have them), a bee's pollen detector, chlorophyll, and every other functional trait.

Again, whether one sees this as a problem depends on whether classification in the life sciences needs to be determinate. It may be that the life sciences can make do with shifting taxonomies of kinds or that it can even benefit from such a thing. However, it is at least *prima facie* strange to claim that the mechanism in the frog that responds to black dots is, literally, the same kind of thing as chlorophyll or, for that matter, thick fur. Yet, until the question of function determinacy receives an answer, the functionalist seems committed to this position.

Before turning to the second argument against individuating kinds by function alone, it is important to note that individuation by adaptation does not face this problem of functional indeterminacy. Because structural properties count significantly in the individuation of adaptations, and because identification of structural properties is not especially problematic, structural properties can serve as an

---

3 Some teleologically minded functionalists have attempted to solve this problem of function indeterminacy. For a valuable discussion of these attempts and the difficulties they face, see Enç (forthcoming).

anchor against functional drift. The frog's perceptual mechanism and chlorophyll cannot be the same kind of adaptation, despite the fact that both have the function to provide energy, because the properties by which they provide energy differ. Of course, one remains free to say that the frog's bug-detection mechanism and chlorophyll have in common the ability to provide energy, and thus generalizations true of energy providers are true of both. Yet, in saying this one does not thereby have to, as the functionalist must, say they are the same kind of thing. They are different things with similar functions. If individuation by adaptation can retain the benefits of a purely functional individuation without having to assert identities between things that seem clearly dissimilar then it is preferable.

Let's turn now to a second reason for skepticism about a purely functional individuation of traits. In presenting this reason, we will see why a strike against multiple realizability is good news for psychologists. It should go without saying that the practice of individuation ought to serve some purpose. I have already argued that the individuation of adaptations is necessary for judgments of convergence and divergence, which are in turn crucial as evidence for the operation and force of selection. But now, having granted that minds are adaptations, we can ask whether conceiving them as such is preferable to conceiving them as purely functional kinds. Should the term 'mind' be limited to those things that are adaptations or should its reference be broadened to include anything that has the function that minds have? The answer to this question, as I have noted, depends on our purposes. But, if our purpose is to understand what minds are and how they work, then it seems clear we are better off treating mind as an adaptation than as a whatever-it-is-that-functions-as-a-mind.

To argue for this conclusion, it pays to introduce terms that distinguish between the kinds that result from the two distinct methods of individuation. I will use the term 'adapted mind' to refer to minds identified as adaptations and the term 'functional mind' to refer to the class of things that includes not only adapted minds but all things with the same or very similar functions as the adapted mind. Just to be clear, if we stipulate that camera eyes are adapted eyes, then it would be false that compound eyes are also adapted *eyes* because they are not, I have argued, the same kind of adaptation as camera eyes. Yet, compound eyes can be functional eyes if they have the same function as camera eyes. Moreover, they can be adapted eyes*, so long as we recognize that eyes* are distinct from eyes. In contrast, the Pleistocene mammalian tiger and Pleistocene marsupial tiger both have adapted sabre-teeth. With these terms in hand, the question before us is why, given the purpose of understanding what minds are and how they work, we should prefer an individuative apparatus that presents us with adapted minds rather than functional minds.

In answer to this question, consider how one might begin to investigate a functional eye. One would choose some particular token from among the great variety of things that can see – say a dragonfly's compound eye. One would then dissect the eye, contemplate the optics that the exposed structural properties of the eye supports, perhaps develop a computer simulation of the compound eye to test one's hypotheses, and then announce what has been discovered about how functional eyes work. Except, of course, one has *not* made a discovery about how functional eyes as a class work. One has learned something only about how one variety of functional eye works. If the goal is to understand how eyes work and by 'eye' is meant a functional eye, then it is hard to see how one could ever meet this goal. If functional eyes can, as the functionalist believes, be realized in an unlimited number of ways, then there should be no expectation that anything of a general nature will be true of all functional eyes – except for the fact that all functional eyes, by definition, see.[4]

In short, the two distinct methods of individuation suggest two distinct kinds of answer to the question "What makes an eye a seeing thing?" When studying adapted eyes, the answer will involve appeal to structural properties. Moreover, what one learns from the study of a token adapted eye projects to all adapted eyes. Meaningful generalizations about adapted eyes – generalizations that go beyond a mere recitation of the function of eyes – become available. On the other hand, when studying functional eyes, a definition suffices to answer the question about what makes them see – functional eyes see because it is seeing that makes them eyes. Thus, keeping in mind that one should allow one's purposes to settle questions about how to individuate kinds, it seems clear that when one's purpose is to understand how

---

4 For a related argument, see Shapiro (2000).

some biological trait works one should prefer a scheme of individuation along adaptive lines to one along mere functional lines. This moral, I claim, is as true for minds as it is for eyes.

Conclusions

One immediate consequence of treating minds as adaptations is a taxonomy of minds that cross cuts more traditional divisions. As we have seen, the adapted mind perspective is more restrictive than the functionalist position. Because minds, if adaptations, are kinds of structures with kinds of functions, there may be adaptations with the same functions as minds but that, nevertheless, are not minds. But also, because there may be psychological homologues in other species that, like the eyes of bats, no longer function as minds, the adapted mind perspective is more restrictive than the type-identity theorist's. Indeed, classification of minds as adaptations adopts the individuative recommendations of both functionalism and identity theory and thus confers the benefits of each on those who wish to pursue a study of adapted mind.

At first blush, the implications of this view of mind might seem difficult to swallow. On the one hand, individuating the mind as an adaptation implies that something with a brain just like ours may not have a mind. On the other hand, it implies that a nonhuman being (e.g., a Martian) with whom we may have perfectly ordinary conversations – conversations about whether Michael Jordan is the greatest basketball player of all time, about where to find the best pizza, about why the dimples on golf balls make them fly farther, etc. – may not, if structurally quite distinct from ourselves, have a mind. However, I think a little reflection shows these consequences to be not too distressing.

Regarding the first consequence, that brains structurally like ours may not realize minds, it should be noted that this is an empirically very unlikely result. The evolution of the eye confirms the intuition that as a structure increases in complexity it becomes more dedicated in function. Thus, as I noted earlier, simple eye spots have evolved numerous times, but there is no reason to assume that on each occasion they were selected for the same effects. Some simple eye spots might have the function to alert their possessor of a looming predator. Others might have the function to orient their possessor in a particular direction. Yet, as eyes increase in structural complexity, it becomes less likely that their specialized machinery – lenses, corneas, irises, retinas – has evolved as a result of distinct selection pressures. The more intricate the structure, the more specialized its function will be. This is why it is easy to conceive of two inventors living in very different climates, one intensely sunny and the other very rainy, who both design an umbrella, while it is very hard to imagine that inventors with distinct purposes would hit upon the same design for a CAT scanner or a computer printer. Similarly, the vast intricacy of the human brain makes it vanishingly improbable that some other selection history could produce another organ just like it. If ever we find an organ structurally similar to our brain, it will be a near certainty that it has been selected to do the same sorts of things.

But what of the Martian who, despite all the appearances of having a mind, does not? In response to this possibility, it becomes important to distinguish minds as kinds of things from what minds do. The claim that minds are adaptations carries with it, I have argued, a commitment to a manner of individuation. Similarly, the claim that firefly lights are adaptations implies something about how *they* are to be individuated. Nonetheless, as we have seen, it is consistent with facts about the individuation of adaptations that distinct adaptations have many of the same functions. We can say of crickets that, despite lacking firefly lights, they have something that does the same thing that firefly lights do, i.e., attract mates. Fireflies and crickets, that is, both have adaptations that have been selected to attract mates. Likewise, we can say of the Martian that it has an adaptation that has been selected to do whatever it is that minds do for human beings. But this no more implies that Martians have minds than does the cricket's ability to attract mates imply that it has a firefly light. The claim that an organism has a *particular* adaptation, e.g., a wing, an eye, a tooth, is quite substantive. If biologists are to rely on such claims to support judgments of convergence and divergence, then these claims must convey more than the modest assertion that an organism has some trait or other that performs a given function. So, assuming that Martian brain structure differs radically from human brain structure, one should deny that both Martians and humans have minds while recognizing that members of both species may exhibit similar mental capacities.

There are further consequences of the perspective on mind I have sketched above. If minds are adaptations, then it is possible to ask of them how significant the role of natural selection has been in their evolution. While it is trivial that natural selection influences the evolution of all adaptations, it may have had a greater hand in the evolution of some adaptations than others. For any adaptation, it is possible to ask how significant nonselective factors were in its evolution. Elliott Sober (1993, 130), for instance, observes that the statement 'The eye is an adaptation' leaves open two questions: (1) how much impact did nonselective forces like mutation and drift have on the evolution of the eye; and (2) given the complexity of the eye, were all of its many parts equally the product of selective forces? A psychology that treats the mind as an adaptation must face the same questions Sober asks about the eye. Accordingly, it seems appropriate for psychology to make use of the same kind of optimality models that biologists have used to assess the prevalence of natural selection in the evolution of a given trait. This, in turn, requires psychologists to become quite explicit about what the functions of the mind are and what selection pressures have contributed to its development.

My purpose here has been to explore the consequences of applying a well-established biological concept to a psychological subject. From the simple fact that minds are adaptations a number of conclusions follow. Minds are not epiphenomenal. They probably are not unique to the human species. They are not multiply realizable. One may object at this point that because these conclusions about minds follow from the nature of adaptation generally, I have not shown anything to be true of minds that is not true of any adaptation. Thus, the objection goes, I have not provided the psychologist with any information that is especially suited to a study of mind. In defence, I would argue that merely recognizing that what's true of any adaptation is also true of the mind marks a profound step forward in how we think of the mind. The mind's undeniable complexity has lent it a mystical pallor that seems to sanction claims no one would dare make about other adaptations. The mind, for all its wondrous abilities, is just another adaptation. This fact, humbling as it may be, provides a sound starting point for an investigation of mind.

References

Cohan, F. 1984. "Can Uniform Selection Retard Random Genetic Divergence Between Isolated Conspecific Populations?" *Evolution* **38**, 495–504.

Dawkins, R. 1982. "Universal Darwinism." In *Evolution from Molecules to Men*. D. Bendall, ed. New York: Cambridge University Press, pp. 403–25.

Dawkins, R. 1996. *Climbing Mount Improbable*. New York: W.W. Norton & Co.

Enç, B. Forthcoming. "The Indeterminacy of Function Attributions." In *Functions: New Readings in the Philosophy of Psychology and Biology*, A. Ariew, R. Cummins, and M. Perlman, eds. New York: Oxford University Press.

Futuyma, D. 1998. *Evolutionary Biology*, 3rd ed. Sunderland: Sinauer Associates, Inc.

Land, M. 1991. "Optics of the Eyes of the Animal Kingdom." In *Evolution of the Eye and Visual System*, J. Cronly-Dillon and R. Gregory, eds. New York: Macmillan, pp. 118–35.

Nilsson, D., and Pelger, S. 1994. "A Pessimistic Estimate of the Time Required for an Eye to Evolve," *Proceedings of the Royal Society of London* B. Vol. 256, pp. 53–58.

Salvini-Plawen, L., and Mayr, E. 1977. "On the Evolution of Photoreceptors and Eyes," *Evolutionary Biology* **10**, 207–63.

Shapiro, L. 2000. "Multiple Realizations," *Journal of Philosophy* **97**, 635–54.

Sober, E. 1993. *Philosophy of Biology*. Boulder: Westview Press.

II. Teleosemantics

A Tale of Two Froggies

COLIN ALLEN

There once was an ugly duckling. Except he wasn't a duckling at all, and once he realized his error he lived happily ever after. And there you have an early primer from the animal literature on the issue of misrepresentation – perhaps one of the few on this topic to have a happy ending.

Philosophers interested in misrepresentation have turned their attention to a different fairy tale animal: the frog. No one gets kissed in this story and the controversial issue of self-recognition is avoided. There are simply some scientifically established facts about ways to get a frog to stick out its tongue. (Who would want to kiss a frog under those conditions, anyway?) Some frogs, it seems, are fairly indiscriminate about sticking out their tongues. Not just flies, but a whole slew of other things will go down the hatch if propelled at just the right velocity and range through a frog's visual field, provoking a tongue-flicking response. Fortunately for us all, frogs seem to be a bit more discriminating about whom they will kiss.

At first sight, the frog's tongue-flicking response seems like an ideal starting point for those who wish to promote evolutionary or "teleological" theories of intentional content. The signals passed from the frog's retina to the frog's brain were undoubtedly honed by the deaths of untold millions of insects snagged by countless generations of amphibians. Those amphibian ancestors whose eyes generated signals that were more reliable guides to the location of food in the environment did better at propagating their genes, all other things being equal, than their cohorts whose eye to brain signals were less reliable. The teleosemanticist identifies the content of frogs' intracranial signals in terms of the environmental conditions that historically corresponded to successful tongue-flicking, namely the presence of frog food – typically flies – in tongue-flicking range. And their descendants live happily ever after.

But this would not be a fairy tale unless there were something to pose a credible threat to this happy ending. Enter villains, armed with BBs (but not shotguns), who find that their amphibian subjects have as much of an eye for lead pellets as for more nutritious fare. Paradise lost, for no longer can frogs flick their tongues with impunity. Too heavy a dose of BBs could very literally sink a frog. But the real moral of the story, according to those whose target is teleosemantics not frogs, is that natural selection doesn't care what the frog's eye tells the frog's brain so long as the environment serves up the right kind of thing with sufficient frequency. Whether the signal sent to the frog's brain says "food" or whether it says "food or BB" doesn't matter. When there are no BBs around, both messages provoke tongue-flicking in exactly the same circumstances and are thus equally adaptive. So, it seems, there is no evolutionary reason to prefer one phrase over the other if you want to specify the content of the frog's eye-to-brain signal and thus there are no grounds for claiming that the frog who swallows a BB is the victim of a misrepresentation.

There are, of course, gaps in this argument against teleosemantics and these gaps have been fruitfully exploited by several defenders of teleosemantics. This is neither the time nor the place to survey all of that fine work, some of it conducted by other contributors to this issue. Instead, I wish to reorient the discussion by examining the role of the English expressions that purport to give the content of the frogs' neural signals. When examined, it will be seen that the so-called disjunction problem collapses into a choice between alternatives that cannot be adjudicated in a practical vacuum.

We begin by focusing on the internal representations of two specific frogs. The first frog whom I will call "frog–then" lived at a time before BBs existed. The second frog, "frog–now," we will suppose to be a direct descendant of frog–then, and has the misfortune of being the first in her lineage to be spotted by scientists hell-bent on feeding a frog some BBs. For the example, let us imagine that frog–then's visual system has been faithfully replicated through the generations to frog–now, and that some signal token s–then that passed from frog–then's eye to brain is neurologically indistinguishable from s–now that passes from frog–now's eye to brain on her first exposure to a BB. They are both tokens of neurobiological type S.

Ignoring the indexical components (i.e., here and now) of the contents of s–then and s–now, either s–then and s–now have the same intentional content, or they do not. (I shall not include the qualification about indexicality anywhere else in this paper; it should be taken as implicit throughout.) If these two token signals have different contents, then it is possible for the content of tokens of type S to change without any structural changes in the organisms producing those tokens. While some content-externalist views might in principle allow this possibility, it is not an option for backward-looking teleosemantic views. There has been no time for a changed selection regime to take effect because, by hypothesis, frog–now is the first of her lineage to have been exposed to a BB. With respect to the environment of selection that matters to teleosemantic accounts of content, frog–then and frog–now are in the same moat.

Proponents of alternative, non-teleological externalist accounts of content have also put forward theories which entail that S tokens have the same content then and now. Thus, for example, Fodor's (1990) principle of *asymmetric dependence* maintains constancy of content because the frogs' tendency to respond to BBs is counterfactually dependent upon the tendency to respond to flies but not conversely; i.e., the frogs' tendency to respond to BBs is causally dependent on their tendency to respond to flies, and not vice versa. Nevertheless, the environment external to frog–now is different from that encountered by frog–then, so one can imagine constructing an externalist theory of content that is sensitive to this fact. While it might be fun to explore the construction of theories that have the consequence that the contents of S tokens are different then and now, this is not the way in which the philosophical discussion of what the frog's eye tells the frog's brain has proceeded. Accordingly, I will limit the present investigation to the consequences of assuming that the contents of s–then and s–now are the same.

Let us, then, call the putative shared content of s–then and s–now "FETFB" (an acronym for Frog's Eye To Frog's Brain; note that FETFB is intended to indicate the signals' content, not the signals themselves). How might one specify FETFB using the English language? An obvious suggestion is this: provide an English expression L such that the content of L is identical to FETFB.

One obvious problem with this proposal relates to the requirement that FETFB, the content of a neural signal, be *identical* to the content of some fragment of English. English and the signals of frog-neuralese are tools with rather different functions, and it would be surprising indeed if any simple phrase of English had exactly the same content as a frog's neural signal. What, then, are we to make of the choice between "food" and "food or BB" for expressing the content FETFB? Sticking to the search for identical contents one could regard "food" and "food or BB" as shorthand for two longer expressions of English that are the genuine candidates for having the content FETFB. To settle which, if either, of the indicated longer expressions has a content that is identical with FETFB, one must determine the difference between their contents; in the absence of the longer expressions themselves, one must attempt to determine what is added to the content of the expression indicated by "food" by attaching the words "or BB."

First, a relatively superficial objection to the use of "BB" in specifying FETFB. Recall that we are operating under the lemma that s–then and s–now have the same content. At the time of frog–then's existence, BBs had not been invented and there was no necessity, metaphysical or otherwise, that BBs would be invented. The planet could have been destroyed that year by a huge comet and no BBs would have ever come to be. If the term "BB" makes a contribution to the intentional content of s–then, then so must names for many other entities that failed to exist then or now. But there are no good empirical reasons to refer to merely possible entities (if entities they be) in specifying the contents of the representations of actual organisms. One does not need to have much of a Quinean streak to draw the line at this point. But just in case the reader lacks a Quinean streak altogether, there is another line of argument available, viz., that if mere possibilia are relevant to the specification of content then we can never know the content of any actual signal for we can never know or specify the full range of objects that would cause the signal to be tokened (except in this unspecific, circular fashion). The utility of content specification for scientific purposes would be undermined if one cannot draw the line so as to exclude the merely possible, for it is of no interest at all to be told that a signal's content is given in terms of its possible causes, and its possible causes are just those things that might cause the signal. Drawing the line so as to exclude the merely potential causes of s–then eliminates reference to BBs as such from the expression of the content of s–then, and hence too of s–now. So, if the choice is directly between the contents indicated by "food" and "food or BBs," then "food" wins going away. But there is a deeper point lurking.

BBs provide a nice, real-world example of the kinds of non-food items at which frogs will stick out their tongues. The point of the disjunction problem is surely not tied to BBs per se, but to a more general class of non-food items whose ingestion by frogs was not nutritious for them. The more interesting distinction to be made in trying to specify the content FETFB is between contents that designate a class F of objects that have both the property of causing the signal and whose ingestion has, on the whole, been good for frogs, and a class G of objects that have the former property but which lack the latter. Construed this way, G is not a class that should raise any Quinean hackles. Frogs being as indiscriminate tongue-flickers as they are, it is virtually certain that members of this class were a part of frog–then's environment, even in the distant past when BBs were not even a gleam in Fodor's eye. The disjunction problem for FETFB may then be construed as the problem of selecting between two ways of specifying the content indicated by the expressions "F" and "F or G."

Given a choice between these ways of expressing the content FETFB, we must still ask what role the word "or" is playing in the second alternative. Given that this topic is known as "the disjunction problem" one could be forgiven for thinking that it is crucial. But it is not. Philosophers' discussions of what the frog's eye tells the frog's brain have (intentionally) been carried on in the absence of any commitment to a functional role for FETFB beyond its involvement in the tongue-flicking response. FETFB is not, for example, required to play any role in inferences such as disjunctive syllogism. (The simplicity of the frog example is considered one of its main virtues for thinking about semantic theories. Its simplicity also underlies the muttered and footnoted comments of many philosophers that teleosemantics might be fine for frogs but is unlikely to scale up to princes.) If disjunction is assumed to play no structural role in the content FETFB, then the content of the English "food or BB" cannot be identical to FETFB (although their extensions may, of course, be the same). Neither can the content of "*F* or *G*" be identical to FETFB insofar as "*F* or *G*" is an abbreviation for a disjunction of English. If the word "or" is to feature in the expression *L* of the schema above, we must give up on the idea that *L* and FETFB will have identical contents. In other words, we must give up on the proposal as it was formulated above.

Once we give up on identity between FETFB and the content of whatever expression of English we choose to represent it, the discussion is stalled unless criteria are provided for determining whether a given expression of English adequately captures FETFB. To my knowledge, no one has provided such criteria. There is an old, sizable, and largely pessimistic literature on the difficulties of using expressions of English to express the mental contents of nonhuman animals, particularly for the purposes of precise prediction of animal behaviour (e.g., Dennett 1969; Stich 1983). Optimists (e.g., Allen 1992) have done little more than attempt to shoot down the arguments of the pessimists and gesture in the direction of how one might come up with qualifications upon qualifications of English phrases to express the contents of animal minds. The arguments against giving precise contents for animal thoughts aren't very good, but the theories that would make content attributions precise aren't available either. My assessment is that there is presently a stalemate on this point.

I do not intend to remedy the situation here. (Indeed I am not sure how to remedy it.) However, some progress might be made by investigating a weaker condition on *L*, that it have the same reference or extension as FETFB. With respect to the original question of whether to gloss FETFB as "food" or "food or BB" what we need to know is this: Do BBs belong in the extension of those signals, or don't they? But focusing on extension renders the question of choosing between "food" and "food or BB" entirely moot. For, as Fodor is fond of pointing out, in frog–then's environment the extensions of these two descriptions are identical. If the only criterion for selecting between these expressions is what they designate in the current environment, then there is nothing to choose between them as expressions of what *s*–then refers to.

This result is, of course, an artifact of the non-existence of BBs in frog–then's environment. Presumably, though, it did not require the intervention of scientists to get frogs occasionally to stick out their tongues at things that aren't so good to eat, so, even discounting the relevance of BBs to frog–then, there is a real distinction between the alternatives previously labelled "*F*" and "*F* or *G*." Notice, however, that the move to consider these alternatives further reinforces the irrelevance of disjunction to the so-called disjunction problem. The disjunction "*F* or *G*," which stands for "signal-causing and nutritious or signal-causing and not nutritious," is logically equivalent, and thus extensionally equivalent, to the simpler phrase "signal-causing." Thus, if extensional equivalence is the only criterion applied, there is nothing to choose between these phrases. That is, from the standpoint of extensionality, the choice between "*F*" and "*F* or *G*" to express the extension of the frogs' neural signal is equivalent to the choice between "nutritious and signal-causing" on the one hand, and simply "signal-causing" on the other. Disjunction has disappeared from the disjunction problem, along with the not-so-ubiquitous BBs, and what is left is the question of whether teleosemantic theories (like other naturalistic semantic theories) have the resources to limit the function of these signals to the representation of anything less extensive than their causes. Surely not even the most ardent critic of teleosemantics can doubt that natural selection does care about this distinction; animals have evolved to learn from their mistakes, after all.

If something beyond mere reference is at stake for *s*–then, then we are owed an account of how our English expressions of content are supposed to map onto Diplasicoelan content. But it doesn't seem possible to do this without begging the question against rival theories of content, for one must produce a theory of content to show how the contents of English and frog-neuralese are related. There is no theory-independent way of settling this matter. Consequently, it is my view that selection of the best theory of content is not a matter for mere philosophical reflection on the consequences of each theory for our intuitive judgments about content. Rather, the theories must be judged in a different way that is based on the (putative) roles of content attribution in the behavioural sciences. The ultimate test of any theory of content will be the success of the sciences that adopt it (see Allen 1995a). Such a "meta-empirical" test means that the viability of a theory of content cannot be subjected directly to experiment but is determined by the empirical successes or failures of entire research programs. Thus, the competition between theories cannot be adjudicated in advance by philosophers, although philosophers certainly play a role in distinguishing the possible forms that naturalistic semantic theories can take.

The tale of froggie neurosemantics is perhaps a useful nursery-primer for philosophers seeking to develop competence in naturalistic semantics. But despite its origins in the scientific literature, it is not a good place to pursue the meta-empirical evaluation of naturalistic semantic theories. The real scientific action lies elsewhere. For whatever reasons, among them perhaps that there is little interest in employing intentional notions to describe such simple systems, there are no scientific controversies about the proper way to gloss the neural signals of frogs and no particular explanatory use to which scientists attempt to put such descriptions. So it is elsewhere that we might expect to get useful feedback about the utility of competing semantic theories, and consequently elsewhere that philosophers might more fruitfully devote their energies.

In my opinion, the much more interesting discussions are those taking place in comparative psychology and ethology about how to gloss the various communicative behaviours of animals, within both natural and artificial systems of communication. There are those comparative psychologists (particularly among chimpanzee researchers) who apply individualistic behavioural criteria – such as whether animals learn from their mistakes and generalize what they learn – to the attribution of content to communicative acts of animals (e.g., Savage-Rumbaugh 1990, who labels language a "cause-effect system"). Kanzi (a bonobo) gets up and puts the hammer in the refrigerator having heard "put the hammer in the refrigerator" even though he has never heard that exact sequence of words before, because he apparently understands the content of the instruction by having generalized from other examples such as "put the hammer in the box" and "put the cup in the refrigerator." When Kanzi later uses the lexigram keyboard to produce a series of words, the content of that sequence is interpreted in light of his individual history of learning to use similar sequences of lexigrams in particular ways, for example to signal his desire for a particular food item or to go to a particular location outdoors. The patterns of explanation in this genre are very familiar to philosophers because they closely follow the pattern of folk-psychological explanations of human behaviour.

Less familiar to philosophers is the pattern of explanation among those ethologists who adopt a "functional" approach to signal content, that glosses the content of signals according to their evolutionary and ecological significance (e.g., Evans and Marler 1995). Such "functional" approaches are typically more concerned with explaining the evolution of patterns of behaviour in a population than with moment-to-moment predictions of the behaviour of individual organisms. In vervet monkeys, individual learning does play a role in the entrainment of specific vocalizations to specific avian predators (Cheney and Seyfarth 1990) whereas the vocalizations of chickens to their aerial predators may be more fixed (Evans and Marler 1995). Both, however, are functionally characterized by ethologists as alarm calls and glossed as conveying the message "avian predator present" to conspecifics. In both species there has evolved a kind of "audience effect" (Marler et al. 1991) such that the signal is emitted only in the presence of conspecifics who are likely to benefit from it. Despite the fact that the presence of a conspecific is part of the normal condition for these signals to be produced, as well as a condition of their efficacy, ethologists have not shown any inclination to gloss these signals as having the conjunctive meaning "avian predator and conspecific present." Here, then, we have a clear case of the signals' content being distinguished from both causes and the conditions under which they enhance fitness. A proper understanding of this practice will require philosophers to pay more attention to the real explanatory goals in the sciences that make use of content attributions.

A further step away from the nursery may be achieved by coming to see alternative semantic theories as complementary rather than antagonistic. Different approaches to content specification may well be compatible, reflecting different but perhaps equally legitimate explanatory goals. I believe that functional approaches correspond best to a "metacausal" explanatory role for intentional properties in the behavioural sciences, meaning that the attribution of such properties figures in explanations of how particular causal relationships between signals and behaviours are established (Allen 1995b; see also Dretske

1988). Other semantic theories may be more suitable for attempts to show that intentional properties are directly causally involved in the moment-to-moment behaviour of organisms. However, the approaches are independent in that it is possible that the metacausal project can be sustained even if, contrary to the wishes of many, more direct kinds of intentional causation cannot be defended (Allen 1995b).

Perhaps this is another story about misrepresentation that lacks a thoroughly satisfactory ending. But I never was much of a fan of fairy tales. Here's an ending with realism. Ethologists can choose between the range of theories of intentional content on offer to see which best fits their explanatory projects. Philosophers can continue to search for ingenious new ways of thinking about content without the burden of having to show that any particular theory defeats allcomers. And frogs can get on with the business of catching a meal, free, it is to be hoped, from the clutches of people with government grants to flick BBs in front of their noses.

Acknowledgment

I am grateful to Scott Kimbrough, Chris Menzel, Eric Saidel, and especially to Jill McIntosh for comments on earlier drafts of this essay.

References

Allen, C. 1992. "Mental Content," *British Journal for the Philosophy of Science* **43**, 537–53.

————.1995a. "Intentionality: Natural and Artificial." In *Comparative Approaches to Cognitive Science*, J.-A. Meyer and H. L. Roitblat, eds. Cambridge, MA: MIT Press, pp. 93–110.

————. 1995b. "It Isn't What You Think: A New Idea about Intentional Causation," *Noûs* **29**, 115–26.

Cheney, D., and R. Seyfarth. 1990. *How Monkeys See the World: Inside the Mind of Another Species*. Chicago: University of Chicago Press.

Dennett, D. C. 1969. *Content and Consciousness*. London: Routledge and Kegan Paul.

Dretske, F. 1988. *Explaining Behavior*. Cambridge, MA: MIT Press.

Evans, C., and P. Marler. 1995. "Language and Animal Communication: Parallels and Contrasts." In *Comparative Approaches to Cognitive Science*, J.-A. Meyer and H. L. Roitblat, eds. Cambridge, MA: MIT Press, pp. 341–82.

Fodor, J. 1990. *A Theory of Content and Other Essays*. Cambridge, MA: MIT Press.

Marler, P., S. Karakashian, and M. Gyger. 1991. "Do Animals Have the Option of Withholding Signals When Communication is Inappropriate? The Audience Effect." In *Cognitive Ethology: The Minds of Other Animals. Essays in Honor of Donald R. Griffin*, C. A. Ristau, ed. Hillsdale, NJ: Lawrence Erlbaum, pp. 187–208.

Savage-Rumbaugh, E. S. 1990. "Language as a Cause-Effect Communication System." *Philosophical Psychology* **3**, 55–76.

Stich, S. 1983. *From Folk Psychology to Cognitive Science: the Case Against Belief*. Cambridge, MA: MIT Press.

CANADIAN JOURNAL OF PHILOSOPHY
Supplementary Volume 27

The Excesses of Teleosemantics

PAUL SHELDON DAVIES

Teleosemantics asserts that mental content is determined by natural selection. The thesis is that content is fixed by the historical conditions under which certain cognitive mechanisms – those that produce and those that interpret (respond to) representational states – were selectively successful. Content is fixed by conditions of selective success. The thesis of this paper is that teleosemantics is mistaken, that content cannot be fixed by conditions of selective success, because those conditions typically outnumber the intentional objects within a given representational state. To defend against this excess, advocates of teleosemantics must attempt to privilege some conditions of success while ignoring others. This results in selective explanations that are *ad hoc*, thereby depriving teleosemantics of the virtues it hoped to inherit from the theory of evolution by natural selection, including its alleged naturalistic credentials.

I. Two Forms of Content Specificity

The contents of some mental states are fine-grained in at least two ways. (1) The objects of one's intentional state – the things or relations represented – are represented under quite specific descriptions. You represent Ortcutt to yourself as a banker, and I represent him as a spy. This is because you and I are ignorant of different properties of the man in question, so that a single object is depicted under distinct descriptions. Call this sort of fine-grainedness *description-specificity*. (2) The objects of any intentional state – the things or relations represented

– are a proper subset of all the things or relations causally involved in the production of that representational state. This is true diachronically and synchronically. I have a visual representation of the goldfinch at my window but not of the egg from which it was hatched. Likewise, my representation of the finch does not include among its contents the retinal image or the neurological processes that produce this representation in me. Very few of the objects involved in the causal history or the current instantiation of a mental state are among the objects represented. Call this sort of fine-grainedness *object-specificity*.

The latter is more basic than the former; object-specificity is more basic than description-specificity. A theory of content must provide principled means for including the objects that appear within the content of a mental state. It also must exclude those that do not appear. A theory thus must specify why the finch is the intentional object of my perception and not, say, the egg from which it came or the neurological processes that underwrite this perception. Having settled this issue, the theory then must specify the description(s) under which I represent the bird to myself. I may represent it as "goldfinch" but I also may represent it under an indefinite number of alternative descriptions, including "bright yellow, sparrow-like bird." Settling upon the right description of an intentional object is relevant only once it is determined that a given object is in fact part of the representational content. So object-specificity is basic.

Saying that object-specificity is basic is not a claim about the phenomenology of our mental lives. I am not saying that we, from the first-person point of view, first notice which objects appear in our representational field and then settle upon some description. The claim is purely theoretical. The obligations of a theory of content can be ordered in this way. If, for any mental state, the theory cannot divide between objects that are intentional and those that are not, then it is a hopeless theory. Discerning the specific description under which an agent represents those objects is pertinent only if we have grounds for thinking that those are the objects of the agent's intentional state.

At any rate, a theory of mental content is adequate only if it accounts for both types of specificity, object and description. My thesis is that appeals to natural selection are far too coarse-grained to account for the object-specificity of mental states. The thesis, more specifically, is that an adequate selective explanation of the historical success of our cognitive mechanisms – those involved in the production and interpretation of representational states – must cite a wide array of ecological conditions that led to such success. The conditions involved are diverse and several, and typically outnumber the intentional objects of the organisms involved, making them far too excessive to account for the object-specificity of mental content.[1]

II. Teleosemantics and the Appeal to Natural Selection

Teleosemantics accounts for object-specificity only if there are principled grounds for classifying as intentional just those objects that in fact appear within the organism's representational field. Teleosemantics must achieve this, moreover, on the basis of considerations from the theory of evolution by natural selection. This additional constraint is important, for teleosemantics is proposed as a naturalistic approach to mental content grounded in the theory of evolution by natural selection, a highly confirmed theory within natural science. It is incumbent upon the advocate of teleosemantics to show how the object-specificity of mental contents is grounded in the relevant sorts of considerations from evolutionary theory.

To illustrate the theory, consider an example from Millikan (1989). Several beavers are milling around their river dam when one espies what he takes to be a predator and immediately slaps the water with his tail with quite specific force and tempo. Upon hearing this signature sound, the others dive underwater for safety. Let us agree that the fleeing beavers, upon hearing the warning, come to believe that there is a predator in the vicinity, and this belief, combined with appropriate motivation, causes them to flee. What in this scenario fixes the content of the beavers' belief? What in the organism or in the organism's relation to its environment makes it the case that its

---

1 This thesis contrasts with that of Fodor (1990, chap. 3). He claims that appeals to natural selection are too coarse-grained to account for the *description-specificity* of mental states. This means that the several attempts to fend off Fodor's objection (e.g., Sterelny 1990) do not touch the objection pressed here.

belief is about predators but not also about additional features of the environment? Why is the belief not also about, say, tail slaps or the water upon which the slaps are produced – or any other objects involved in the production of the beavers' representational state? This is not to inquire about the description under which a given object is represented. It is to inquire about the grounds upon which certain objects in the beavers' environment are included in the content of their mental representations.

Teleosemantics asserts that the content of any type of mental state is fixed by just those conditions integral to the selective success of past tokens of that type. This, at any rate, is the central tenet of Millikan's (1984; 1989) version, one of the most detailed accounts available.[2] The claim, more precisely, is the following:

> (T) Mental state S has representational content *that P* if and only if P was a Normal condition for the performance of the proper function of the mechanism(s) that interpret(s) S.

Content is specified by a specific "Normal condition" – or a specific set of such conditions – for fulfilling the "proper function" of mechanisms that "interpret" S. Let me explain.

The beaver sentry produces a representation – a sound representing, presumably, the presence of predators – and those that heed the warning possess a certain mechanism that responds to and interprets this representation. This interpretive mechanism works along the following lines: The auditory system receives the sound as input and, after translating this signal into some internal medium, inputs the resulting message to the interpreting mechanism. This mechanism, by virtue of some innate or acquired rule, processes the message and outputs a signal to certain behaviour-inducing mechanisms, which initiate escape behaviour.

The innate or acquired rule with which this interpreting mechanism processes such messages is a direct product of its own selective history. If the rule is innate, the history of the population is relevant; if the rule is acquired, all that matters is the developmental history of the

---

2 See also Papineau (1987; 1993).

individual organism. It is presumed that the process of selection that drives evolution in ontogenesis is sufficiently similar to the process that drives evolution in a population. For innate rules, past instances of the interpreter mechanism processed messages according to this rule and such processings were selectively advantageous; organisms that lacked this mechanism, or organisms in which the mechanism processed differently, did not fare as well reproductively; in consequence, since this mechanism was heritable, it was selected for the processing of messages according to this rule. The selective story for acquired rules is supposed to be analogous, though applied to individual organisms throughout their development rather than generations of organisms within a population.

The general claim, then, is that the interpreter mechanism was selected for the processing of messages according to this innate or acquired rule, which is just to say that this mechanism today has what Millikan calls the "proper function" of interpreting messages according to the given rule.[3] But proper functions are acquired only under certain conditions of selective success. Certain historical conditions are such that, had they not obtained, the given mechanism would not have been selectively successful. Perhaps the most obvious condition in the case of the beaver's interpreting mechanism is the presence of a predator. Consider the difference between beavers that had the interpreting mechanisms with those that did not. Those that had it, upon receipt of certain inputs, were caused to dive for safety, and those that did not have it were not. Under what conditions would this difference between having and not having such a mechanism make a difference in reproductive output? When moving toward safety, as opposed to not so moving, made a difference in reproductive output – namely, when a predator was in fact present. The presence of a predator, therefore, is a condition of success – what Millikan

---

3 Millikan (1989) is explicit that only the interpreter mechanism is relevant to content: "… a good look at the consumer [i.e., interpreter] part of the system ought to be all that is needed to determine not only representational status but representational content" (reprinted in Millikan 1993, 88). A year later, however, Millikan modifies her view, claiming that the function of the *producer* mechanism, in addition to the function of the interpreter, is required. See section V below for discussion.

calls a "Normal condition" – for the performance of the mechanism's proper function.

Teleosemantics thus asserts that the type of belief enjoyed by the fleeing beavers has the specific content "predator in the vicinity" if and only if:

(i) the beavers have a mechanism the proper function of which is to process and respond to the signature acoustic signal produced by a specific type of tail slap, and

(ii) the Normal condition for the performance of this mechanism's proper function is the presence of a predator.

A token of this type of belief, I assume, has the specified content if and only if it is interpreted (or consumed) by an instance of the relevant interpreter mechanism. This, in outline, is the teleosemantic approach to content.

III. Excess Normal Conditions

It is clear, however, even in the beaver case, that the conditions set forth in (T) are excessive to a fault – they cannot capture the object-specificity of the fleeing beavers' belief. An adequate explanation of the selective success of the beavers' interpreting mechanism must cite several ecological conditions. And, as we shall see, while each of these conditions contributed substantially to the mechanism's selective success, virtually none was among the objects of the beavers' mental state. More generally, explanations of success in selection are adequate to the extent they specify salient features of the environment and the population. The problem is that the range of such features is typically far broader than the range of objects that appear in the mental contents of the organisms involved.

To see the problem, consider the diversity of Normal conditions involved in even simple cases of evolution by natural selection. Consider, for example, the case of the peppered moth *Biston betularia*, studied by Kettlewell (1973). Prior to 1850 in the Manchester, England area, roughly ninety-nine percent of the moths in the local population had light-coloured wings. This was a consequence of the fact that lichen grew on the tree trunks upon which the moths roosted, camouflaging those that were similarly coloured while exposing those with dark coloration to predatory birds. But the selective regime changed dramatically with the onset of the industrial revolution. Heavy coal soot settled upon trees, killing lichen and darkening trunks, with the result that dark moths were camouflaged while light ones were exposed. By 1900, only one per cent of the population had light-coloured wings; the fortunes of dark-coloured and light-coloured moths had reversed. In Millikan's terms, then, dark coloration acquired the proper function of providing camouflage from predatory birds. Hence, the evolution due to selection of melanism.

This selective explanation appeals to various conditions of selective success. It appeals to those features of the organism and those of the selective regime that led to the success of dark coloration. Perhaps the most obvious is the presence of predatory birds. Had the birds skipped town or found a better food source, there would have been no new selective discrimination between dark and light coloration and hence no evolutionary change. In that case, dark coloration would not have acquired the proper function of providing camouflage. But equally obvious is the presence of dark tree trunks. Had the tree trunks remained light in coloration, there would have been no change in selective discrimination and hence no redistribution in the relative frequency of dark coloration. In that case, dark coloration would not have acquired the proper function it did. So the Normal conditions for dark coloration include at least these two features, predatory birds and dark tree trunks.

In general terms, a feature of the environment is a condition of selective success so long as it affects members of the population in such a way that there is discrimination between variants of one or more traits. In the moth case, the presence of predatory birds elicited competition between dark and light coloration that resulted in selection. The presence of birds thus discriminated between dark and light moths. But responsibility for selection does not fall entirely to the birds. The birds occupied the moth's niche prior to the onset of selection for dark coloration. It was only when industrial soot darkened the tree trunks upon which the moths roosted that selection for dark coloration set in. So an adequate selective explanation of dark coloration must cite both the presence of the birds and the presence of darkened tree trunks.

Features of the environment that discriminate in this way between variants of organismic traits are features that trigger a *selective response* within the population. We may identify such features on the basis of the following:

> (SR) Environmental feature *F* is an integral part of the selective regime acting on population *P* if and only if there is differential reproduction within *P* caused by differences between organisms in the success with which they respond to or satisfy *F*.

The way to identify a Normal condition is to identify features of the environment that provoke a selective response – that satisfy (SR) – for such are the conditions of selective success. If some feature provokes competition between variants of some trait, then that feature of the environment must be cited in explaining the subsequent selective success, in which case it is a Normal condition. Otherwise, it is non-Normal. This way of identifying Normal conditions is grounded in the theory of evolution by natural selection, in considerations involved in adequate explanations of selective success. Advocates of teleosemantics thus must endorse (SR). Or, if there are sound objections to (SR), advocates nevertheless must endorse some mechanism for identifying conditions of selective success that accurately reflects the constraints on adequate selective explanations.

As we have seen, an adequate selective explanation in the moth case must cite not only the presence of predatory birds, but also the presence of darkened trees, and the conditions set forth in (SR) make clear why this is so. Darkened trees triggered a selective response in the population insofar as there was differential reproduction caused by differences between moths with dark wings and moths with light wings. The difference, of course, was that moths with dark-coloured wings better satisfied the demand for camouflage by better blending with the darkened tree trunks.

Now consider the beaver case again. Surely the presence of predators is *one* condition of selective success, as Millikan claims, since predators satisfy (SR). But as in the case of the peppered moth, the presence of predators does not suffice; an adequate selective explanation must cite further conditions that led to success. Suppose, for example, that not just any sort of tail slap triggers the interpreting mechanism that causes beavers to flee. Suppose that the slap must be produced with a specific force and tempo, that there is a *signature* acoustic signal that triggers the interpreting mechanism. Slaps that are significantly softer or louder and slaps that are significantly slower or faster fail to produce the signature acoustic signal. For good measure, let us also assume that the signature sound involves a splashing noise, in which case slaps upon tiny puddles, downed trees, or dry ground likewise fail to trigger the interpreting mechanism. Slaps thus produce the signature sound only if produced upon sufficiently large bodies of water.

In this case, then, at least three features of the beavers' ecology are candidate conditions of selective success. The interpreting mechanism is triggered only if, in addition to (1) the presence of predators, there exists (2) a tail slap with appropriate force and tempo and (3) a sufficiently large body of water upon which the slap is produced. Features (2) and (3) are analogous to the presence of darkened tree trunks in the case of the peppered moth. Just as a change in the coloration of the tree trunks triggered the selective regime that resulted in the evolution of melanism, so too variations in the force and tempo of tail slaps and variations in the quantity of water in the vicinity result in new selective regimes affecting the population. They do so, at any rate, in conjunction with one another and the presence of predators. When beavers fail to slap with appropriate force or tempo, or when a drought or a new dam or sheer haste prevents beavers from slapping upon sufficiently large bodies of water, possession of the interpreting mechanism confers no selective advantage. In such unhappy circumstances, beavers with the interpreting mechanism are subject to predation at the same rate as those that lack the mechanism. It is only when the tail slaps produced are appropriate and only when there is sufficient water in the vicinity that there is selective discrimination between organisms with the mechanism and those without it. So (2) and (3), along with (1), satisfy (SR), and hence all three are among the Normal conditions for the proper functioning of the interpreting mechanism.

Teleosemantics thus forces us to attribute to the fleeing beavers the rather bloated belief that there are predators in the vicinity *and* sufficient water in the vicinity *and* a tail slap with such-and-such force and tempo. This, of course, is hardly plausible. Neither the presence of a certain kind of tail slap nor the presence of water is relevant to an intentional explanation of the fleeing behaviour that ensues. But both conditions *are* relevant to an explanation of the selective success of the beavers' interpreting mechanism. This illustrates the excesses of teleosemantics. It is this sort of excess, derived from rudimentary constraints on explanations of selective success, that renders the theory powerless to account for the object-specificity of content.

IV. Adequate Selective Explanations

There are several skeptical reactions to this line of argument. Three deserve comment. All are concerned with the conditions of adequacy for selective explanations. Perhaps the most worrisome is that selective explanations are not nearly so clear-cut as my argument suggests. In particular, my appeal to (SR) may give the false impression that any proposed selective explanation can be evaluated as adequate or as inadequate with no attending vagueness. It is na ve to think that the conditions of adequacy on selective explanations are precise; it is na ve to think that (SR) can distinguish neatly between features of the environment that are conditions of success and those that are not. In consequence, it is likewise na ve to think that a decisive refutation of teleosemantics (or any theory) can be based upon (SR).

I agree with the substance of this objection. Under certain conditions, it is indeed hard to know whether a given condition satisfies (SR). But this hardly impugns the force of my argument against teleosemantics. Two considerations are relevant. No doubt there is no clear line between all the features of the environment responsible for the selective response and all the features not responsible. But surely the existence of such vagueness does not prevent us from identifying *some* of the features responsible for a selective response. If this were not the case, evolutionary biologists would despair of ever producing adequate selective explanations. Yet there are plenty of such explanations available, including the evolution of melanism in the peppered moth population. And in the case at hand – fleeing beavers – it is likewise clear that vagueness does not undermine our explanation. It is clear that at least *some* features of the environment satisfy (SR), including the presence of appropriate tail slaps and the presence of sufficient water. This is clear because beavers flee only in response to the signature acoustic signal; they do not dive for safety in the presence of other sorts of tail slaps. Since the presence of sufficient water and an appropriate slap are (by hypothesis) integral to production of the signature signal, they, by their very presence, and in concert with the presence of predators, trigger a selective response. At any rate, if we are unwilling to say that sufficient water and appropriate slaps are triggers of a selective response, we should be equally unwilling to say it of predators – and I take it for granted that we *are* willing to say it of predators. I conclude, therefore, that worries about vagueness in no way diminish my thesis that teleosemantics suffers a fatal excess of conditions satisfying (SR).[4]

But suppose I am mistaken. Suppose the application of (SR) to signature slaps or sufficient water is vague. That does not show that the general form of my argument fails, for it does not rule out the possibility that an alternative example will raise the problem of excess Normal conditions. This seems a genuine possibility when we consider examples involving mentally more complex agents such as normal adult human beings. Moreover, if the application of (SR) is vague in this way, then that is a problem for *advocates* – not critics – of teleosemantics. After all, advocates of teleosemantics assert that content is fixed by the conditions of selective success. If the above objection is correct, if (SR) fails to specify with sufficient precision the conditions of selective success, then there is little hope of teleosemantics ever accounting for the object-specificity of mental contents. This assumes, of course, that (SR) is the correct or at least the best means available of distinguishing Normal from non-Normal conditions. That is an assumption I embrace. Unless there are ways to improve (SR) that eliminate all such vagueness, the problem of vagueness, such as it is, belongs to advocates of teleosemantics.

A second skeptical reaction to the argument of the previous section is that the problem of excess Normal conditions is really just the old problem of distinguishing explanatory causes from mere background causes, in which case teleosemantics can be excused for

---

4 There are, of course, additional conditions integral to the beavers' success. I mention one presently.

not having solved it. Pietroski, in an otherwise powerful criticism of teleosemantics, asserts that

> This distinction between background and explanatory [i.e., Normal] conditions is neither perfectly sharp nor completely satisfactory. But this is hardly a strong point against Millikan's account, as opposed to other (say, causal) accounts. (Pietroski 1992, 272)

I agree with the analogy. The problem of excess Normal conditions is structurally analogous to the problem of distinguishing between explanatorily salient causal factors and those that are merely in the background. But I do not agree that this excuses the problem of excess Normal conditions. First, as I have explained, evolutionary biologists *do* apply (SR) to good effect, in which case the distinction between background and Normal conditions *is* sufficiently sharp and satisfactory. We thus have strong *prima facie* reason to accept the constraints imposed by (SR). And, of course, advocates of teleosemantics have even stronger reason to accept it, since they take themselves to be giving a theory of content grounded in evolutionary theory. Second, we must remember *why* teleology was introduced into the debate about content in the first place. It was hoped that appeal to conditions of selective success would justify the claim that certain conditions in the world were genuinely explanatory and thus constitutive of content. It was asserted that teleosemantics improves on causal accounts *in precisely this regard* – Millikan (1989; 1990; 1991) is explicit on this point. Since teleosemantics is *supposed to* solve the problem that has dogged causal accounts – since it supposed to be *better* than those accounts – the fact that it is *no worse* is hardly a compelling defence.

A third skeptical worry suggests that I have misconstrued Millikan's account. On my construal, the content of the beavers' belief is fixed by the Normal conditions for the proper functioning of the interpreting mechanism (but see section V below for modification of this view). That much is unobjectionable. But I also claim that the presence of appropriate tail slaps and sufficient water are among the Normal conditions for the interpreting mechanism. It is here that the objection is lodged. The presence of appropriate slaps and sufficient water, it is suggested, are Normal conditions for the proper functioning of the relevant *producer* mechanism but *not* for the co-operating *interpreter* mechanism. The producer is the mechanism that causes the sentry beaver to slap its tail in response to what he takes to be a predator, while the interpreter is the mechanism that causes the other beavers to flee. Since these are distinct mechanisms, their conditions of selective success are likely distinct as well. Indeed, the producer mechanism can discharge its proper function only when it produces an appropriate type of slap and only when there is sufficient water. But once discharged – once the signature acoustic signal has been issued – the Normal conditions for that mechanism lapse. Now it is up to the interpreter to do its job, and for that a *different* set of Normal conditions applies. In particular, the interpreting mechanism responds to the signature signal; it does not respond to the *production* of that signal, but to the *signal* itself. So the Normal conditions for production need not be among the Normal conditions for interpretation of the signal. Hence the argument I have levelled against teleosemantics fails on the grounds that it conflates distinct sets of Normal conditions.[5]

But this cannot be right. For one rather central condition of the interpreter's selective success is the *presence of the producer mechanism*. The Normal conditions for the functioning of the beavers' interpreting mechanism include the presence of predators, to be sure, but they also include the presence of the producer mechanism with which it co-operates. In fact, it is likely that the interpreter and the producer mechanisms co-evolved as a result of their mutually supporting selective success. If so, then the presence of each mechanism is among the Normal conditions for the functioning of the other. And this means that the conditions integral to the selective success of each mechanism are likewise among the Normal conditions of the other. So, while I agree that the presence of an appropriate tail slap and the presence of sufficient water are Normal for the functioning of the producer, I disagree that this entails that they are not Normal for the functioning of the interpreter. On the contrary, since they are Normal for the producer, they must be Normal for the interpreter.

This interdependence between producers and interpreters is, I

---

5 I am grateful to Colin Allen and Mohan Matthen for raising this objection during the conference mentioned below in footnote 6.

believe, embedded in Millikan's view, especially the more recent statements. She asserts, for example, that:

> Being "built" by natural selection is sufficient for proper function, being maintained by natural selection is independently sufficient, and having been utilized by other structures built or maintained by natural selection is also independently sufficient for proper function. (Millikan 1993, 49)

Suppose, then, that trait T has proper function F because ancestral tokens were selected for task F. Suppose further that ancestral tokens of some other trait T^* performed task F^*, where this performance was utilized by ancestral tokens of T in the course of T's being selected for task F. On Millikan's view, then, tokens of T^* today have the proper function of performing F^* *by virtue of being utilized* by ancestral tokens of T. That means that current tokens of T^*, like current tokens of T, have Normal conditions for the fulfillment of their proper function. But surely the Normal conditions for T^* are *among* the Normal conditions for current tokens of T. Since the ancestral performance of F^* by tokens of T^* contributed to the selective success of ancestral tokens of T, then surely the conditions of T^*'s selective success are among the conditions of T's selective success. I take it, therefore, that Millikan would agree with my response to the present objection – that the Normal conditions of the producer are among those of the interpreter.

One could, I suppose, insist that Millikan has things wrong and that she should not allow that the presence of the producer is among the Normal conditions for the functioning of the interpreter. But I think Millikan is right in this regard. Applying (SR) shows that the presence of the producer mechanism is among the conditions of selective success for the interpreter. Historically, the presence of this mechanism – along with the presence of predators, appropriate tail slaps, and sufficient water – triggered a selective response between beavers with the interpreting mechanism and beavers without it. An adequate selective explanation of the interpreter must cite the efficacy of the producer, as well as the efficacy of any other mechanisms with which the interpreter co-evolved. This shows, incidentally, that the teleosemantic content attributed to the fleeing beavers is not simply "the presence of predators *and* the presence of an appropriate tail slap *and* the presence of sufficient water," but also "the presence of the producer mechanism." The excesses of teleosemantics are extensive indeed.

V. A Failed Response

Millikan (1990) attempts to solve the problem of excess Normal conditions, but her proposal does not work. She addresses the problem in the course of discussing the snapping behaviour of frogs. Some mechanism within the frog produces a visual representation of a nearby fly; this representation is translated into an internal code and delivered to the bug detector mechanism; this detector, *qua* interpreter, processes the incoming representation according to some rule and, in consequence, sends a signal to the tongue-snapping mechanism, causing it to fire. Hence, the frog eats. All of this, we may suppose, was selectively efficacious in ancestral frogs, in which case the bug detector now has the proper function of processing and responding to such representations. A plausible Normal condition for the fulfillment of this function is the presence of flies, in which case the Millikanian content of this particular frog belief is "there is a fly present."

Now, Millikan acknowledges that there are other candidate Normal conditions in this case, including the "presence of surround air and [the] presence of a stable platform under the snapping frog" (Millikan 1990, in Millikan 1993, 127). She thus is obligated to argue that these conditions are not relevant to the detector's selective success and hence not among the Normal conditions. I will assess her argument for that claim presently. But first notice that it is quite easy to agree with Millikan that the presence of surround air and a stable base beneath the frog are conditions that selective explanations probably rightly ignore. This is so, at any rate, *if* neither satisfies (SR). But it does not follow from this that the problem of excess Normal conditions is solved. The problem is not resolved by simply noticing that there are *some* conditions that do not qualify as Normal. What needs to be shown is that teleosemantics provides principled grounds for distinguishing Normal from non-Normal conditions in all pertinent cases. We need principled reasons, for example, for thinking that an appropriate tail slap or sufficient water in the beaver case fails to satisfy (SR) – or fails to satisfy some other, defensible account of Normal conditions.

131

Millikan's response is to modify her theory. In addition to the interpreter or consumer mechanism, we now must pay heed to the function of the producer mechanism as well:

> This is where the function of the representation *producer* needs to be brought in. The representation producer has been designed by selection to produce representations for the consumer *that* correspond to conditions in the world *by* the rule of correspondence that figures in the most proximate normal explanation of the consumer's success. To be very explicit, the producer's job is to produce not just a representation – graphically, a "shape" – but to produce a correspondence, a certain relation *between* "shape" and world. Obviously, if this is the producer's function, there must be a way that it sometimes *effects* this function. But ... the frog's bug-detection system [does not] help to *effect* that its firings coincide with the presence of surround air and the presence of a frog-supporting platform. So it cannot be a *function* of these systems to produce these correspondences, hence these correspondences are not relevant to mental semantics. (Millikan 1993, 127–28)

The argument in this passage in not entirely perspicuous, but I take the main moves to be the following:

(1) Producer mechanisms have the proper function of producing representations (shapes, sounds, etc.) that correspond to certain conditions in the environment.

(2) Producer mechanisms have the proper function of producing a correspondence relation between certain representations (shapes, sounds, etc.) and certain conditions in the environment.

(3) In order to have the proper function of producing such correspondence relations, producer mechanisms must effect (do) something that produces those relations.

(4) The relevant mechanism in the frog does not effect a correspondence between snapping behaviour and the presence of surround air or the presence of a stable platform, in which case it cannot have the associated proper function.

(5) Therefore, since the frog mechanism cannot have the proper function of producing a correspondence involving the presence of air or a stable platform, these conditions are not genuine Normal conditions.

Proper functions accrue to producer mechanisms only if they "effect" correspondences between certain outputs and certain conditions of the environment. But, presumably, no producer mechanism can effect a correspondence involving the presence of air or the stability of the earth's surface because there is nothing that such a mechanism can do to produce or otherwise influence its relations to those features. The production of these relations, then, is not a proper function of producer mechanisms, in which case the question concerning Normal conditions does not arise.

This is Millikan's attempt to distinguish Normal from non-Normal conditions. But her argument, to the extent I understand it, is unsound. The main claim is that the producer mechanism has the function of producing correspondence relations (premise 2) precisely when it has the capacity to "effect" its relations to the specified features of the environment in ways that lead to selective success (premise 3). Returning to the beaver case, then, we may grant that the firing of the sentry mechanism has the proper function of effecting a correspondence between itself and certain conditions of selective success. The question, of course, is, What are these conditions? Well, Millikan is committed to the following two claims:

(a)   the sentry mechanism effects a correspondence between its own firings and the presence of predators, and

(b)   the mechanism does not effect a correspondence between its firings and the presence of sufficient water, nor between firings and slaps produced with signature force and tempo.

The problem for Millikan's argument, however, is that (a) appears false and, to the extent (a) can be made plausible, (b) appears false. I begin with (a).

Premise (1) of Millikan's argument, as reconstructed above, asserts that the producer mechanism has the proper function of producing representations that correspond with certain conditions in the environment. Let us grant the claim. Premise (2), however, is a dubious strengthening of (1). It is dubious because it inflates the functional powers of organismic traits in a manner that is difficult to justify. It is one thing to say that a producer mechanism produces representations that correspond (co-vary) with certain conditions in the environment. That is just to say that the mechanism has the function of producing representations that are functional – representations that co-vary with certain features of the environment and thereby accomplish some work within the organismic system. Premise (1) thus can be true even though the powers of the mechanism are limited to the production of representations. The correspondences that occur between representations and certain features of the environment may have been historically accidental but nevertheless sufficiently regular to result in selective success. Premise (2), by contrast, is much stronger. The claim is that the mechanism has not only the function of producing representations, but also the function of producing correspondence relations between representations and certain features of the environment. The claim, so far as I understand it, is that the mechanism has the function of non-accidentally bringing about correspondences between its own firings and the occurrence of some quite specific feature of the environment. If this were the case, the production of the correspondence would have to be something the mechanism controls in some manner or other; it would have to be a consequence of something the mechanism directly "effects." But, if this is a correct interpretation of premise (2), on what grounds should we believe that a mechanism as simple as the beaver's sentry is endowed with any such powers?

This is not to question the capacity of the mechanism to produce certain representations under certain conditions. It is to question, rather, the alleged capacity to control the production of a correspondence between representations and some highly specific feature of the environment. On what grounds do we attribute to the mechanism the "effecting" of any such correspondence relation? Indeed, on what grounds do we justifiably attribute to the mechanism the capacity to "effect" anything at all – *especially* when "effecting" is so fine-grained as to rule in the presence of one causal factor (predators) and rule out the presence of other, closely related factors (signature slaps, sufficient water, etc.)? At the very least, we need evidence for the existence of this rather remarkable capacity to "effect" such correspondences. As it is, we have no justification, either in terms of the beaver's psychology or its selective history, to attribute to its sentry mechanism the capacity to so "effect." Statement (a) must be set aside.

It is difficult to fully assess the claim that producer mechanisms effect correspondences because we do not know with any precision what "effecting" refers to. We could try to fill the gap by explicating the concept on Millikan's behalf, but that is unlikely to save her argument. This brings me to claim (b). If we grant the sentry mechanism the capacity to "effect" a correspondence between firings and predators, we should, by parity of reasoning, grant it the capacity to "effect" a correspondence between firings and sufficient water, and between firings and signature slaps. Whatever "effecting" comes to, if the sentry mechanism accomplishes it with respect to predators, what prevents it from producing the same result with respect to all the other features of the selective regime that played a proximate, causal role in the mechanism's selective success? Whatever the beaver's mechanism "does" to effect a correspondence between firings and predators is, presumably, something it can "do" to effect a correspondence between firings and sufficient water and firings and signature slaps. And if the mechanism cannot do it in the latter case, why think it can in the former? After all, the presence of water and the presence of appropriate tail slaps worked *in concert with* the presence of predators; *all* of these conditions are equally immediate and proximate, and, had even one been absent, the sentry mechanism would not have been selected for. An adequate selective explanation of the sentry's selective success must cite them all. There is, in consequence, no justification for thinking that the capacity to "effect" a correspondence will somehow provide the theoretical resources with which to isolate just one of these three conditions as the real and true Normal condition.

The failure to explicate and defend the relevant notion of "effecting" is not a trivial omission. But neither is it a surprising omission, given the extraordinary work it is assigned. After all, the appeal to the effecting abilities of the producer mechanism is supposed to solve a central problem for any theory of content, namely, the object-specificity of content. Indeed, the capacity to effect correspondences, on Millikan's view, is nothing more, though nothing less, than the capacity to specify the objects of our representational states. We thus are being asked to believe that producer mechanisms, like the sentry in the beaver, contain the entire solution, or at least the crux of the solution, to the problem of object-specificity. And we are being asked to believe this with no account of the crucial capacity and no argument concerning its reality. We are being told, in essence, that our representational states have object-specificity because the thing that produces those states gives it to them. That, of course, may be true, but we need evidence that mechanisms as simple as the beavers' sentry are in fact endowed with such striking powers.

At any rate, the burden is on Millikan to explain how the capacity to "effect" correspondences can save teleosemantics from an excess of Normal conditions. Short of that, we have a rather stark choice. We can identify Normal conditions by way of (SR), as I suggest, or we can do so by way of the capacity to effect correspondences, as Millikan suggests. As we have seen, (SR) has the virtue of being anchored in the theory of evolution by natural selection. It also has the virtue of being clear enough to employ in actual biological theorizing. The notion of effecting, by contrast, appears devoid of any such virtues.

VI. Conclusion

The inability to eliminate excessive Normal conditions undermines the teleosemantic attempt to naturalize mental content. The proposed naturalization is plausible only if the appeal to evolutionary theory is consistent with our best available understanding of that theory. But Millikan's appeal is not consistent in this way. She restricts the range of Normal conditions to fit neatly the semantic stories she wishes to tell, but such restrictions are at odds with the requirements, expressed in (SR), on adequate selective explanations. Teleosemantics, in consequence, fails to account for the object-specificity of mental content. Its excesses undo it. [6]

---

6 My thanks to Jillian McIntosh for inviting me to present an earlier version of this paper at *Naturalism, Evolution, and Intentionality: An Interdisciplinary Conference in the Philosophy of Mind* in April of 1998. Thanks to her tireless efforts, the conference was productive and pleasant. I am additionally grateful to Jillian for comments on the penultimate draft of this paper. I am also grateful to the philosophy department at the University of Western Ontario for hosting the conference. I first floated the idea for this paper in conversation with Christopher Gauker while I was a Charles P. Taft Postdoctoral Fellow at the University of Cincinnati. My thanks to Chris for his spirited skepticism. My thanks too to the University of Cincinnati philosophy department for their warmth and collegiality and to the Taft Memorial Foundation for support of my work. Finally, thanks to my home institution for additional support.

References

Davies, P. S. 2000. "The Nature of Natural Norms: Why Selected Functions are Systemic Capacity Functions," *Noûs* **31**, 85–107.

———. 2001. *Norms of Nature: Naturalism and the Nature of Functions.* Cambridge, MA: MIT Press.

Fodor, J. A. 1990. *A Theory of Content and Other Essays.* Cambridge, MA: MIT Press.

Kettlewell, H.B.D. 1973. *The Evolution of Melanism: The Study of a Recurring Necessity.* Oxford: Oxford University Press.

Millikan, R. G. 1984. *Language, Thought, and Other Biological Categories.* Cambridge, MA: MIT Press.

———. 1989. "Biosemantics," *Journal of Philosophy* **86**, 281–97.

———. 1990. "Compare and Contrast Dretske, Fodor, and Millikan on Teleosemantics," *Philosophical Topics* **18**, 151–61.

———. 1993. *White Queen Psychology and Other Essays for Alice.* Cambridge, MA: MIT Press.

Papineau, D. 1987. *Representation and Reality.* Cambridge, MA: Basil Blackwell.

———. 1993. *Philosophical Naturalism.* Cambridge, MA: Blackwell.

Pietroski, P. 1992. "Intentionality and Teleological Error," *Pacific Philosophical Quarterly* **73**, 267–82.

Sterelny, K. 1990. *The Representational Theory of Mind: An Introduction.* Cambridge, MA: Basil Blackwell.

CANADIAN JOURNAL OF PHILOSOPHY
Supplementary Volume 27

Teleosemantics and the Epiphenomenality of Content

ERIC SAIDEL

The naturalistically inclined philosopher of mind faces two related challenges: (1) show how mental content could be part of the natural world, and (2) show how content can be one of the factors responsible for producing (causing) behaviour, that is, show that content is not epiphenomenal. One might pursue the first goal with the intent of showing that mental content is epiphenomenal, but it is more likely that the philosopher concerned with showing how content can be naturalized also expects content to be causally efficacious. Indeed, why pursue the first challenge while holding that content is epiphenomenal? Thus these two challenges overlap: show how content can be naturalized without making content epiphenomenal.

One apparently promising approach to these challenges is the family of theories that appeal to evolution by natural selection (or to some analogous process) in order to naturalize content. I argue that these theories, teleosemantic approaches to the mind, fail to meet this combined challenge. Even if they succeed in naturalizing content, they fail by making content epiphenomenal. The problem is that teleosemantic theories make the determinants of content distinct from the state that is supposed to be doing the causal work. Teleosemantic theories face what Kim (1991) calls the "soprano" problem.[1] According

---

1 Imagine a soprano sings the syllable "break" at the appropriate volume and pitch, causing a crystal glass to shatter. The glass shatters because of pitch and volume of the sound and not because of its meaning. (The example is Dretske's.)

to teleosemantics, the content of a mental state is determined by its history, but the causal work the state is doing now is determined by those (physical) properties that are present now. This opens teleosemantics to the soprano problem; the historical properties of the state – its content properties – are epiphenomenal. I argue that the soprano problem so thoroughly infects teleosemantics that even the solutions teleosemanticists propose for the soprano problem succumb to it.

This essay proceeds as follows: I consider three versions of teleosemantics, those presented by Dretske (in §1), Millikan (in §2), and Neander (in §3),[2] and argue that each of these theories has the consequence of making the content of a representation epiphenomenal insofar as it is determined by the teleological function of that representation. In §4, I argue that any theory that looks to evolution by natural selection to provide intentionality will face this fate. In the concluding section, I argue that this result should be noteworthy to all philosophers who think that there may be minds, whether they think mental properties are epiphenomenal or not.

1. Structuring Causes

Dretske's goal in his 1988 book *Explaining Behavior: Reasons in a World of Causes* is to show "how reasons – our beliefs, desires, purposes, and plans – operate in a world of causes, and to exhibit the role of reasons in the *causal* explanation of human behavior." He suggests further that some of the things we do are *"causally* explained ... by the reasons we have for doing them." (p. x, his emphasis) Furthermore, Dretske is careful to make clear that in referring to reasons, he is referring to their content. He wishes to show how a reason's explanation of behaviour can be both the correct (causal) explanation of behaviour and consistent with a bio-chemical (also causal) explanation of behaviour.

---

2 See Dretske (1988; 1995), Millikan (1984; 1993a), and Neander (1995). I consider these theories because they are sufficiently distinct to be interesting and because they are representative of the teleosemantic theories that are offered by other philosophers. Other philosophers who favour teleosemantics include David Papineau (1987), and Kim Sterelny (1990).

Dretske does this, in part, by arguing that the explananda that are explained by reference to representations are instances of internal events causing bodily movements, rather than instances of bodily movements *simpliciter*. When I walk to the fridge, my bodily motion is an event that is caused by some event(s) internal to me. This internal event is generally thought to be representational in nature. However, Dretske doesn't look to the content of this representation to be a cause of my bodily movement. He allows that the representation causes the bodily movement in virtue of its formal properties, and not in virtue of its semantic properties. Instead, it is that internal event's causing of the bodily movement that itself is caused by the content of the representation.

The best way to conceptualize Dretske's account is by looking at how Dretske symbolizes this complex event. Allowing the bodily motions to be represented by M, and the neural/representational cause of those motions to be C, the complex event is then: $C{\to}M$ (where the arrow symbolizes causation). Dretske notices that there are two sorts of causes of $C{\to}M$. One he calls the "triggering" cause: What caused C, which then caused M? Clearly some other neural events. The other is what Dretske calls the "structuring" cause: What caused my body to be wired in such a way that C would cause M? The answer to this question, Dretske argues, is the content of C.

In order to evaluate this proposal, we need to look next at how Dretske thinks content is determined. For Dretske, the content of a representation is determined by the (teleological)[3] function of that representation. In addition, Dretske is careful to distinguish between

---

3 The philosophical literature is rife with claims that functions are best understood either as capacities inherent in an object or as capacities that an object is supposed to have. See Wright (1973), Neander (1991), and Godfrey-Smith (1994) for arguments in favour of the latter view; see Cummins (1975) and Bigelow and Pargetter (1987) for arguments favouring other views. For an argument that the etiological (latter) view does not tell the full story of biological functions, see Walsh (1996). And for a general overview of the debate, see Enç and Adams (1992). Etiology is thought to provide objects with normative functions: a heart, for example, *should* pump blood, otherwise it is *malfunctioning*. Thus, etiology-based theories make the normative character of mental states dependent upon the teleological nature of biological functions. Thus, those philosophers wishing to ground intentionality by appeal to biological functions generally support an etiological understanding of biological functions.

systems (and their functions) and states of those systems (and their functions). This instance of $C{\rightarrow}M$ is an instance of a particular token event of C occurring, which occurrence then causes (triggers) M. But C, the token, is a state of a system, which itself is the product of selection. Call this system S. S is an indicator of F (roughly, it is reliably correlated with F), and it is because it indicates F that it has been selected as a cause of M. This selection is what has structured the event of $C{\rightarrow}M$. The triggering cause of $C{\rightarrow}M$ is the event that caused this tokening of C; the structuring cause of $C{\rightarrow}M$ is the selection of the system S to be hooked up so that states of S would be causes of M. S was selected because it is an indicator of F. S indicates F and it is this fact that causes Cs, states of S, to be causes of M.

S is a system that indicates F by tokening Cs, but according to Dretske, this alone does not make Cs representations of F. Indicating a property does not make a state a representation of that property. When we take the number of rings of a tree to represent a tree's age, the representational power of the tree's rings is dependent upon our ability to represent. Dretske is interested in something other than that: representations that do not derive their content from some other intentional system. For Dretske, the difference between tree rings and representations generated by some system lies in the function the system has. The tree rings do not have the function of indicating the age of the tree; however, S does have the function of indicating F. Being an indicator is not sufficient to make a system a generator of contentful representations; instead the system must have indicating as its function.

So: S indicates F by generating Cs, and because S indicates F, S has been recruited (i.e., appropriately coupled with other systems) so that the states it generates, Cs, can be causes of M. One consequence of this is that Cs now mean F. Thus, it is S's representing F that is the structuring cause of the complex event $C{\rightarrow}M$. Content does not explain the triggering of this event, but it does explain why the organism is structured so that C causes M. Put differently, there are (at least) two sorts of why-questions we may ask about the event of M: "Why did C cause M now, rather than at some other time?" and "Why did C cause M, rather than some other event?" The answer to the first question will cite the triggering cause of *C*; the answer to the second question will cite the structuring cause of *C*→*M*.[4]

---

4 I argue below that this proposal fails to accomplish what it sets out to; it does not succeed in making reasons causes, even structuring causes. In a sense, then, it is too conservative about meanings. Interestingly enough, if this proposal were to succeed in making reasons causes it seems that it would be too liberal about meanings: many organisms (and artifacts) have systems that have been recruited as causes because of what they indicate. We might reasonably balk at attributing to all of these organisms action for a reason. For example, deciduous trees presumably have a system that senses the presence of autumn. States of this system cause the tree to lose its leaves. Furthermore, this system is hooked up the way it is, so that when it generates these states, they cause the tree to lose its leaves, because these states are indicators of autumn. Thus, according to Dretske's account, the content of this state, that it is fall, is a structuring cause of the behaviour the tree is performing (i.e., the tree's internal states causing it to lose its leaves). Reasons are causes for trees just as much as they are for human beings. Of course, that's approximately where we started: the worry was that reasons were just as much causes of human behaviour as they are of tree behaviour (i.e., not at all); Dretske's view fails to be satisfactory if he is forced to declare that reasons are just as much causes of tree behaviour as they are of human behaviour. Dretske considers a similar example (1988, 89ff.) and argues that this is not a problem for his view because, while natural selection is responsible for trees with such a structure surviving, natural selection is not the cause of the structure of the individual trees (but see Sober 1995). Notice, though, that this defence rules out any explanation by reference to content when a structure was formed in a previous generation. Thus, it is not unlikely that there is an evolutionary explanation for the discomfort many people feel in the presence of snakes, but Dretske's claim suggests that if this is so, then their behaviour is not appropriately explained by reference to their discomfort. Moreover, this blocks content explanations in the case of mass-produced artifacts. We may be tempted to suggest, as Dretske does (1988, 87–88), that thermostats have the structure they do because of the (contentful) plans of their designer. But this would be a mistake: thermostats have the structure they do because they are produced by machines which cause them to have the structure they do, in the same way that the genotype of the trees causes them to have the structure they do. If the genotype screens off natural selection in the case of the trees, then the specifications of the thermostat-producing machine screens off the plans of the designer in the case of the thermostat. So much the worse for both.

For example, suppose my thermostat is rigged so that when the temperature drops below a certain threshold, it opens my garage door. We ask why the thermostat opened the garage door, but this question is ambiguous: we may wish to know why the thermostat opened the garage door now, rather than at some other time; or we may also wish to know why the thermostat opened the garage door, rather than starting the furnace. The answer to the former question is that the temperature dropped below the threshold at which the thermostat was set. This question demands an answer in terms of a triggering cause. The answer to the latter question will have to do with the way the electrician wired the system. This question demands a structuring cause explanation. Dretske urges us to think that questions about behaviour (bodily movements) are similarly ambiguous. For example, upon seeing me retrieve a beer from the fridge, you may wonder why I did so. You may be wondering why I got a beer from the fridge now, rather than ten minutes ago. This is a demand for a triggering cause. I explain my actions by telling you that I want a beer now, whereas I did not want a beer ten minutes ago. (However, it is not the content of my desire that caused the behaviour; in this case, the desire is a triggering cause, and as such it was merely its formal properties that caused the behaviour. See the paragraph immediately below.) Or you may be wondering why I attempted to retrieve the beer from the fridge rather than from the dishwasher. Here the right explanation has to do with the content of the belief(s) that caused my behaviour: I believed that beer was in the fridge and not in the dishwasher. This explanation is an explanation in terms of the structuring cause of my behaviour: I am structured so that the presence of a belief that there is beer in the fridge (in concert with desire for a beer) causes me to look in the fridge rather than the dishwasher because my beliefs that beer is in the fridge are indicators of the presence of beer in the fridge, and because of this the system that generates those beliefs was recruited as a cause of my beer-retrieving movements.[5] Thus, the role content plays is as part of the structuring, not the triggering, cause of behaviour.

---

5 In order for mental states to do any causing, there must be both motivational states and descriptive states. Dretske takes this into account. (However, see Stampe 1990.) I ignore such details in my exposition of his account as they do not affect the points I wish to make.

Unfortunately, this strategy does not manage to avoid the soprano problem. Note, first, that the role content might play on this theory isn't the role we might naively think content plays in causing our behaviour. According to Dretske's account, my belief that there is a beer in the fridge may be a structuring cause of my beer-retrieving behaviour, but the content of that token belief is inert in this (and every) causal exchange. This is because, according to Dretske, the contents of mental states play a role in structuring the mind/brain so that tokens of a particular mental state type can cause bodily movements appropriate to the content of that mental state type. They don't play a role in causing a particular behaviour (bodily movement). The content of the belief is causally inert; once the system of which that belief is a state has been recruited, the content has no role to play. Dretske might object to this argument[6] by claiming that a structuring cause can explain token events: the fact that the thermostat is wired to the garage door in the way that it is helps explain why the change in ambient temperature causes the garage door to open on a particular occasion. Similarly, my being structured (wired) in the way that I am helps explain why my belief that there is beer in the fridge is a cause of my going to the fridge to get a beer. However, structuring causes explain only the *structure* that gave rise to the behaviour; while they are certainly part of the causal antecedents of the behaviour, their role is limited to structuring the agent such that the triggering cause has the effects it has. The content of my occurrent belief, that there is beer in the fridge, plays no role in the production of my current bodily movements; the role that content plays, Dretske tells us, is to cause a particular structure to be in place, but that structure is already in place when I have the occasion to have this particular belief.

That said, content cannot play even the restricted role Dretske envisions for it. C, a state of S, has the content F because S has the function of indicating F. S gets the function of indicating F by being selected to cause M because S indicates F. Is the content of S a structuring cause of $C \rightarrow M$? No. That S is an indicator of F is a structuring cause of $C \rightarrow M$, but being an indicator of F is not the same

---

6 As he does to a similar argument put forth by Lynne Rudder Baker (1991). See Dretske (1991a).

as having the content that F; it is only when S has been recruited because S indicates F that Cs acquire the content F, but that happens at the same time that the structure $C{\rightarrow}M$ is wired up. That is, S may acquire the function of indicating F, but its having that function is not a cause of $C{\rightarrow}M$; its indicating F is.

Consider the beer-retrieval story again. Suppose I am in brain state C generated by brain system S. S generates Cs when there is beer in the fridge. That is, S is an indicator of the presence of beer in the fridge (F), and it indicates the presence of beer by tokening C. Because of this correlation between Cs and the presence of beer in the fridge, S is recruited to be a cause of M, my movements toward the fridge that end in my retrieving a beer from the fridge. Before S is recruited to be a cause of M, S lacks the function of indicating beers in the fridge, and thus Cs lack content. Once S is recruited as a cause of M, S gains the function of indicating that there is beer in the fridge, and thus Cs gain the content "there is beer in the fridge." I am in C which (in concert with some of the other states that I also instantiate) causes me to M, retrieve a beer. What is the structuring cause of C's causing me to retrieve a beer? That is, what structures my brain so that the tokening of C causes me to M? Clearly, according to Dretske's story, the fact that S was recruited to be a cause of M. Good enough. What caused S to be recruited to be a cause of M? The fact that S is an indicator of the presence of beer in the fridge. What about the content of the states that S produces? That must be inert in the structuring cause explanation of $C{\rightarrow}M$ because there was no such content when the structure coupling Cs and M was built.

This objection to Dretske's account is not wholly novel, and Dretske has responded to similar objections several times, so it is worth looking at what he has to say.[7] Dretske points out that when C has a meaning it does so because it is a token of a type, N, and that earlier tokens of N (earlier Cs) were indicators of F, and were recruited to

---

7 Previous authors who have raised similar objections include Baker (1991), Kim (1991), Horgan (1991), and Stampe (1990). For Dretske's reply I am following Dretske (1990; 1991b); I have changed his symbols for consistency with the symbols I use here.

cause M because they were indicators of F. So, "the fact that C ... represents F (has this content property) is, on this account of meaning, a fact about earlier tokens of N. It is, if you will, an *historical* fact about the role of N in the causal re-organization of the system in which its tokens occur. It is the fact that earlier tokens of N – because of what *they* (not C) indicated, because *they* successfully indicated F – shaped the causal role of subsequent tokens of N ...." Furthermore, "[t]o attribute a meaning to a token internal state is ... to describe the *source* of its causal efficacy" (1991b, 215).

However, this way of putting things only makes the difficulty more clear: the fact about earlier tokens of N that is supposed to describe the source of C's causal efficacy is that they were indicator states, not states with meaning. When the meaning of C is cited in an explanation of C's causing M, in a structuring cause explanation, what is being referred to is the fact that previous Cs were indicators of F. It is this fact that is supposed to explain how current Cs are causes of M. But nowhere does this explanation mention that current Cs have the function of indicating F. That's because even though current Cs may indeed have that function, that fact is irrelevant to Cs being causes of M; what is relevant is that previous Cs were indicators of F, something they did without having the function of indicating F, therefore something they did without representing F. The soprano problem is present even in Dretske's attempt to avoid it. The soprano problem is that by making content depend on distal events while causation depends on proximal events, teleosemantics apparently makes content irrelevant to causation. Dretske attempts to avoid this by making the explanandum a distal event as well. But, this distal event (the structuring cause of $C{\to}M$) is explained by events proximal to it, while the content of C is determined by events distal from the structuring cause of $C{\to}M$.

Thus, if the content of a representation is determined by its having the function of indicating, then content is epiphenomenal. Although it's cleverly disguised, the soprano problem is what's troublesome here. The content of the representation is determined by its function which is in turn determined by its relation to events – namely its being recruited as a cause of some movement because of its correlation with some state of affairs – but, because its content depends on this relation and not on more proximal factors, the content is powerless to produce the structure that Dretske wants it to produce.[8]

2. Normalizing Explanations

Unlike Dretske, Millikan does not wear on her sleeve her commitment to the thesis that mental content can be causally efficacious. On the contrary, she even suggests that it is not possible for content to be a cause of behaviour: "On the account of this essay, the semantic category of a thought is determined relative to its biological functions, which depend in turn on its history, upon its place relative to certain prior events. But having a history is not, of course, an attribute that has 'causal powers.' Hence reasons cannot be, as such, causes" (1993b, 186[9]).

However, like Dretske, Millikan is clearly committed to the reality of semantic content. Her efforts in explicating and defending a theory whereby semantic content is naturalized and misrepresentation is

---

8 There are two residual issues here:

> (1) Isn't this explanatory exclusion (see Kim 1991) and not the soprano problem? No. The problem is not that the formal properties of the representation can explain all its effects without recourse to the semantic properties that apparently supervene on the formal properties. The problem is that the semantic properties are determined by events in such a way that they (the semantic properties) are not present when the important causation is going on. The soprano problem is not that we think that it might be the content of the word "break" that is causing the crystal to shatter; the soprano problem is that the content is irrelevant once the volume and pitch are established. That is the problem here: once the relationship between C and M is established, then it doesn't matter what the content C has; as the content of C is irrelevant in establishing that relationship, it is epiphenomenal.
> (2) Perhaps, one might think, even though content is not causally responsible for the structure $C \rightarrow M$, it might be causally relevant. However, it is hard to see how that might be: the structure is established independently of the content of C (the same events that cause C to have the content it does cause the structure $C \rightarrow M$ to be established); there is no room for C's content to play any role.

9 Page numbers refer to the article as it appears in Millikan's 1993a.

made possible suggest, at the very least, that she thinks that the content of mental representations plays an important role in the mind. Despite her claim that reasons cannot be causes, Millikan's entire program is based on a supposition that is based on the causal powers of mental states: "If ... mental intentional states ... are members of ... [teleofunctional] categories, then they are ... intentional states not by virtue of their powers but by virtue of what they are supposed to be able to do" (1984, 17).

The distinction between these two quoted passages should be clear. It may be the case that mental states get their content by being states that are supposed to do something, but what allows them to fulfill their functions is not what determines their content, so their content is not what is supposed to do the work. This is the same puzzle that Dretske attempts to avoid. If Millikan's claim is that whatever work mental states do is in virtue of their form rather than their content, then her account also falls victim to the soprano problem. Thus, the crucial question for Millikan is what role content plays on her account.

Millikan suggests that representational systems have three main components: the representation producer, the representation, and the representation consumer. Each of these has been shaped by (a historical process that could be, but need not be) natural selection to play a particular role. The producer's role is to produce representations that the consumer can use. These representations are useful only if they inform the consumer about the world. Thus, the representations must (if the system is to work properly) correspond with the world. But, not any correspondence will do; the representations must correspond according to the rule of correspondence that the consumer is using. For example, the slap of a beaver's tail corresponds to danger (at the time and place of the slap); the consumers of this representation – other beavers – are able to interpret the slap correctly because the correspondence between the signal and conditions in the world follows the rule of correspondence they are using. (A different rule of correspondence might be that the slap corresponds to danger in five minutes.) The function of the representation producer is thus to produce representations that "are true *as the consumer reads the language*" (1989, 88, Millikan's italics).[10] One might think that the function of the representations is to correspond to conditions in the world, but, as Millikan is careful to point out, this correspondence is not something the representations effect, but something that is effected by the representation producer. Instead, each representation has the function of causing the representation consumer to "behave" in ways appropriate to the content of that representation.[11]

Content, according to this picture, is determined by "there being a certain condition that would be *normal* for performance of the consumer's functions" (1989, 89; see also 91). By "normal" Millikan means to pick out those conditions that were relevant for selection. For example, the normal condition for performance of the vomiting reflex is a condition in which there is poison in the stomach, for "[i]t is only under these conditions that this reflex has historically had beneficial effects" (1989, 87).[12] This is so even though most vomiting occurs without the presence of poison in the stomach. This correspondence between the representation and the world needs to hold in order that the well-functioning consumer achieves what it was selected to achieve.

A particular representation producing system is present because its ancestors enjoyed a sufficient level of success at generating representations which then caused the representation consumers to cause behaviour with the result being the better survival and reproduction of the representation producing systems. An explanation

---

10 This isn't quite correct. Consumers today may not read the language as consumers of the same type did when selection for producers occurred. Thus, the producer may have the function of producing representations that use a particular correspondence rule that the consumer no longer uses. This possibility is accounted for in Millikan's talk of the correspondence rule that is part of a normal explanation (see below) for the presence of the tail slap in the beaver's behavioural repertoire.

11 See Millikan (1990, 128).

12 We might wonder about the determinacy of this description. Surely the proper functioning of the vomit reflex requires normal conditions other than the presence of poison in the stomach. See Davies (this volume) for these sorts of worries. For the purposes of this paper, I assume that such difficulties are surmountable.

of the presence of the representation producing and consuming systems is one that cites those conditions under which it was beneficial to possess those traits. Those are the "normal" conditions; the conditions in which the representations produced by the producer corresponded to the world according to that rule of correspondence used by the consumer. The content of the representation is determined by the normal conditions. Thus, a particular bee dance has the content, "flowers over there," because the conditions in which that dance was selected for were conditions in which that dance was correlated with the world by a particular rule of correspondence, and according to that rule of correspondence there are flowers over there.[13]

Notice, however, that the content of the bee dance is not what causes the bees to fly off. In part, this is because the content of the representation (the bee dance) is determined by historical events to which the consumers of the representation (the other bees) are not sensitive. Still, one may be tempted to claim that the content is efficacious because the content is determined by the correspondence rule, and the correspondence rule is used by the bees in order to interpret the dance. But we should be careful here: it is not how the representation corresponds to the world that is efficacious; instead, it is the representation's formal properties that are doing the causal work; the correspondence rule merely shows how those formal properties correspond with certain conditions.

Millikan recognizes this point. It is to this that she refers when she claims that "reasons cannot be, as such, causes" (1993b, 186). For it is not *qua* reasons that representations are causes, but *qua* structures with particular formal properties that they are causes.[14] Nonetheless, she thinks that reasons explanations do explain something. She calls

---

13 It is not necessary that the particular dance the bee is currently performing be a replica of dances that were selected for. What is important is that the dance is a symbol which corresponds to the world according to rules of correspondence which are part of normal explanations for the persistence of dances in the bees' phenotype. Thus, this particular dance may be a novel combination of various simpler symbols all of which are part of the bees' repertoire because of the contribution similar symbols made to the survival of the bees' ancestors either individually or as part of other dances.

14 This, of course, is the soprano problem.

reasons explanations "normalizing explanations."[15] Normalizing explanations explain by subsuming a phenomenon under a pattern of norms for a teleological system; for example, we explain why a dishwasher is filling with soapy water by saying that it is doing so in order to wash the dishes. This involves, among other things, classifying the phenomenon as an "outcome of a teleofunctional process" (1993b, 188), and to classify the explanandum thus is to explain it. "What is it doing? It's washing dishes, not making soup or just dirtying the water" (ibid.). As we have seen, on Millikan's account, a mental state has the function of adapting the system of which it is a part so that the system can perform its function. Mental states accomplish this by taking part in inference processes. They create models of the environment, the organism's desired end-states, and the manipulations of the environment of which the organism is capable in order to find a solution to the problem of reaching those end-states. Thus, a normalizing explanation of our behaviour starts with the recognition that "the making of good practical and theoretical inferences corresponds to normal ... functioning for beliefs and desires ..." and this allows us to conclude, "[a]ccordingly, explanations of behaviors by reference to reasons for action are normalizing explanations" (1993b, 190).

Why did I go to the kitchen? Because I wanted a beer and I believed there was one in the fridge, which I believed was in the kitchen. What makes this a normalizing explanation? The presence of the beliefs and the desire are explained by their evolutionary history: it was the presence of similar beliefs and desires in certain circumstances in the past that accounts for their presence in this present circumstance. Those normal conditions include the participation in an inference which caused the organism that had the similar mental states to move in ways appropriate to their content, i.e., the way in which

---

15 Millikan borrows this term from Pettit (1986) and claims that her views are parallel to his (1993b, 187), but for Pettit normalizing explanations are similar to Dennett's stances: they are interpretations of behaviour which entail assuming that the person behaving is rational and then fitting the behaviour within norms for behaviour. Given that Millikan is such a staunch realist, this seems an odd position for her to endorse. I assume that she is borrowing the term from Pettit and not the anti-realism.

they corresponded to the world according to the normal rule of correspondence. Thus,when we explain my beer-retrieval behaviour with reference to my beliefs and desires,we are citing those normal conditions and we are showing how my behaviour accords with those norms.

We do well to wonder just how normalizing explanations work. Why should we think that there is no conflict between normalizing explanations and mechanistic explanations?[16] Why should we think that the appeals to content made in the normalizing explanations should be taken literally? Millikan claims that normalizing explanations "connect with" causal explanations because those objects with teleofunctions have a "normal" way of performing their functions. We can analyze this "normal" way, find the physical structure that in normal conditions realizes the object that has a teleofunction, and analyze how that physical structure works (*à la* Cummins 1975). The normalizing explanation points to, without citing or elaborating, this sort of explanation by analysis. (As Millikan puts it: "normalizing explanations may thus circumscribe quite specific physical explanations without detailing them," 1993b, 190). So we can explain why I went to the kitchen to get the beer by citing my beliefs and desires without knowing anything about the physiological bases of those mental states.

This doesn't help much, however. Consider the idea that the teleofunctional object has a normal physical structure. Remember that Millikan uses "normal" to refer to conditions that are required by an evolutionary explanation of the presence of the object with a teleofunction, but which might not be satisfied this time. It's certainly

---

16 One obvious response to this question is to wonder why we might think that there may be a conflict; normalizing explanations are not causal explanations so why would they come into conflict with mechanistic explanations? I assume here that explanations are either causal or pragmatic. Pragmatic explanations may be perfectly satisfactory as explanations, but they give us no reason to believe that the entities cited in the explanation have a secure place in the world. On the other hand, causal (realist) explanations do give us such a reason. As we are interested in the ontological status of mental states, only a causal explanation will do. If normalizing explanations are a variety of pragmatic explanation, rather than a variety of causal explanation, then they have no claim on our ontology.

possible that the object be realized by some other physical structure while continuing to satisfy its function, but that seems unlikely. Instead, if the object is not realized by its normal physical structure, but is realized differently from those of its ancestors that were selected because they achieved some end, then it is unlikely that the object will be able to achieve that end. Thus, when the normalizing explanation succeeds in being explanatory, that is because the normalizing explanation is simply one way of referring to the physical structure that realizes the object and does the actual causal work. The normalizing explanation ends up being explanatory just because it points to properties that do the causal work. (Nor does it help to suppose that the teleofunctional object might be multiply realized. If that were so, then it would simply be more clear that the normalizing explanation merely explains by making reference to whatever physical structures realize the teleofunctional object. The only difference in supposing that the object is multiply realized is that one must then suppose that a functional analysis will not culminate in a description of the "elements normally composing the system," for there will be no such elements.)[17]

It isn't enough for an explanation of my beer retrieval behaviour to cite beliefs and desires that *would* lead to my going into the kitchen to retrieve a beer, *if* I had those beliefs and desires; I must actually have those beliefs and desires,and they must be efficacious in this

---

17 Millikan claims that her theory "does not imply that, given a certain species, there is a classically understood type-type identity relation between, say, normally constituted and normally functioning beliefs and desires about x on the one hand, and certain physiological structures on the other." (1993b, note 9.) I don't see how this denial is consistent with her claim that "[a]n exhaustive analysis of the way, given its history, that any functional item operates when operating normally arrives eventually at a description of normal physical structure for such a device ..." (1993b, 190). If the normal physical structure is that physical structure which was present in those circumstances in which the functional item performed in such a way as to positively affect the fitness of the organism in which the functional item was present, and thereby lead to the selection of that functional item, and if Millikan is using "normal" here in her usual technical sense, then the latter citation suggests precisely that there is a type-type identity relation between normally constituted and normally functioning mental states and certain physiological structures.

transaction.[18] When we use a normalizing explanation, i.e., a belief-desire explanation, to explain behaviour, we are merely referring to those properties doing the causal work. The normalizing explanation seems to be explanatory only because lurking behind it is a causal explanation. But then, when we explain my beer-retrieval behaviour by citing the mental states that led to that behaviour, we may be placing that behaviour in a context in which we can understand certain patterns of my behaviour, but insofar as that context is historical, it is not explanatory. The context is explanatory only if it refers to physical structures (those physical structures that are the normal realizers of the mental states cited in the explanation) that are present and efficacious in the present case. But then the explanation is parasitic on the presence of those physical structures and the historical relations alluded to by the normalizing explanation do no explanatory work. My mental states do not cause me to behave as I do because of their historical relations to certain normal conditions; they cause me to behave as I do because of their current causal powers, and those causal powers are due to their formal properties, not their semantic properties. No matter what role the content of beliefs and desires play in that normalizing explanation, in the causal explanation the content is inefficacious. This is the soprano problem: if content is to depend upon a historical relation, then there's going to be a difficulty in finding events that are causally sensitive to that historical relation.[19]

---

18 See Davidson (1963)

19 But what of the explanation of the dishwasher's filling with soapy water? That explanation sounds right; the dishwasher is filling with soapy water in order to wash the dishes. Notice, however, the contrasting explanations Millikan offers: making soup or dirtying the water. These are teleological explanations; they are answers to the question: Why was the dishwasher designed to fill with soapy water? In this case, we want an explanation that cites the goals of the designer. That's why this explanation sounds right. Millikan's goal, however, is to provide a naturalistic account of the mind; in non-artifactual cases, we do not want an explanation that cites the goals of the designer. Why is the plant growing toward the sun? In order to absorb more of the sun's rays, or because the hormone auxin is deactivated on the side of the plant closest to the sun, thus causing the other side of the plant to elongate and the plant to bend toward the sun? In this

This problem arises because while Millikan claims that reasons explanations are normalizing explanations, her analysis of normalizing explanations makes them a species of mechanistic explanations. If the processes cited by the normalizing explanation depend upon the processes cited by the mechanistic explanation, then those aspects of the normalizing explanation that fail to supervene on the processes cited by the mechanistic explanation are going to be inert, both causally and explanatorily. This includes those aspects secured by teleofunctions, namely the content.

One might wish to save Millikan's account by making the normalizing explanation and the mechanistic explanation complementary rather than coincidental; if the normalizing explanation explains something other than what the mechanistic explanation explains, then perhaps the content can play a role. This would fail within the context of Millikan's theory just as it did in the context of Dretske's theory. That's because in order to get the processes referred to by the normalizing explanation to do any causal work, they have to supervene on some mechanistic processes, and, whatever mechanistic processes they supervene on, those will not include the historical processes needed to bring content into the causal picture. Once again, teleosemantics distances content from the causal transactions mental states enter into, and thus leads to epiphenomenalism.

3. Minimalist Teleosemantics

Unlike most teleosemanticists, Karen Neander (1995) does not claim that she is attempting to provide a theory according to which content is efficacious.[20] Accordingly, the argument I present here should not be

---

case, the latter explanation is preferable, although we don't want to dismiss the former out of hand: those ancestors of this plant that turned toward the sun were better able to survive and reproduce, and were thus selected for, because they absorbed more of the sun's rays. Thus, an explanation of the presence of this type of phenomenon in the population will cite the advantage for plants of absorbing more of the sun's rays.

20 Neander seems to suggest that content plays a role in shaping the inferences that shape our behaviour. As discussed below, she suggests that perceptual

taken to show that her theory fails to satisfy her goals for it, but merely that if mental content is determined in the way that Neander claims it to be and it is teleosemantic, then that content is epiphenomenal. (Neander's theory is importantly different from the others considered here: her theory is open to the possibility that the semantic content of a mental state may be determined by something other than that state's teleofunction.)

Neander calls those theories according to which content is teleofunctional "High Church" theories of teleosemantic representation. Think of the familiar story of the frogs, flies, and bee-bees. When a frog perceives a fly it attempts to catch and eat it. Apparently, though, the frog cannot distinguish between a fly and any other similarly sized dark object moving through its visual field; researchers have successfully fed frogs bee-bees. What, we may ask, do the frogs see the small dark objects as? Flies; bee-bees; black specks; small, dark, moving things? The High Church answer to this is that their visual experience is an experience of flies. Roughly, the reasoning is that the frog is equipped with a fly-detector and that when the fly detector malfunctions and detects things that are not flies it detects them as flies, and thus its detections carry the content, "fly." Neander calls this position the "High Church" account because it adopts a high level of description of what the detector is doing: the detector is detecting flies by detecting small dark moving things. Neander prefers the Low Church approach according to which teleofunctional content is minimal: the detector is detecting small dark moving things. When the detector fires, it has the content "small dark moving thing," not "fly." It is on this basis that Neander wishes to build a naturalized semantics.

As Neander is well aware, there are several apparent problems with the Low Church approach. Most prominent is that it appears to

---

recognition is an inferential process, "specifically, an abductive inference in the light of background knowledge" (134), but knowledge can affect an inferential process only if content can affect that inferential process. However, Neander also claims (in personal communication) that she thinks that content is inefficacious. In either case, I argue below that inasmuch as her theory makes content depend on teleofunction, content will turn out to be inefficacious.

make it impossible for the frog to misrepresent. Cognitive systems sometimes misrepresent; any theory that makes misrepresentation impossible is *prima facie* incorrect. One might worry that if the content of the frog's representation is merely, "small dark moving thing," then the frog is unable to misrepresent, for whatever causes the frog to token that state, whether it be a fly or a bee-bee, it will be a small dark moving thing. (Or, to put this worry differently, we might be concerned that according to Neander's theory the frog is functioning properly when it is stuffing itself on bee-bees.) Neander points out, however, that while, on her account, frogs are not misrepresenting when they respond to bee-bees as they do to flies, they are still able to misrepresent: if a snail – a small, dark, (relatively) stationary object – causes a frog to token the "small dark moving thing" state, then the frog is misrepresenting.

This response has the appearance of simply forestalling the worry, for the consequence remains that if the frog's perceptual system is functioning properly, the frog is unable to misrepresent. (That is, the frog is functioning properly when it is stuffing itself on bee-bees.) The frog can misrepresent by tokening the state "small dark moving thing" in response to a snail, but doing so requires a malfunction in the frog's perceptual system. However, Neander claims, this fact – that when functioning properly the frog will not be able to misrepresent – is irrelevant; all that is important is that there are conditions under which the frog can misrepresent.

This is plausible; Neander has provided a story according to which frogs are able to represent and misrepresent. Still, there is a wide gulf between the sort of frog misrepresentation that Neander is talking about and the human misrepresentation that teleosemanticists wish to naturalize. If Neander is right, the frog can misrepresent only if it is malfunctioning. Human beings misrepresent all the time, even when functioning perfectly well. For example, even though my visual system is functioning perfectly well, I might see a skinny cow in the distance and represent it as a horse. Furthermore, on Neander's account, the content of my visual representation is something like, "thin dark four-legged creature." So whence comes the misrepresentation? Neander's suggestion is that the misrepresentation is a product of the correctly represented visual state (my visual system is not malfunctioning) and an inference which oversteps the evidence of "the less than compelling perceptual data" (133).[21]

I think this is a promising view, well worth more attention than this essay allows. For the purposes of this essay, it is enough to highlight the nature of the determinants of semantic representation that Neander endorses. My representation of the cow as a horse is the result of an inference. The inference moves from the representation of the cow as something that looks a particular way to the representation of the cow as a horse. There are two representations implicated here. In the first, pre-inference, representation, I represent the cow as something that looks a particular way. Call this *Rt*. In the second, post-inference, representation, I represent the cow as being a horse. Call this *Rs*. *Rt* is not a misrepresentation; *Rs* is. Following Neander's analysis of the frog's apparent misrepresentation, teleosemantics accounts for the content of *Rt*. However, *Rt* is not the proximal cause of any of my behaviour; *Rs* is. If teleosemantic content is to cause my behaviour, then teleosemantics must account for the content of *Rs*. According to Neander, this does not happen directly, for the content of *Rs* is fixed by an inference, not by natural selection or some analogous process. Nonetheless, the content of *Rs* may still be teleofunctional, either because the inference to *Rs* from *Rt* is itself a product of natural selection, or because the inference is somehow controlled by the teleofunction of *Rt* (which might make *Rt* a distal cause of my behaviour), or because the complex representation that results from the inference, namely *Rs*, is a construction of simpler, teleofunctional representations.

Notice, however, that on the first two alternatives, the evolutionary history is doing no work. If the mechanism responsible for the inference from *Rt* to *Rs* has its own teleofunction, that function is

---

21 Notice the parallel between Neander's solution to the contemporary misrepresentation problem and Descartes' solution to his misrepresentation problem. God, Descartes tells us, guarantees that when our perceptual systems are functioning properly they will accurately portray the world; it is only when our judgment o'erleaps our clear and distinct ideas that we make mistakes. Evolution, Neander tells us, guarantees that when our perceptual systems are functioning properly they will generate accurate representations; it is only when our inferences o'erleap faulty data that we misrepresent.

not what is causing it to infer Rs from Rt; the formal properties of the mechanism and of Rt are responsible for the inference (this is the soprano problem). Similarly, if the inference is governed by Rt, it is the formal properties of Rt that are doing the causal work, not its historical/evolutionary properties (again, this is the soprano problem). In neither of these cases is the content of Rs teleosemantic; it is a product of the occurrent causal powers of Rt and the occurrent causal powers of the mechanism that infers Rs from Rt. The third alternative does appear to make the content of Rs teleosemantic: the content of the complex representation is composed of the contents of the simpler teleosemantic representations that make it up. Rs is composed of several Rts, each of which has teleosemantic content, and each of which contributes its content to determining the content of Rs.[22] But this doesn't help us with the soprano problem. Inasmuch as this content is teleosemantic, the content of Rs is a historical property of the various Rts that make up Rs, and thus unable to do any causal work in bringing about my current behaviour.

Thus, according to Neander's account, to the extent that content is a product of the teleofunction of the representation, it's not causally efficacious.

4.   Teleosemantics and the Epiphenomenality of Content

Each of the three distinct teleosemantic theories of content examined here make the content of a representation, to the extent that it depends on the function of the representation, epiphenomenal. Can there be a teleosemantic theory of content that allows for the causal efficacy of content? No matter what we think content is causally responsible for, if the content of a representation is determined by its history, then that state cannot cause anything in virtue of its having the content it has. This is because the causal powers the representation has are determined solely by its intrinsic physical properties and not by its extrinsic historical properties (which includes the pattern of selection that has led to the presence of that state). This can be seen easily by

---

22   See Dretske (1996) for a similar suggestion.

considering replicas. Any state in me – that, let us suppose, has the appropriate historical / evolutionary properties – has the same causal powers as its physically identical counterpart in a replica of me that lacks the appropriate history. The individual states – in me and in my replica – have the same causal powers. Thus, the evolutionary history of a state does not affect its causal powers. This point is recognized explicitly by Millikan and implicitly by Dretske. Both, consequently, look elsewhere for the causal role of content.

Their failures to find a causal role for content elsewhere are instructive. While Dretske and Millikan look in different places to find a role for content, they fail to find such a role for similar reasons. Dretske thinks content can cause the mechanisms which cause bodily movement to have particular structures, but this fails because the causes of these structures are the determinants of content, rather than the content itself. Millikan thinks that content can be part of a normalizing explanation, but this fails because insofar as normalizing explanations rely on content, they fail to be explanatory, and the degree to which they are explanatory is the degree to which they are supported by the sort of mechanistic explanations that make historical properties irrelevant. In both of these cases, the hope is that content can cause something other than those bodily movements that are part of behaviour. But here we face the same problem that faces the simpler idea that content may cause bodily movements: if content is a product of evolutionary history, then whatever event or state of affairs the contentful state is supposed to bring about could be brought about by a physically similar state which lacked that evolutionary history. No matter what content is supposed to cause, if content is teleofunctional, we can run the same thought experiment to show that it is some aspect of the representation other than its content that is doing the causal work. Following the Millikan-Dretske path to making content efficacious does not work; content ends up being epiphenomenal.

Neander's approach, on the other hand, may show the promise of making content efficacious, but this comes at the cost of abandoning telesemantics; representational content, on Neander's theory, does not depend on the evolutionary history of the representation.

Thus: teleosemantic content can not cause bodily movements, nor can it cause anything else that might be part of the process of behaviour.

5. Concluding Remarks

I have argued that teleosemantics not only fails to show how mental content can be causally efficacious, but it makes content causally inert. Should this result have any effect on our assessment of teleosemantics as a theory? It may seem that epiphenomenalism about mental content is consistent with teleosemantics: we might wish to naturalize content even though we suspect, or believe, that content is epiphenomenal, and think that teleosemantics provides a promising avenue for naturalizing content. Or so it seems.

I suspect that what misleads us into believing that this is a viable alternative is the typical sort of event that we consider when we consider the causal efficacy of content: my believing that there is beer in the fridge, coupled with my desire to drink a beer, is what causes me to head for the kitchen. When we consider the possibility that content might be epiphenomenal, we think that it may be the case that the content of these states is not what is actually causing my body to move from here to there; the states that are causing my body to move may be doing so in virtue of something other than their content. However, there's another way in which content can be efficacious: my belief that there's beer in the fridge also apparently causes in me an awareness (a belief that another belief is present) that I believe that there's beer in the fridge. Certainly, the epiphenomenalist must admit that I am apparently aware of the content of my belief. But if content is epiphenomenal, then content must be unable to have this effect as well. Perhaps some versions of epiphenomenalism are consistent with this phenomenon, but not teleosemantic epiphenomenalism. For me to be aware of the content of my mental state is for me to have a mental state with the content, "I have a mental state with the content that P," for some proposition P. But the content of the state cannot cause in me an awareness that I am in a state with content P, for, according to teleosemantics, that P is the content of that mental state is a fact about the history of that mental state, and, as I have argued here, that history is epiphenomenal with respect to the effects of that mental state. There are other paths to awareness of the content of a mental state: one may reflect on the history of the mental state, or one may infer from some behaviour the cause of that behaviour. But these are not available to the teleosemanticist: both reflections on the history of a state and observations of behaviour are themselves contentful and so cannot be grist for any inference for the teleosemanticist.

Because teleosemantics does not have recourse to content-based inferences about the content of one's own mental states, it is left then for the teleosemanticist to assert that the formal properties of my mental states are independently sufficient to cause in me an awareness of the content of those mental states. The best face that the teleosemanticist can put on this is to claim that in those cases in which an agent really does know the content of her mental states (for certainly we are mistaken some of the time), that knowledge is caused not by the content of those mental states but is the result of selection for awareness of those mental states. For example, Dretske might claim that there is an indicator for the presence of states with content *P*, and that indicator has been recruited to cause some movement *M* when states with content *P* are present. Or Millikan might claim that under normal conditions it was beneficial to ancestors of this organism to have certain other mental states present when states with content *P* were present. Thus, the apparent awareness of the content of one's mental states would be a result of selection for the presence of the second-order state whenever the first-order state was present.

The teleosemanticist putting forward this account has work left to do. How is it possible that there be an indicator of the presence of a state with some content if content is epiphenomenal? Indicators, one would hope, do their indicating by being causally connected with whatever property they are indicating. But nothing can be causally connected with content if content is epiphenomenal. Similarly, how might there be selection for the coincidence of states with particular contents if content is epiphenomenal? These are promissory notes that, I fear, would remain unpaid.

The other alternatives facing the teleosemanticist are even less attractive. She might suggest that the formal properties of mental states are sufficient to determine their content. But this is to give up on the teleosemantic program. Or she might suggest that because our awareness of our mental states can depend only on their formal properties and those properties are not sufficient to determine their content, we thus constantly run the very real risk of being wrong about the content of our own mental states. But this is a very big bullet to bite.

So: unless we're eliminativists, we should view the epiphenomenality of teleosemantic content as a reason to give up teleosemantics. And if we're eliminativists, we shouldn't be pursuing any sort of naturalized semantics, teleofunctional or not.[23]

23 I owe a great debt to Jill McIntosh for her careful reading of several drafts of this paper. The quality is clearly improved as a consequence of her effort. I am also indebted to Larry Shapiro and Elliott Sober for their comments on an early draft of this paper.

References

Baker, Lynne Rudder. 1991. "Dretske on the Explanatory Role of Belief," *Philosophical Studies* **63**, 99–111.

Bigelow, John, and Pargetter, Robert. 1987. "Functions," *Journal of Philosophy* **83**, 181–96.

Cummins, Robert. 1975. "Functional Analysis," *Journal of Philosophy* **72**, 741–65.

Davidson, Donald. 1963. "Actions, Reasons, and Causes," *Journal of Philosophy* **60**. Reprinted in Donald Davidson, *Essays on Actions and Events*. Oxford: Oxford University Press, 1980.

Davies, Paul Sheldon. This volume. "The Excesses of Teleosemantics."

Dretske, Fred. 1988. *Explaining Behavior.* Cambridge, MA: MIT Press.

———. 1995. *Naturalizing the Mind.* Cambridge, MA: MIT Press.

———. 1990. "Reply to Reviewers," *Philosophy and Phenomenological Research* **50**, 819–39.

———. 1991a. "How Beliefs Explain: Reply to Baker," *Philosophical Studies* **63**, 113–17.

———. 1991b. "Dretske's Replies." In *Dretske and his Critics.* Brian McLaughlin, ed. Cambridge, MA: Basil Blackwell, pp. 180–221.

———. 1996. "How Reasons Explain Behaviour; Reply to Melnyk and Noordhof," *Mind and Language* **11**, 223–29.

Enç, Berent, and Fred Adams. 1992. "Functions and Goal-Directedness," *Philosophy of Science* **59**, 635–54.

Godfrey-Smith, Peter. 1994. "A Modern History Theory of Functions," *Noûs* **28**, 344–62.

Horgan, Terence. 1991. "Actions, Reasons, and the Explanatory Role of Content." In *Dretske and his Critics.* Brian McLaughlin, ed. Cambridge, MA: Basil Blackwell, pp. 73–101.

Kim, Jaegwon. 1991. "Dretske on How Reasons Explain Behavior," in *Dretske and his Critics.* Brian McLaughlin, ed. Cambridge, MA: Basil Blackwell, pp. 52–72.

Millikan, Ruth Garrett. 1984. *Language, Thought, and Other Biological Categories.* Cambridge, MA: MIT Press.

———. 1989. "Biosemantics," *Journal of Philosophy* **86**, 281–97. Reprinted in Millikan (1993a).

———. 1990. "Compare and Contrast Dretske, Fodor, and Millikan on Teleosemantics," *Philosophical Topics* **18**, 151–61. Reprinted in Millikan (1993a).

———. 1993a. *White Queen Psychology and Other Essays for Alice.* Cambridge, MA: MIT Press.

———. 1993b. "Explanation in Biopsychology." In *Mental Causation.* John Heil and Alfred Mele, eds. Oxford: Oxford University Press. Reprinted in Millikan (1993a).

Neander, Karen. 1991. "Functions as Selected Effects: The Conceptual Analyst's Defense," *Philosophy of Science* **58**, 168–84.

———. 1995. "Misrepresenting and Malfunctioning," *Philosophical Studies* **79**, 109–41.

Papineau, David. 1987. *Reality and Representation.* New York: Blackwell.

Pettit, Philip. 1986. "Broad-Minded Explanation and Psychology." In *Subject, Thought, and Content*, Phillip Pettit and John McDowell, eds. Oxford: Oxford University Press.

Sober, Elliott. 1995. "Natural Selection and Distributive Explanation: A Reply to Neander," *British Journal for the Philosophy of Science* **46**, 384–97.

Stampe, Dennis. 1990. "Desires as Reasons - Discussion Notes on Fred Dretske's 'Explaining Behavior: Reasons in a World of Causes'," *Philosophy and Phenomenological Research* **50**, 787–93.

Sterelny, Kim. 1990. *The Representational Mind.* New York: Blackwell.

Walsh, Denis. 1996. "Fitness and Function," *British Journal for the Philosophy of Science* **47**, 553–74.

Wright, Larry. 1973. "Functions," *Philosophical Review* **82**, 139–68.

CANADIAN JOURNAL OF PHILOSOPHY
Supplementary Volume 27

Monsters Among Us[1]

TIMOTHY SCHROEDER

1. The Threat

There are monsters that scare children and monsters that scare grown-ups, and then there are monsters that scare philosophers of mind. This paper is concerned with this third sort of monster, whose primary representative is the zombie – a living being, physically just like a person but lacking consciousness. Though zombies act like normal people and appear to have normal brains, everything is blank inside. Unfortunately, the term 'zombie' covers a narrower class of deficits than is convenient, failing to cover apparently normal human beings lacking propositional attitudes. Davidson's (1987) "Swampman" is supposed to be an example of such a creature, so I will dub individuals who are apparently normal but lack all propositional attitudes 'swampfolk,' though this is non-standard terminology. In what follows, I will refer to both zombies and swampfolk as 'monsters,' and will similarly designate animals lacking in consciousness or propositional attitudes.[2]

---

1 This paper draws on Chapter 4 of my unpublished doctoral dissertation, *Foundations of Mental Representation*. Thanks to Fred Dretske, Patricia Smith Churchland, and Peter Godfrey-Smith for helpful comments on ancestors of the present work.

2 In this terminological framework, zombies are imagined to lack only consciousness, swampfolk are imagined to lack only propositional attitudes, and there is no special word to designate just those creatures lacking both. Nothing hangs upon the assumption that these dissociations are possible, in any interesting sense of 'possible.'

What makes monsters scary to philosophers of mind is the chance their theories will hold it physically possible that monsters exist (logical possibility being another matter[3]). It is a widely shared intuition that monsters are *not* physically possible, and any theory that says otherwise is wrong. Philosophers whose intuitions revolt at the thought of monsters typically make them theoretical impossibilities: this is the strategy pursued with regard to swampfolk by externalists like Fodor (1990; 1994) and all internalists about mental content, and with regard to zombies by most philosophers working on consciousness. Not everyone is afraid of philosophical monsters, however. Millikan (1984; 1993; 1996), Neander (1996), Papineau (1987; 1996) and Sterelny (1990) allow that swampfolk are physically possible,[4] while Dretske (1995) and Lycan (1987) allow that zombies are also possible.[5] These authors are forced to be fearless because each employs evolution in explaining mental representation and each takes the propositional attitudes or consciousness to be analyzable in terms of mental representations.[6] For anything to have a mind, according to

---

3 How to understand various senses of 'possibility' is a vexed question which I do not intend to address here, but a few words are in order. I take 'logical possibility' to name a species of possibility in which possibility is characterized by the formal satisfiability of a statement of the logical possibility, after translation into some appropriate formal system. The existence of zombies is thus a logical possibility, but this shows little of deep philosophical interest. Physical possibilities, on the other hand, are characterized by their compatibility with the actual laws of physics, whatever those might be (*not* current physical theory). If there are intelligible intermediate notions of possibility, such as metaphysical or conceptual possibility, I take them to be entailed by physical possibility, and so showing that monsters are physical possibilities (on certain theories, as will be done in what follows) will also show that they are metaphysical or conceptual possibilities (on those theories).

4 Millikan (1996) casts some doubt upon this.

5 Dretske and Lycan aren't alone in their intuitions that zombies are physically possible – Tye (1995) also accepts their possibility, at least for simple beings, and Devries (1996) argues at length for it. These authors do not hold evolution to be the source of intentionality, however, and so they are not within the scope of this work.

6 Lycan (1987) skips the intermediate stage of analyzing representation.

these authors, it must have an evolutionary history giving its brain representational functions; not everything that looks or moves just like a person need have an evolutionary history, and so, they conclude, monsters are a physical possibility. These theorists, whom I will call 'ET theorists' (for 'evolution-derived teleology'), reject the intuition everyone else shares.

What is one to make of this battle of intuitions? The teratophobes have a powerful appeal, and it is tempting to complain that ET theorists are just being perverse. In this paper, I will go beyond the usual complaints by showing ET theories have a consequence unappreciated by their authors, a consequence which may be intuitively unacceptable even to the ET theorist who thinks monsters are possible: I will show that ET theories imply not only the possibility of monsters, but also their actuality. Because of the tremendous plasticity displayed by the mammalian brain, structures sometimes systematically engage in activities for which they did not evolve. Hence, ET theorists are committed to the claim that, insofar as people possess such deviant neural structures, they are monstrous.[7] The obvious response, following Millikan's (1984) discussion of adapted functions, will be shown to fail to cover the most extreme cases of plasticity (described below). Finally, I will suggest where the ET theorist must look if she wishes to remain a teleosemanticist without appeal to evolution.

Would the actuality of monsters be more damning to the ET theorist than their physical possibility? An analogy with moral theory will be helpful here. While it might be hard to accept, it ought not be ruled out *a priori* that, under extraordinary circumstances, it would be morally imperative to knowingly kill an innocent person. No doubt a very strong theory would be needed to support such a claim, but such a theory is an epistemic possibility. Yet any theory holding it to be morally imperative that under perfectly ordinary circumstances I kill my innocent elderly neighbour is intolerable regardless of other intuitive benefits it might provide. There are few moral certainties, but one is that the unmotivated killing of elderly neighbours is immoral.

---

7 Seager (1997) has recently suggested that this sort of argument threatens Dretske's (1995) representationalism, but he does not go on to consider the various ins and outs of the argument. See 95ff.

Just so, there are few certainties in the philosophy of mind, and one might believe that, in extraordinary circumstances, a living being could come about which would be monstrous. This, the ET theorist holds, is an epistemic possibility. Yet it still seems obvious that one has never met a monster in daily life, and a theory that says otherwise is even harder to believe than one saying that under incomprehensibly improbable conditions, one might. If the facts of neural plasticity entail that, according to ET theories, there are monsters among us, that is a serious reason to worry about such theories.

2. Neural Plasticity

By 'plasticity' I mean to pick out a collection of phenomena typically so identified by working neuroscientists, including changes in synaptic strengths, changes in the number of synaptic connections, and growth of new axonal or dendritic branches. Work over the last half-century has made it clear that the self-modifications of which the mammalian brain is capable are extraordinary, exceeding anything one might have guessed. For example, amazing cases of the plasticity of neural structures subserving perception are found in experiments by Métin and Frost (1989) and Roe et al. (1990). (For a review, see Sur et al. 1990.) Surgical procedures allowed an infant ferret's or hamster's optic nerve to synapse with neurons in either the auditory or somatosensory relay nucleus of the thalamus, inducing nonstandard thalamic structuring. The deviant thalamic nuclei, now innervated by optic nerves, caused the cortex to which they projected to take on many properties of a visual cortex. Investigation of the modified cortex revealed a fairly regular retinotopic map, with irregularly sized but recognizably well-organized receptive fields, in which different cells displayed different orientation sensitivities and so on. In other words, to all appearances the experimental animals had somewhat deformed visual cortices where one would expect their auditory or somatosensory cortices to be. This restructuring was also manifested at the behavioural level – the experimental animals behaved as though they possessed (defective) sight. It would thus appear that cortical structures selected for their contribution to hearing or touch sensitivity came to represent visual properties, and thus (according to ET theorists) must have come to have biological functions regarding visual properties. Yet it would appear that no such functions exist – the evolutionary functions for these modified cortical structures would be functions regarding auditory or tactile properties. The ET theorist seems forced to say that the visual capacities of these animals were monstrous. Recent work (reviewed in Kaas 1991; Weinberger 1995) has shown that adult mammalian brains are also open to significant reorganization, albeit to a lesser degree, so the problem for the ET theorist threatens to be a fairly common one.

For striking examples of plasticity in propositional attitude-forming mechanisms, one need look no further than studies of human subjects whose centres of language function shifted in location from left to right hemisphere. A review of studies on left hemispherectomy patients and language by Piacentini et al. (1988; also Witelson 1987; but see Bullock et al. 1987) concluded that, although most humans are born with a left hemisphere specialized for language, those receiving left hemispherectomies within the first several years of life go on substantially (if incompletely) to recover from the loss of the language centre, the recovery being made possible by changes in the right hemisphere. This movement of language functions from one hemisphere to the other during childhood is not restricted to complete hemispherectomy patients – individuals with epileptic foci in the left hemisphere have unusually high rates of right-hemisphere language dominance (Helmstaedter et al. 1994; Rausch and Walsh 1984), suggesting that the disturbances of language function in the left hemisphere caused such functions to be relocated in some cases to the right hemisphere.

In these hemispherectomy and epilepsy subjects, it is the capacity for language comprehension and production, rather than a sensory capacity, that has been relocated, but the implications are similar. Structures in the left hemisphere of most individuals have evolutionary functions regarding language. However, in the cases just mentioned, we saw right hemispheres take on language functions. It should be noted that the parts of the right hemisphere taking over from the left are not "backup cortex" with the function of propping up the left hemisphere in case of injury, but have functions of their own regarding visual memory which they fail to perform properly in these cases (Helmstaedter et al. 1994). So in these cases of shift in the language-dominant hemisphere, it seems that a brain structure with one function, regarding visual memory, comes to take on other functions, regarding language. Again, the ET theorist seems forced to hold that the capacities in question, because they do not involve evolution, are monstrous.

3. Adapted Functions

Discussion so far suggests evolution cannot play a constitutive role in perception or the formation of the propositional attitudes, on pain of declaring a number of actual creatures to be partial monsters. But Millikan (1984) anticipates such objections and addresses them by appealing to the existence of adapted functions. Millikan's favourite example is that of chameleon skin-pigment mechanisms. A chameleon's skin-pigment mechanism has the function of making the chameleon's skin green if the chameleon is on a green surface, but the mechanism did not evolve to make the chameleon's skin that particular colour. Rather, the mechanism evolved to match the colour of the chameleon's skin to the colour of the surround, whatever that might be. Evolution provides the function "make the skin the same colour as x," as it were, and context provides the x. According to Millikan, the functions that brain structures have are often adapted functions in this sense. The Millikanian response to gross plasticity thus holds that the forces driving cortical plasticity are merely contextual factors which help to specify the adapted function of each plastic neural structure. Although Millikan is the only ET theorist who has stressed the importance of adapted functions, no other ET theorist holds a view incompatible with their existence, and so Millikan's answer to the objection can be everyone's answer to such cases.

The answer, though sound in general, must be stretched somewhat here. Consider the people subjected to hemispherectomies, or the rodents in which visual cortices are induced outside the occipital lobe. These cases seem to show that parts of the cortex can have the job of doing things very different from the things they usually do – they do not just adapt, as the chameleon's skin does, to variations within a narrow range of possibilities. Under pressure from examples of neural plasticity, it appears necessary to hold that the cortex (at least) is *all* adapted functions, and that only the genetic code has unadapted functions. Or perhaps the neural mechanisms of plasticity have unadapted functions, and everything else in the cortex has adapted functions assigned to them by the mechanisms of plasticity. Millikan seems willing to make such a move if pressed; consider Millikan (1984, 48):

> ... however flexible the human nervous system is, containing systems that are instructed or programmed by other systems that are instructed or programmed by still other systems, still there must come an end to the flexibility. Both the outermost systems and principles involved and the kinds of flexibility possible in programming more inner systems must be inherent in the basic brain – the original product of evolutionary design.

This might appear to conflict with other views of Millikan's, such as her claim that "the brain is a highly differentiated organ containing numerous structures with highly specialised functions" (Millikan 1993, chap. 2), but the conflict is merely apparent. The highly specialized functions of the brain are highly specialized *adapted* functions, on this view, and so their existence is compatible with holding that the "outermost systems and principles" of neural plasticity are the only brain structures with unadapted (direct) functions.

The response just considered is problematic, however, for Millikan's definitions of 'direct' and 'adapted' proper functions appear not to permit it. Millikan's (1984, 28) definition of 'direct proper function' runs as follows:

> Where *m* is a member of a reproductively established family *R* and *R* has the reproductively established or Normal character *C*, *m* has the function *F* as a direct proper function iff:
>
> (1) Certain ancestors of *m* performed *F*.
> (2) In part because there existed a direct causal connection between having the character *C* and performance of the function *F* in the case of these ancestors of *m*, *C* correlated positively with *F* over a certain set of items *S* which included these ancestors and other things not having *C*.

(3)   One among the legitimate explanations that can be given of the fact that m exists makes reference to the fact that C correlated positively with F over S, either directly causing reproduction of m or explaining why R was proliferated and hence why m exists.

Adapted functions, by way of contrast, are functions the performance of which need not explain why the structure having the function exists (i.e., clauses 2 and 3 may not be met). In the case of the chameleon, the chameleon's skin may have the function of producing a particular pattern of colours even though no chameleon has ever before produced that pattern, and so having that pattern is not something which can explain why the skin having that function exists.[8]

Consider now the claim the ET theorist must make: no modified neural structure offered as a counter-example to the ET theorists has its function as a direct function, but only as an adapted function given by its environment plus the genome (and any stable mechanisms of neural modification). This claim does not appear sustainable, given the above definition of direct proper function. Take, for instance, the aforementioned case of the ferret whose optic nerve was re-directed to the auditory relay centre of its thalamus, so that visual input came to drive its auditory cortex in such a way that its auditory cortex took on many of the properties of a visual cortex (including enabling optical control of behaviour). Was this auditory cortex a structure which had response (of various specific sorts) to sounds as its direct or adapted evolutionary function? Taking the particular modified auditory cortex to be m, normal auditory cortex structuring to be C, and the function F of m to be responding to sounds (in various specific ways), we find that (1) ancestral instances of the modified cortex responded to sounds in certain regular ways; (2) having normal structuring was what enabled ancestral auditory cortices to respond to sounds in these regular ways – they did not do so when (because of deformity) they were radically mis-structured; and (3) part of the reason the modified cortex exists is that ancestral cortices responded to sounds as they did by having a normal structure, thus promoting the reproduction of

---

8 A full discussion of adapted functions is found in Chapter 2 of Millikan (1984).

similar cortices. Hence, responding to sonic stimuli is a direct function of the ferret's auditory cortex. If, in our particular ferret, the structure evolved to respond to sonic stimulation is in fact responding to visual stimulation, that does not affect the fact that (according to the ET theorist) the relevant cortex is supposed to respond to sonic stimulation, and hence represents it. This, however, is problematic for the ET theorist. The ferret's modified cortex is strikingly similar to a visual cortex and strikingly dissimilar to an auditory cortex in its structure, operation, and in its behavioural consequences. The ferret appears able to see, not hear; neurologically, it appears to have a (defective) visual cortex, not an auditory cortex. According to the ET theorist, then, the ferret is a monster.

Similar things may be said regarding individuals subjected to hemispherectomies. The ET theorist needs to hold that, in the individuals in question, the new language centre (created out of what would have been a structure involved in visual recognition) has no direct evolutionary functions, but only adapted functions. This does not seem likely to be the case. About ninety per cent of all people have language functions lateralized exclusively in the left hemisphere (Kolb and Wishaw 1996), suggesting that, at least in these people, that hemisphere's structure has a character C unlike that of the counterpart structure in the right hemisphere. This character C has evidently been selected for enhancing language comprehension and production (F), and the fact that it has enhanced such processes is part of the reason that language centres exist in the left hemisphere. Similarly, the corresponding region of the right hemisphere, which has the capacity to become a (very imperfect) speech centre, has a different character, C^*, which has been selected because it enhances that region's capacity to aid visual recognition (F^*). So the right hemisphere has direct functions regarding visual recognition, not speech (in at least ninety percent of all humans).

It is easy to be tricked into thinking that, simply because the brain exhibits enormous plasticity, neural functions must generally be adapted functions, but this is too much. In the past, individuals needing hemispherectomies, individuals with serious epileptic foci, individuals with large-scale cortical damage and their like did not derive any evolutionary benefit from the adaptability of their brains. In general, they died without offspring. The brain having adaptability under extreme conditions has only recently come to have any significance for evolution; only with the advent of successful neurosurgery, anticonvulsive drugs and so on has the full adaptability of the brain been of use, evolutionarily speaking. For most of evolutionary history, neural plasticity has had only limited functions regarding development, the fine-tuning of the senses and the formation of the usual range of beliefs and desires. The capacity of the brain for radical reorganization after radical insult has long been a mere exaptation.

The point may be pressed by recalling H. G. Wells' *The Island of Doctor Moreau*. In Wells' story, Moreau is able to turn large mammals into upright-walking, tool-using, speaking beings through repeated surgical modifications and through the natural adaptability of the animals' bodies. Moreau grafts bone, reconnects muscles, re-routes neurons and so on and allows natural healing to do the rest. If we grant to Wells the premise of the story, that the body is almost limitlessly malleable given a skilled surgeon and the tremendous recuperative powers of many animals, we still do not come to the conclusion that Moreau's animals' bodies are performing their adapted proper functions in giving their possessors, e.g., upright stance. The reason is that such horrific procedures are outside the scope of normal explanations (in Millikan's sense) of how tissue plasticity and resilience contribute to survival. The fact that there are circumstances under which such malleability might lead to a leopard having upright stance, or an opposable digit, does not make it true that such novel features would have adapted functions. Brain hemispherectomies and debilitating epileptic foci are like Moreau's surgeries in this way: though they are an occasion for displays of tremendous plasticity, they are abnormal occasions and tell us nothing about brain functions. To hold otherwise is to be forced to hold that Moreau's creatures' bodies perform their biological functions as well, which is clearly absurd.

4. Learning to the Rescue?

Recall what moved the ET theorist to appeal to evolution in the first place: the ET theorist holds that in order for brain structures to exhibit intentionality, there must be something they are supposed to do, and evolution is the likely source of such "natural norms." Yet we have found that appeals to evolutionary functions are even more problematic than the ET theorist expected. Is there any way to give up on evolution but remain a teleosemanticist? There is: it is entirely within the principles explicitly endorsed by Dretske (1988), Millikan (1984), and Papineau (1987) to hold that the mechanisms of plasticity are also sources of functions on their own, whether they have evolutionary histories or not. More carefully, these authors see certain evolution-like mechanisms of learning (a subset of the mechanisms of plasticity) as sources of functions.

ET theorists treat (their preferred form of) learning similarly to the way they treat evolution. They see both as historical processes by means of which structures come to have functions because they were selected for doing certain things. The most significant difference between learning and evolution, according to these authors, is that learning operates on a much shorter time scale – the fact that one is carried out via neurons, the other via DNA, is not of philosophical significance. Some learning is indeed suggestively like a selective process – operant conditioning generally takes this form. Some learning is not – observational learning, for instance, or rote memorization. But this need not stand in the way of one particular sort of learning serving as the foundation of mental content.[9]

To see that Millikanian ET theorists really can do without appeals to evolution, recall again Millikan's (1984) definition of 'proper function' quoted earlier. If we take m to be the tokening of some internal representation type, we can see that learning mechanisms alone could suffice to make m meet Millikan's conditions (1) to (3), and hence have a full-blown function. It might be the case, as Dretske (1988) puts it, that m has the function of carrying the information that P, because (1) ancestors of m (i.e., earlier tokens) did so, because (2) m's having

---

9 Millikan attempts to forestall this line of argument. She writes that without appeal to evolutionary functions, "the animal's learning patterns have no functional explanation at all" (1984, 47). This may be true, but ET theorists do not need to argue that learning patterns have functions. They set out to argue that semantically significant neural states are structures with functions, and they may have functions whether or not the systems giving them functions have functions themselves.

character *C* (say, its being connected to certain sensory inputs) made it able to perform *F* (say, carry the information that *P*) better than other brain structures lacking *C*, and because (3) it is the fact that *m* had its information-carrying capacity, plus the fact that learning mechanisms select structures for having such capacities, that explains (in part) why there is now a token of *m* being produced. So although it may be against the spirit of Millikan's work to abandon evolution, it is no contravention of the law's letter.

If the mechanisms underlying the neural plasticity we have been discussing turned out to be learning mechanisms of the sort Dretske, Millikan and Papineau take to give rise to natural functions, that would seem to solve their problems. ET theorists could give up on evolution as the source of psychologically significant functions and embrace learning as the source instead – or could they?

Because learning as ET theorists conceive it is like evolution, only faster, the same problems with evolutionary theories are bound to arise for learning theories, only on shorter time scales. If lightning strikes a swamp and out walks Swampman, he will not have a learning history any more than he will have an evolutionary history – he will be a swamp-person and a zombie (assuming representationalism is the right account of both propositional attitudes and the senses) for quite some time thereafter. Indeed, if nothing of note happens to Swampman, and the mechanisms of neural "recruitment" (to use Dretske's 1988 phrase) are not called upon, Swampman may go for some dull hours or days of life without having any mind at all. In a like fashion, there is no reason to think that Swampman will attain full mentality all at once. On the contrary, the mechanisms of neural recruitment are likely to operate at different times on different brain regions in response to different experiences. If Swampman stumbles, some sort of "error signal" will no doubt lead to the recruitment of some superior attentional mechanism or something similar, and hence lend original intentionality to that part of the brain, while having no effect on, say, Swampman's "language" centres.

Those unmoved by Swampman as a counter-argument to ET theories will be no more moved by Swampman as a counter-argument to what we might call LT (for learning-based teleological) theories. Can the same arguments mounted against ET theories from actual cases be mounted against LT theories? To the best of my knowledge, there is not yet enough evidence at the neurological level to do so. That is, there is not yet enough evidence regarding how neural systems interact to say whether selective learning processes generally work in a fashion that would routinely produce swampfolk and zombies if they were the sole underpinning for original intentionality. However, something can be said. As Millikan has argued (1993, chap. 1), nothing can be said to have been selected unless it was, at some point, an option presented amongst alternatives. The nose has not, in recent times, been selected for the holding of glasses because, at least in recent times, people have not occasionally been born without noses and therefore been unable to wear glasses. If one thinks of the mechanisms of neural learning as a system providing functions through its selection of certain structures, it must be thought of as selecting those certain structures over alternative structures. Now think of a person born lucky in some neural respect – say, born with her primary auditory cortex already set up in just the way a normal adult's primary auditory cortex is set up. To the extent that the region of cortex is initially found in a state requiring no selection, it will never feel selective forces acting on it. But then the newborn will grow up monstrous – unable to form auditory representations, but behaviourally just like hearing people, because of her "bad luck" at birth. The possibility of such a monstrous child, whose apparent good luck turns out to be bad according to the LT theorist, seems to me another good argument against LT theories. Those who favour the hypothesis of an innate deep grammar should also take note that the neural encoding of one's deep grammar could not be a meaningful structure if it is born as-needed, and thus not modified through selective procedures.

5. From Design to Control

LT theories and ET theories are both problematic, then. Does this mean that there is no hope for a theory of mind which appeals to natural norms in explaining mentality? Perhaps, but perhaps not. In this final section, I will attempt to show what a would-be teleosemanticist could do to preserve a teleological approach without falling back on evolution or some related phenomenon.

Everyday representations and the norms involved in their creation seem to fall into two types. First, there are representations whose features are supposed to correspond to some distal state of affairs (or co-vary with them, or indicate them – hereafter I will write 'correspond' for convenience) because someone *designed* them to do so. Street maps are designed so that lines on them correspond to street positions, thermometers are designed so that mercury height varies with temperature, characters in allegorical works of fiction are designed to have features in common with certain actual people, and so on. In general, objects given certain features by a designer in the belief and hope that those features would enable the object to stand in correspondence to some distal object's properties are objects which are *supposed* to correspond to some distal object's properties because of their design – they are representations whose normative component is derived from design.

The second sort of representation, much neglected by teleosemanticists, is that which gets its normativity from some sort of control.[10] Suppose I take a saltshaker and a peppershaker and begin to move them about in illustrating how a bicycle crash happened. In doing so, I create a representation of the crash using objects that were not designed for that purpose. Nonetheless, by moving them about, intending that their movements correspond to the movements of the cyclists, I make it true that they are supposed to correspond to the cyclists' movements, and so represent them. Another example of representations featuring control-like norms can be found in improvisational theatre, in which actors control their movements in ways intended to correspond with the movements made by people in love, people fighting, etc., independent of the intentions of any designer (such as a playwright).

A fact worthy of the teleosemanticist's attention is that evolution (and selectionist forms of learning) is a design-like process. Of course, evolution is not literally a designer – it does not choose mutations because it foresees benefits. Nonetheless, evolution is as design-like a

---

10 An exception is Dretske (1988), although Dretske's classificatory scheme cross-cuts the present one.

11 Even adapted functions have something which is fixed about them.

process as there is to be found in the sub-intentional world; Dawkins (1986) presents this view forcefully. And it is precisely this kinship with the processes of design which is problematic for ET theorists, for all design-like processes are historical processes, processes in which norms get fixed when a representation comes into being, and stay fixed throughout the representation's lifespan.[11] ET and LT theorists are stuck saying that having a mind requires having a certain sort of history, which just seems untenable. What the teleosemanticist needs is not a design-like source of norms for her theory, but a control-like source of norms. Control-derived norms exist just as long as control or relevant intentions to control exist: if a saltshaker's movements represent the movements of a cyclist because of the way I am using the saltshaker, they do so as soon as, but only so long as, I move the saltshaker for that purpose. Once I put the saltshaker down and cease to concern myself with it, it stops representing – there is no longer any movement it is supposed to make, no relation in which it is supposed to stand. Control-derived norms ignore history in a way that design-derived norms do not. Thus, if teleosemantics could discover control-like norms in our heads of a sort sufficient to create mental representations, it could eliminate appeals to history in its account of mentality. If teleosemantics is to work, perhaps its proponents should stop thinking of mental representations as structures designed by evolution and begin thinking of mental representations as structures controlled by the mechanisms of plasticity.

How would a control-based teleosemantic theory of mind look? To a first approximation, it would hold that to be a mental representation is to be a structure whose features are supposed to correspond to some particular state of affairs (type), this being the core of all teleosemantic theories. But it would go on to say that neural structures have these functions precisely because there are mechanisms of neural regulation, governance, or control which causally drive neural structures towards instantiating correspondences with particular states of affairs. Just as a person can control a saltshaker so as to make it correspond to a bicycle's movements, so (such a theory would say) structures in the brain can control other structure's features, driving them so as to make them correspond to various things in the world. And just as the history of the saltshaker is irrelevant to its control-given function, so long as the control actually exists, so the history of the neural structure would be irrelevant to its control-given function, so long as the control exists. Finally, if the control exists, then whether the controlling structure evolved to exert this control is itself quite irrelevant. Thus, such a theory would retain the fundamental teleosemantic premise while excising any mention of history from the theory.

It is an open question whether this strategy would actually pay off for the teleosemanticist, but there are some reasons for cautious optimism. The principal problem awaiting the teleosemanticist is the discovery of natural, sub-intentional analogues of control-based norms, and the principal reason for hope is that work on this subject has already been begun, in philosophical discussions of cybernetics. From the birth of cybernetics in the 1940s until the mid-1970s, a number of philosophers attempted to analyze what it is to be a feedback-governed system and attempted to put such analyses to use in characterizing intentional action and biological function, Braithwaite (1968), Nagel (1961), and Rosenblueth et al. (1943) being well-known examples. While it is true that these theories all had a number of problems, it may be time for teleosemanticists to turn their attention back to them, for they may offer an escape from historical accounts of the mind while holding on to the normativity of the mental. They appear to provide a chance for teleosemantics to escape the theoretical perils of monsters, and for that reason they deserve new attention from everyone interested in the teleosemantic project.

References

Braithwaite, R. 1968. *Scientific Explanation: A Study in the Function of Theory, Probability and Law in Science.* London: Cambridge University Press.

Bullock, D., J. Liederman, and D. Todorovic. 1987. "Reconciling Stable Asymmetry with Recovery of Function: an Adaptive Systems Perspective on Functional Plasticity," *Child Development* **58**, 689–97.

Clark, S., T. Allard, W. Jenkins, and M. Merzenich 1988. "Receptive Fields in the Body-Surface Map in Adult Cortex Defined by Temporally Correlated Inputs," *Nature* **332**, 444–45.

Davidson, D. 1987. "Knowing One's Own Mind," *Proceedings and Addresses of the American Philosophical Association.* Vol. **60**, pp. 441–58.

Dawkins, R. 1986. *The Blind Watchmaker: Why the Evidence of Evolution Reveals a Universe Without Design.* New York: W.W. Norton and Co.

Devries, W. 1996. "Experience and the Swamp Creature," *Philosophical Studies* **82**, 55–80.

Dretske, F. 1988. *Explaining Behavior: Reasons in a World of Causes.* Cambridge, MA: MIT Press.

———. 1995. *Naturalizing the Mind.* Cambridge, MA: MIT Press.

Fodor, J. 1990. *A Theory of Content: And Other Essays.* Cambridge, MA: MIT Press.

———. 1994. *The Elm and the Expert.* Cambridge, MA: MIT Press.

Garraghty, P., and J. Kaas. 1991. "Large-Scale Functional Reorganization in Adult Monkey Cortex after Peripheral Nerve Injury," *Proceedings of the National Academy of Sciences* (USA). Vol. **88**, pp. 6976–80.

Helmstaedter, C., M. Kurthen, D. Linke, and C. Elger. 1994. "Right Hemisphere Restitution of Language and Memory Functions in Right Hemisphere Language-Dominant Patients with Left Temporal Lobe Epilepsy," *Brain* **117**, 729–37.

Kaas, J. 1991. "Plasticity of Sensory and Motor Maps in Adult Mammals," *Annual Review of Neuroscience* **14**, 137–67.

Kolb, B. and I. Wishaw. 1996. *Fundamentals of Human Neuropsychology: 4th ed.* New York: Freeman.

Lycan, W. 1987. *Consciousness.* Cambridge, MA: MIT Press.

Métin, C. and D. Frost. 1989. "Visual Responses of Neurons in Somatosensory Cortex of Hamsters with Experimentally Induced Retinal Projections to Somatosensory Thalamus," *Proceedings of the National Academy of Sciences (USA)*. Vol. **86**, pp. 357–61.

Millikan, R. 1984. *Language, Thought, and Other Biological Categories.* Cambridge, MA: MIT Press.

———. 1993. *White Queen Psychology and Other Essays for Alice.* Cambridge, MA: MIT Press.

———. 1996. "On Swampkinds," *Mind and Language* **11**, 103–17.

Nagel, E. 1961. *The Structure of Science: Problems in the Logic of Scientific Explanation.* New York: Harcourt, Brace & World.

Neander, K. 1996. "Swampman Meets Swampcow," *Mind and Language* **11**, 118–29.

Papineau, D. 1987. *Reality and Representation.* Oxford: Basil Blackwell.

———. 1996. "Doubtful Intuitions," *Mind and Language* **11**, 130–32.

Piacentini, J. and Hynd, G. 1988. "Language after Dominant Hemispherectomy: Are Plasticity of Function and Equipotentiality Viable Concepts?" *Clinical Psychology Review* **8**, 595–609.

Rausch, R., and G. Walsh. 1984. "Right-Hemisphere Language Dominance in Right-Handed Epileptic Patients," *Archives of Neurology* **41**, 1077–80.

Roe, A., S. Pallas, J. Hahm, and M. Sur. 1990. "A Map of Visual Space Induced in Primary Auditory Cortex," *Science* **250**, 818–20.

Rosenblueth, A., N. Wiener, and J. Bigelow. 1943. "Behavior, Purpose and Teleology," *Philosophy of Science* **10**, 18–24.

Seager, W. 1997. "Critical Notice of Fred Dretske, Naturalizing the Mind," *Canadian Journal of Philosophy* **27**, 83–109.

Sterelny, K. 1990. *The Representational Theory of Mind: An Introduction.* Cambridge, MA: Basil Blackwell.

Sur, M., S. Pallas, and A. Roe. 1990. "Cross-Modal Plasticity in Cortical Development: Differentiation and Specification of Sensory Neocortex," *Trends in Neurosciences* **13**, 227–33.

Tye, M. 1995. *Ten Problems of Consciousness.* Cambridge, MA: MIT Press.

Weinberger, N. 1995. "Dynamic Regulation of Receptive Fields and Maps in the Adult Sensory Cortex," *Annual Review of Neuroscience* **18**, 129–58.

Wells, H. G. 1996. *The Island of Doctor Moreau.* Jefferson, N.C.: McFarland.

Witelson, S. 1987. "Neurobiological Aspects of Language in Children," *Child Development* **58**, 653–88.

III. Vision

CANADIAN JOURNAL OF PHILOSOPHY
Supplementary Volume 27

Why Vision is More than Seeing

MELVYN A. GOODALE

1. Introduction

Vision is so closely identified with visual phenomenology that we sometimes forget that the visual system does more than deliver our experience of the world. Vision also plays a critical role in the control of our movements, from picking up our coffee cups to playing tennis. But the visual control of movement has, until recently, been relatively neglected. Indeed, traditional accounts of vision, while acknowledging the role of vision in motor control, have simply regarded such control as part of a larger function – that of constructing an internal model of the external world. Even though such accounts might postulate separate 'modules' for the processing of different visual features, such as motion, colour, texture, and form, in most of these accounts there is an implicit assumption that, in the end, vision delivers a single representation of the external world – a kind of simulacrum of the real thing that serves as the perceptual foundation for all visually driven thought and action.

Over the last ten years, the idea of a monolithic visual system has begun to be challenged. Vision is no longer regarded as a single system delivering a 'general-purpose' representation of the external world. Instead, vision is seen as consisting of a number of separate systems in which the input processing of each system has been shaped by the output mechanisms it serves. In particular, it has been suggested that the visual control of actions – from saccadic eye movements to skilled grasping movements of the hand and limb – depends on visual mechanisms that are functionally and neurally separate from those mediating our perception of the world. In the following pages, I will argue that this distinction between vision for action and vision for perception can help us to understand the complex organization of the visual pathways in the human brain. Before examining the intricacies of human vision, however, it might be useful to examine the origins of vision and the role that vision plays in the life of simple organisms.

2. The Evolution of Visuomotor Control

Vision did not evolve to enable organisms to perceive. It evolved to provide distal control of their movements. Take the case of *Euglena*, a single-cell organism that uses light as a source of energy. Euglena has been shown to alter its pattern of swimming as a function of the ambient light levels in different parts of the pond or puddle in which it lives. Such phototactic behaviour ensures that the Euglena stays longer in regions of its environment where sunlight is available for the manufacture of food (Gould 1982). But no one would seriously argue that the Euglena 'perceives' the light or even that it has some sort of internal model of the outside world. Such a 'representational' account is not necessary. The simplest and most obvious way to understand the Euglena's behaviour is in terms of a simple input-output device in which the amount of light is transformed into changes in the rate of swimming. Of course, a mechanism of this sort, although driven by light, is far less complicated than the visual systems of multicellular organisms. But even in more complex organisms, such as vertebrates, much of vision can be understood entirely in terms of the distal control of movement without reference to experiential perception or any general-purpose representation of the outside world.

In simple vertebrates, the visual control systems for different kinds of behaviour depend on relatively independent neural substrates. In other words, with the evolution of a new pattern of behaviour came a new visuomotor control system. Thus, in present-day amphibians, such as the frog, visually guided prey-catching and visually guided obstacle avoidance are separately mediated by different pathways from the retina right through to the effector systems producing the movements (Ingle 1973; 1982; 1991). The visual control of prey-catching depends on circuitry involving retinal projections to the optic tectum in the midbrain while the visual control of locomotion around barriers depends on circuitry involving retinal projections to particular pretectal nuclei in the thalamus. Each of these retinal targets projects in turn to different premotor nuclei in the brainstem and spinal cord. In fact, accumulating evidence from studies in both frog and toad suggest that there are at least five separate visuomotor *modules*, each responsible for a different kind of visually guided behaviour and each having distinct processing routes from input to output (Ingle 1991; Ewert 1987). The outputs of these different modules certainly have to be coordinated, but in no sense are they guided by a single general-purpose visual representation in the frog's brain. (For a discussion of this issue, see Goodale 1996, Milner and Goodale 1995, and Goodale and Humphrey 1998.)

Although there is evidence that the same kind of visuomotor modularity found in the frog also exists in the mammalian brain (for review, see Goodale 1996), the very complexity of the day-to-day living in many mammals, particularly in higher primates, demands much more flexible organization of the circuitry. In monkeys (and thus presumably in humans as well), many of the visuomotor circuits that are shared with simpler vertebrates appear to be modulated by more recently evolved control systems in the cerebral cortex (for review, see Milner and Goodale 1995). This 'Jacksonian' circuitry (Jackson 1875), in which a layer of cortical control is superimposed on more ancient subcortical networks, makes possible much more adaptive visuomotor behaviour. Of course, the basic subcortical circuitry has also changed to some extent and new visuomotor control systems involving both cortical and subcortical structures have emerged. But even though these complex visuomotor control systems in the primate brain are capable of generating an almost limitless range of visually guided behaviour, as we shall see later, there is evidence that these visuomotor modules are functionally and neurally separate from those mediating our perception of the world.

3. The Emergence of Visual Perception

As interactions with the world became more complicated and subtle, direct sensory control of action was not enough. With the emergence of cognitive systems and complex social behaviour, a good deal of motor output has become quite arbitrary with respect to sensory input. Many animals, particularly humans and other primates, behave as though their actions are driven by some sort of internal model of the world in which they live. The representational systems that use vision to generate such models or percepts of the world must carry out very different transformations on visual input from the transformations carried out by the visuomotor modules described earlier. For one thing, the neural codes that generate such perceptual representations are not linked directly to specific motor outputs but access these outputs via cognitive systems involving memory, semantics, spatial reasoning, planning, and communication. The perceptual representations generated by these systems allow us to experience a world beyond our bodies, to share that experience with other members of our species, and to plan a vast range of different actions. But even though perception allows us to choose a particular goal, the actual *execution* of an action that is carried out to realize that goal may nevertheless be mediated by dedicated visuomotor modules that are not dissimilar in principle from those found in frogs and toads. In other words, vision in humans and other primates (and perhaps other animals as well) has two distinct but interacting functions: (1) the perception of objects and their relations, which provides a foundation for the organism's cognitive life, and (2) the control of actions directed at (or with respect to) those objects, in which separate motor outputs are programmed and controlled on-line.

4. Dorsal and Ventral Streams

Beyond primary visual cortex (or V1, as it is sometimes called), visual information is conveyed to a bewildering number of higher-order visual areas (for review, see Zeki 1993 and Allman 1999). Despite the complexity of the interconnections between these different areas, two broad "streams" of projections from V1 have been identified in the

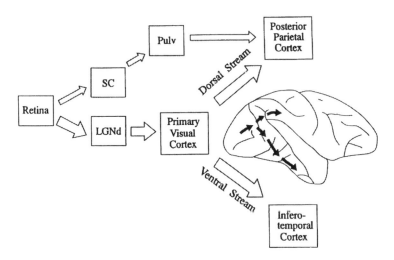

Figure 1.

Major routes whereby retinal input reaches the dorsal and ventral streams. The diagram of the macaque monkey brain (right hemisphere) on the right of the figure shows the approximate routes of the cortico-cortical projections from primary visual cortex to the posterior parietal and the inferotemporal cortex, respectively. LGNd: lateral geniculate nucleus, pars dorsalis; Pulv: pulvinar; SC: superior colliculus. Adapted with permission from Goodale et al. (1994).

macaque monkey brain: a ventral stream projecting eventually to the inferotemporal cortex and a dorsal stream projecting to the posterior parietal cortex (Ungerleider and Mishkin 1982). These regions also receive inputs from a number of other subcortical visual structures, such as the superior colliculus, which sends prominent projections to the dorsal stream (via the thalamus). A schematic diagram of these pathways can be found in Figure 1. Although one must always be cautious when drawing homologies between monkey and human neuroanatomy (Crick and Jones 1993), recent neuroimaging work suggests that the visual projections from the primary visual cortex to the temporal and parietal lobes in the human brain may involve a separation into ventral and dorsal streams similar to that seen in the macaque brain (for review, see Tootell et al. 1996).

In their original 1982 account of the division of labour between the dorsal and ventral streams, Ungerleider and Mishkin argued that the two streams play different but complementary roles in the processing of incoming visual information. The ventral stream, according to them, plays a critical role in the identification and recognition of objects, while the dorsal stream mediates the localization of those same objects. Some have referred to this distinction in visual processing as one between object vision and spatial vision – "what" versus "where." Support for this idea came from work with monkeys. Lesions of inferotemporal cortex in monkeys produced deficits in their ability to discriminate between objects on the basis of their visual features but did not affect their performance on a spatially demanding "landmark" task (Pohl 1973; Ungerleider and Brody 1977). Conversely, lesions of the posterior parietal cortex produced deficits in performance on the landmark task but did not affect object discrimination learning (for a critique of these studies, see Goodale 1995; Milner and Goodale 1995). Although the evidence for the original Ungerleider and Mishkin proposal initially seemed quite compelling, recent findings from a broad range of studies in both humans and monkeys has forced a re-interpretation of the division of labour between the two streams. As will be detailed in subsequent sections, David Milner and I have offered an account of the two streams that emphasizes the differences in the requirements of the output systems that each stream serves.

5.   Vision for Perception and Vision for Action

David Milner and I have suggested, in contrast to Ungerleider and Mishkin (1982), that both streams process information about object features and about their spatial relations. Each stream, however, uses this visual information in different ways (Goodale and Milner 1992). In the ventral stream, the transformations focus on the enduring characteristics of objects and their relations, permitting the formation of long-term perceptual representations. Such representations play an essential role in the identification of objects and enable us to classify objects and events, attach meaning and significance to them, and establish their causal relations. Such operations are essential for accumulating a knowledge base about the world. In contrast, the transformations carried out by the dorsal stream deal with the moment-to-moment information about the location and disposition of objects with respect to the hand or other effector being used and thereby mediate the visual control of skilled actions, such as manual prehension, directed at those objects. As such, the dorsal stream can be regarded as a cortical extension of the dedicated visuomotor modules that mediate visually guided movements in all vertebrates. The perceptual representations constructed by the ventral stream interact with various high-level cognitive mechanisms and enable an organism to select a particular course of action with respect to objects in the world while the visuomotor networks in the dorsal stream (and associated cortical and subcortical pathways) are responsible for the programming and on-line control of the particular movements that action entails.

This division of labour between the two cortical visual pathways requires that different transformations be carried out on incoming visual information. Consider first the task of the perceptual system in the ventral stream. To generate long-term representations of objects and their relations, perceptual mechanisms must be 'object-based'; i.e., constancies of size, shape, colour, lightness, and relative location need to be maintained across different viewing conditions. Some of these mechanisms might use a network of viewer-centred representations of the same object (e.g., Bülthoff and Edelman 1992); others might use an array of canonical representations (e.g., Palmer, Rosch, and Chase 1981); still others might be truly 'object-centred' (Marr 1982). But whatever the particular coding might be, it is the identity of the object, not its disposition with respect to the observer that is of primary concern to the perceptual system. This is not the case for the visuomotor mechanisms in the dorsal stream and other related structures that support actions directed at that object. In this case, the underlying visuomotor transformations have to be viewer-centred; in other words, both the location of the object and its disposition and motion must be encoded relative to the observer in egocentric coordinates, that is in retinocentric, head-centred, torso-centred, or shoulder-centred coordinates (Xing and Andersen 2000). (One constancy that must operate, however, is object size; in order to scale the grasp during prehension, the underlying visuomotor mechanisms must be able to compute the real size of the object independent of its distance from the observer.) Finally, because the position and disposition of a goal object in the action space of an observer is rarely constant, such computations must take place *de novo* every time an action occurs (for a discussion of this issue, see Goodale and Haffenden 1998). In other words, the action systems of the dorsal stream do most of their work on-line; only the perception systems of the ventral stream can afford to work off-line. To summarize then, while similar (but not identical) visual information about object shape, size, local orientation, and location is available to both systems, the transformational algorithms that are applied to these inputs are uniquely tailored to the function of each system. According to our proposal, it is the nature of the functional requirements of perception and action that lies at the root of the division of labour in the ventral and dorsal visual projection systems of the primate cerebral cortex.

6. Neuropsychological Evidence for Perception and Action Streams

In the intact brain, the two streams of processing work together in a seamless and integrated fashion. Nevertheless, by studying individuals who have sustained brain damage that spares one of these systems but not the other, it is possible to get a glimpse into how each stream transforms incoming visual information.

6.1 Perception without Action

It has been known for a long time that patients with lesions in the superior regions of the posterior parietal cortex can have problems using vision to direct a grasp or a reaching movement towards the correct location of a visual target placed in different positions in the visual field, particularly the peripheral visual field. This particular deficit is often described as *optic ataxia* (Bálint 1909). But the failure to locate an object with the hand should not be construed as a problem in spatial vision; many of these patients can, for example, describe the relative position of the object in space quite accurately, even though they cannot direct their hand towards it (Jeannerod 1988; Perenin and Vighetto 1988). Moreover, sometimes the deficit will be seen in one hand but not the other. Problems in the visual control of locomotion and the production of voluntary saccades have also been observed

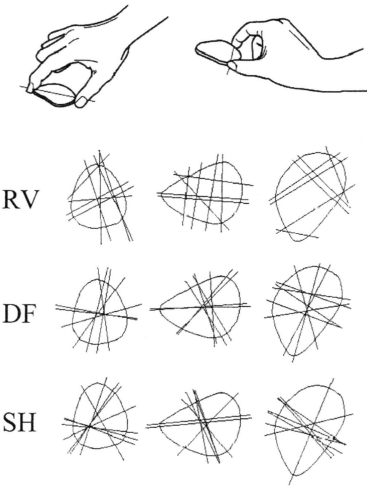

Figure 2.

Grasp lines (joining points where the thumb and index finger first made contact with the shape) selected by the optic ataxia patient (RV), the visual agnosic patient (DF), and the control subject (SH) when picking up three of the twelve shapes used in the study. The four different orientations in which each shape was presented have been rotated so that they are aligned. Notice the similarity between the DF's grasp lines and those of the control subject, and how their grasp lines differ from those of RV who often chooses very unstable grasp points. The illustrations at the top of the figure illustrate grasps in which 'good' and 'poor' grasp points have been selected (left and right respectively). Adapted with permission from Goodale and Humphrey (1998).

following damage to the posterior parietal region (for review, see Milner and Goodale 1995). It should be pointed out, of course, that these patients typically have no difficulty using input from other sensory systems, such as proprioception or audition, to guide their movements. Their deficit is neither 'purely' visual nor 'purely' motor but is instead a visuomotor deficit.

Some of these patients are unable to use visual information to rotate their hand or scale the opening of their fingers when reaching out to pick up an object, even though they have no difficulty describing the size or orientation of objects in that part of the visual field (Jakobson et al. 1991; Jeannerod 1988; Jeannerod, Decety, and Michel 1994; Goodale et al. 1993; Perenin and Vighetto 1988). Similarly, as Figure 2 illustrates, patients with damage to this region can also show deficits in the selection of stable grasp points on the surface of objects of varying shape (Goodale et al. 1994). These results show that the visuomotor disturbances accompanying damage to the posterior parietal cortex need not be limited to deficits in the spatial control of movements but can extend to object features such as size, shape, and orientation. Nevertheless, it is worth emphasizing once more that the deficits are visuomotor in nature not perceptual; the patients have no trouble discriminating between objects of different size or shape or between objects placed in different orientations.

The various visuomotor deficits that have been described in patients with damage to the posterior parietal region are quite dissociable from one another. Some patients are unable to use visual information to control their hand postures but have no difficulty controlling the direction of their grasp; others show the reverse pattern. Some patients are unable to direct their gaze towards a target object, but have no difficulty directing a well-formed grasp in its direction; others may show no evidence of an oculomotor deficit but be unable to guide their hand towards an object under visual control. Indeed, depending upon the size and locus of the lesion, a patient can demonstrate any combination of these visuomotor deficits (for review, see Milner and Goodale 1995). Different sub-regions of the posterior parietal cortex, it appears, are critical for the visual control of different motor outputs. A particular motor act, such as reaching out and grasping an object, presumably would engage visuomotor mechanisms in a number of these different areas, including those involved in the control of saccades, visual pursuit, reaching with the limb, and grasping movements of the hands and fingers (for a discussion of the different components of manual prehension, see Jeannerod 1988). Just how such mechanisms are coordinated is not well-understood – although some models have been proposed (e.g., Hoff and Arbib 1992). In any case, it is clear that the visual control of each of the constituent actions will require different sensorimotor coordinate transformations, and there have been some attempts to specify how the posterior parietal cortex might mediate such transformations (e.g., Flanders, Tillery, and Soechting 1992; Stein 1992). But again, even though patients with damage to the posterior parietal region may show a variety of different visuomotor deficits, they can often describe (and thus presumably perceive) the intrinsic visual features and the location of the very object they are unable to grasp, foveate, and/or walk towards.

6.2 Action without Perception

The fact that patients with damage to posterior parietal cortex can perceive objects but cannot grasp them provides one piece of evidence that there are separate neural substrates for perception and action in the human brain. It also suggests that the superior regions of the posterior parietal cortex, the human homologue of the monkey dorsal stream, are critical for the visual control of action. But even more compelling evidence for separate visual systems for perception and action comes from patients who show the opposite pattern of deficits and spared visual abilities. Take the case of DF, for example.

DF is a woman, now in her late forties, who had the misfortune at age thirty-four to suffer irreversible brain damage as a result of near-asphyxiation by carbon monoxide. When she regained consciousness, it was apparent that DF's visual system had been badly damaged by the anoxia. She was unable to recognize the faces of her relatives and friends or identify the visual form of common objects. In fact, she could not even tell the difference between simple geometric shapes such as a square and a triangle. At the same time, she had no difficulty recognizing people from their voices or identifying objects placed in her hands; her perceptual problems appeared to be exclusively visual. Even today, more than ten years after the accident, she remains quite unable to identify objects or drawings on the basis of their visual form.

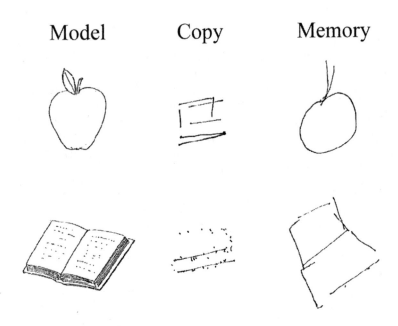

Figure 3.

The patient DF's attempts to draw from models and from memory. DF was unable to identify the line-drawings of an apple and an open book shown on the left. In addition, her copies were very poor. Note that she did incorporate some elements of the line-drawing (e.g., the dots indicating the text in the book) into her copy. When she was asked on another occasion to draw an apple or an open book from memory, she produced a respectable representation of both items (right-hand column). When she was later shown her own drawings, she had no idea what they were. Adapted from Servos, Goodale, and Humphrey (1993).

The damage in DF's brain is quite diffuse, a common pattern in cases of anoxia. Nevertheless, certain areas of her brain, especially those in the posterior region of her cerebral cortex, appear to be more severely damaged than others. Magnetic resonance imaging carried out just over a year after her accident showed that the ventrolateral regions of her occipital lobe are particularly compromised. Primary visual cortex, however, appears to be largely spared in DF (for details, see Milner et al. 1991).

DF's perceptual problems are not simply a case of being unable to associate a visual stimulus with meaningful semantic information. For example, while it is true that she cannot find the right name or semantic association for the objects depicted in the simple line drawings illustrated in the left-hand column of Figure 3, she is also completely unable to draw what she sees when she looks at the line drawing. Moreover, her inability to copy drawings is not due to a problem in controlling the movements of the pen or pencil. When she is asked to draw a particular object from memory, she is able to do so reasonably well, as the drawings on the right-hand side of Figure 3 illustrate.

Nor is DF's inability to perceive the shape and form of objects in the world due to deficits in basic sensory processing (Milner et al. 1991). She remains quite capable of identifying colours, for example. In addition, perimetric testing carried out quite early after her accident showed that she could detect luminance-defined targets at least as far out as thirty degrees into the visual periphery. Her spatial contrast sensitivity was also normal above five cycles per degree and was only moderately impaired at lower spatial frequencies. Of course, even though she could detect the presence of the spatial frequency gratings in these tests, she could not report their orientation. In fact, DF has great problems describing or discriminating the orientation and form of any visual contour, no matter how that contour is defined. Thus, she cannot identify shapes whose contours are defined by differences in luminance or colour, or by differences in the direction of motion or the plane of depth. Nor can she recognize shapes that are defined by the similarity or proximity of individual elements of the visual array. Nevertheless, information about the spatial distribution of the visual array appeared to reach her primary visual cortex. Thus, when she was shown a high-contrast reversing checker-board pattern in an electrophysiological assessment carried out just after the accident, the initial components of the evoked response appeared to be quite normal suggesting that her primary visual cortex was working normally. In short, DF's deficit seems to be "perceptual" rather than "sensory" in nature. She simply cannot perceive shapes and forms – even though the early stages of her visual system would appear to have access to the requisite low-level sensory information.

What is most remarkable about DF, however, is that despite her profound deficits in form vision, she is able to use visual information about the size, shape, and orientation of objects to control a broad range of visually guided movements. DF will reach out and grasp your hand if you offer it when you first meet her. She is equally adept at reaching out for a door handle – even in an unfamiliar environment. She can walk unassisted across a room or patio, stepping easily over low obstacles and walking around higher ones. Even more amazing is the fact that she can reach out and grasp an object placed in front of her with considerable accuracy and confidence – despite the fact that moments before she was quite unable to identify or describe that same object.

These dissociations between DF's perceptual abilities and her ability to use visual information to control skilled movements are also evident in formal testing (Goodale et al. 1991). For example, when she is presented with a series of rectangular blocks that vary in their dimensions but not in their overall surface area, she is unable to say whether or not any two of these blocks are the same or different. Even when a single block is placed in front of her, she is unable to indicate how wide the block is by opening her index finger and thumb a matching amount. Nevertheless, when she reaches out to pick up the block using a precision grip, the opening between her index finger and thumb is scaled in flight to the width of the object, just as it is in subjects with normal vision.

A similar dissociation can be seen in DF's processing of the orientation of objects (Goodale et al. 1991). Thus, even though she cannot discriminate between objects placed in different orientations on a table in front of her, she can rotate her hand in the correct orientation when she reaches out to grasp one of the objects. When presented with a large 'slot' in a vertical surface, she is unable rotate a hand-held card to match the orientation of that slot (see Figure 4). But again, when she attempts to insert the hand-held card into the slot, she rotates the card in the appropriate way as she moves it towards the slot (Figure 4). She can also use information about the shape of an object to locate stable grasp points on its surface when she picks it up (Goodale et al. 1994). Thus, when grasping an object like those illustrated in Figure 2, DF will place her finger and thumb so that a line joining the opposing points of contact passes through the object's centre of mass. And, in contrast to the patient with posterior parietal damage whose performance is also illustrated in Figure 2, DF chooses points on the object's boundary where her fingers are the least likely to slip – such as points of high convexity or concavity – just like the control subject with normal vision

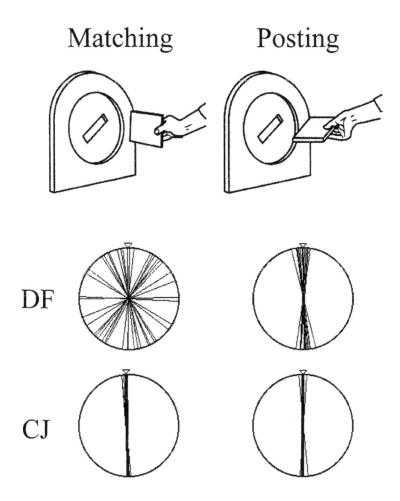

Matching   Posting

DF

CJ

Figure 4.

Polar plots of the orientation of the hand-held card on the perceptual matching task and the visuomotor posting task for DF and an age-matched control subject (CJ). The correct orientation on each trial has been rotated to vertical. Note that although DF was unable to match the orientation of the card to that of the slot in the perceptual matching card, she did rotate the card to the correct orientation as she attempted to insert it into the slot on the posting task.

does. Needless to say, DF is quite unable to tell these objects apart in a same-different discrimination. In short, DF can use visual information about the size, orientation, and shape of objects to program and control her goal-directed movements even though she has no meaningful perception of those object features.

DF's failure to recognize the identity of common objects on the basis of their shape means that she does not pick up familiar objects in a functionally appropriate way. In other words, rather than grasping a knife by its handle in readiness to use it to cut something, she is just as likely to pick it up by its blade. Nevertheless, even though her grasp might be inappropriate in terms of the object's function, the orientation of her wrist and the opening of her hand correspond beautifully to the object's size, shape, and orientation (Carey, Harvey, and Milner 1996).

As I mentioned earlier, these spared visuomotor skills are not limited to reaching and grasping movements; DF can also walk around quite well under visual control. When she was tested more formally, we found that she is able to negotiate obstacles during locomotion as well as control subjects (Patla and Goodale 1997). Thus, when obstacles of different heights were randomly placed in her path on different trials, she stepped over these obstacles quite efficiently and the elevation of her toe increased linearly as a function of obstacle height, just as it does in neurologically intact individuals. Yet when she was asked to give verbal estimates of the height of the obstacles, the slope of the line relating estimated and actual obstacle height was much shallower in her case than it was in normal subjects. Similar dissociations between perceptual judgments about the pitch of the visual field and its effect on eye position have also been observed in DF (Servos, Matin, and Goodale 1995).

To summarize: Even though DF's brain damage has left her unable to perceive the size, shape, and orientation of objects, her visuomotor outputs remain quite sensitive to these same object features. There appears to have been an interruption in the normal flow of shape and contour information into her perceptual system without affecting the processing of shape and contour information by her visuomotor control systems. But where is the damage in DF's brain? If, as was suggested earlier, the perception of objects and events is mediated by the ventral stream of visual projections to inferotemporal cortex, then DF should show evidence for damage relatively early in this pathway. Certainly, the pattern of damage revealed by the MRI is consistent with this interpretation; the major focus of cortical damage is in the ventrolateral region of the occipital cortex, an area that is thought to be part of the human homologue of the ventral stream. At the same time, as was mentioned earlier, her primary visual cortex, which provides input for both the dorsal and ventral streams, appears to be largely intact. Thus, although input from primary visual cortex to the ventral stream has been compromised in DF, input from this structure to the dorsal stream appears to be essentially intact. In addition, the dorsal stream, unlike the ventral stream, also receives important visual input from the superior colliculus via the pulvinar, a nucleus in the thalamus (see Figure 1). Indeed, recent work by Perenin and Rossetti (1996) suggests that this collicular-pulvinar route to the dorsal stream may be able to support object-directed grasping movements even without input from V1. They tested a patient who was completely blind (by conventional testing) in one half of his visual field following a medial occipital lesion that included all of V1. The patient could not see any objects in his blind field. Nevertheless, when he was persuaded to reach out and grasp objects placed in his blind field, he showed some evidence of sensitivity to the size and orientation of objects. Thus, there are at least two routes whereby information could reach the dorsal stream in DF: from the superior colliculus (via the pulvinar) and from the lateral geniculate nucleus (via primary visual cortex). Either or both of these pathways could be continuing to mediate well-formed visuomotor responses in DF.

One must be cautious, however, about drawing strong conclusions about anatomy and pathways from patients like DF. Her deficits arose, not from a discrete lesion, but from anoxia. As a consequence, the brain damage in DF, while localized to some extent, is much more diffuse than it would be in a patient with a stroke or tumour. Thus, while the striking dissociation between perceptual and visuomotor abilities in DF can be mapped onto the distinction between the ventral and dorsal streams of visual processing that David Milner and I proposed (Goodale and Milner 1992), that mapping can be only tentative. The proposal is strengthened, however, by observations in patients like those described in the previous section whose pattern of deficits is complementary to DF's and whose brain damage can be confidently localized to the dorsal stream.

In summary, the neuropsychological findings can be accommodated quite well by the proposal that the division of labour between the ventral and dorsal streams of visual processing is based on the distinction between visuomotor control and the more visuocognitive functions of vision. Moreover, this new way of looking at the organization of the visual system is also consistent with the story that is emerging from anatomical, neurophysiological, and behavioural work in the monkey – as well as from functional neuroimaging studies (PET and fMRI) of activity in the normal human brain.[1]

7. Different metrics and different frames of reference for perception and action

Although the evidence from neurological patients discussed earlier points to a clear dissociation between the visual pathways supporting perception and action, one might also expect to see evidence for such a dissociation in neurologically intact individuals. In other words, the visual information that is used to calibrate and control a skilled motor act directed at an object might not always match the perceptual judgments that are made about that object.

The reference frame and the metrics of visual perception appear to be largely relative. The use of relative or scene-based metrics means that we can construct a detailed representation of the real world without having to compute the absolute size, distance, and geometry of each object in the scene. To have to compute the absolute metrics of the entire scene would in fact be computationally impossible, given the rapidity with which the pattern of light changes on our retina with each and every movement of our eyes. It is far more economical to compute just the relational metrics of the scene, and even these computations do not always need to be precise. The reliance on scene-based frames of reference means, for example, that we can watch the same scene unfold on a small television or on a gigantic movie screen without being confused by the changes in scale.

---

1 Interested readers are directed to Goodale and Humphrey (1998), Milner and Goodale (1995), Jeannerod (1997), and Snyder, Batista, and Andersen, (2000) for a discussion of the neurophysiological work in monkeys and to Goodale and Humphrey (1998) for a review of the neuroimaging literature.

Although we can use this perceptual representation to make inferences about objects in the world, the scene-based metrics of perception are not enough for the control of action directed at those objects. To enable us to pick up the cup of coffee on our breakfast table, our brain has to know more than the fact that the cup is closer to us than the box of cornflakes and further away than the toast. Our brain needs to compute the position of the cup with respect to our hand – and its real size. In other words, it needs to use absolute metrics set within an egocentric frame of reference.

If there really is a difference between the frames of reference used by the

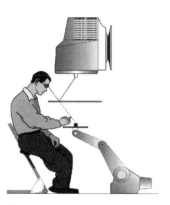

Figure 5.
Simple illustration of the virtual workbench showing the relationship between the virtual and real objects. Adapted with permission from Hu and Goodale (2000).

perception and action systems, it should be possible to demonstrate this difference in the laboratory. The advent of virtual reality displays, where the experimenter has exquisite control over the way in which objects are presented to the observers, has made this kind of experiment a practical possibility. Artificial 'objects' of different sizes can be created and shown to the observer without the possibility of familiarity with particular real objects obscuring the interpretation of the experiment. In addition, it is a simple matter to control the precise period for which the virtual object is visible on the screen.

In a recent experiment using this technique, undergraduate volunteers were shown a series of three-dimensional virtual images of target blocks, each of which was paired with an image of another block that was always either ten per cent wider or ten per cent narrower than the target block. The blocks were never visible for more than half a second. The target blocks were always marked with a red spot. Just as in our previous studies with brain-damaged patients, the observers can be asked in a task of this kind to do either of two things. They can be asked to reach out and grasp the target block – or they can instead be asked to indicate manually the size of the same target block using their finger and thumb. To ensure a natural grasp, the display was designed so that there was a real but unseen block in the same location as the virtual target (see Figure 5).

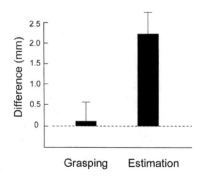

Figure 6.

Mean values of the difference in perceptual estimates of size and the difference in maximum grip aperture when subjects either estimated the size or grasped the 'larger' and 'smaller' objects in experiment by Hu and Goodale (2000). In fact, the target object was the same size in both cases; it was simply accompanied by a larger companion object in one case and a smaller object in the other. To calculate the difference score, the estimate (or grip aperture) for the target accompanied by the larger object was subtracted from the corresponding value for the same target accompanied by the smaller object. (Error bars represent the standard error of the mean difference).

The reason for having two blocks, a target and a companion block, was to induce a 'size-contrast effect.' It was anticipated that the observer's perception of the target's size would be unavoidably influenced by the presence of a larger or smaller companion. In fact, this is exactly what happened. The observers consistently judged a target block accompanied by a large block as smaller than when it was accompanied by a small block. In contrast, however, when they reached out to *grasp* that same target object, they opened their hand to an identical degree whichever companion the target block was paired with (see Figure 6). In other words, the scaling of grip size to the size of the target object was not at all subject to the size-contrast effect that was so compelling during perceptual judgments.

This result is an important one. It confirms that the scene-based coding of size that is such a ubiquitous feature of our perceptual experience does not apply at all to the visual coding of size that is used to guide the action of grasping. Of course, it makes good sense to have a visuomotor system that works with real size rather than relative size, and therefore it should perhaps not be so surprising that the system is immune to the size-contrast illusion.

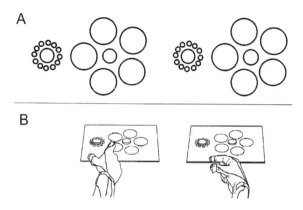

Figure 7.

The 'Ebbinghaus' illusion. Panel A: In the standard version of the illusion, the target circles in the centre of the two arrays appear to be different in size even though they are physically identical as shown in the left-hand figure. For most people, the circle in the annulus of smaller circles appears to be larger than the circle in the annulus of larger circles. The right-hand figure shows a version of the illusion in which the target circle in the array of larger circles has been made physically larger than the other target circle. The two target circles should now appear to be perceptually equivalent in size. Panel B: An illustration of the two tasks performed by each subject using a three-dimensional version of the Ebbinghaus illusion. Light emitting diodes were attached to the finger, thumb and wrist to allow for optoelectronic tracking. The grasping task is illustrated on the left. In this illustration the subject's hand is pictured in-flight on the way to the target disk. The right-hand drawing illustrates the manual estimation task. The heel of the subject's hand rested on the table and the subjects opened their thumb and index finger by an amount that matched the perceived size of the target disk. Adapted with permission from Goodale and Humphrey (1998).

The insensitivity of the grasping system to the relative size of objects in the scene has also been demonstrated in experiments that have used pictorial illusions, such as the Ebbinghaus Illusion. In this familiar illusion, which is illustrated on the left-hand side of Figure 7a, two target circles of equal size, each surrounded by a circular array of either smaller or larger circles, are presented side by side. Subjects typically report that the target circle surrounded by the array of smaller circles appears larger than the one surrounded by the array of larger circles, presumably because of the difference in the contrast in size between the target circles and the surrounding circles. In another version of the illusion, shown on the right-hand side of Figure 7a, the target circles can be made to appear identical in size by increasing the actual size of the target circle surrounded by the larger circles. But despite the clear effect that these displays have on the perception of object size, they have little or no effect on the scaling of target-directed grasping movements. In our own lab, for example, we tested undergraduate volunteers with a version of the illusion in which two thin 'poker-chip' disks were arranged as pairs on a standard Ebbinghaus annular circle display (Aglioti et al. 1995; Haffenden and Goodale 1998). Trials in which the two disks appeared perceptually identical but were physically different in size were randomly alternated with trials in which the disks appeared perceptually different but were physically identical. Even though students showed robust perceptual illusions – even in a matching task in which they opened their index finger and thumb to match the perceived diameter of one of the disks – their grip aperture was correlated with the real size of the disk when they reached out to pick it up (see Figures 7b and 8). Similar dissociations have been observed with other perceptual illusions, such as the Müller-Lyer and Ponzo illusions (for review, see Haffenden and Goodale 2000).

The calibration of grasp does fall victim to size-contrast illusions, however, when a delay is inserted between viewing the objects and initiating the grasp movement. Thus, when observers were forced to wait for five seconds before picking up the target object that they had just seen in the virtual reality display described earlier (Hu and Goodale 2000), the scaling of their grasp was now influenced by the presence of the companion block. Just as they did when they made perceptual judgments, they opened their hand wider when the target block was accompanied by a small block than when it was accompanied by a large block. This intrusion of the size-contrast effect into grip scaling after a delay is of course exactly what we had predicted. The visuomotor system in the dorsal stream operates only in real time and cannot handle a delay. After a delay, the calibration of the grasp depends on a memory derived from perceptual processing in the ventral stream, and so becomes subject to the same size-contrast illusions that perception is prone to. These findings dovetail nicely with the observation that grip scaling in DF (the patient with damage to the ventral perception pathway) falls completely apart when a two-second delay is introduced between viewing a target block and initiating the action (Goodale, Jakobson, and Keillor 1994). Her spared visuomotor system, like the visuomotor system

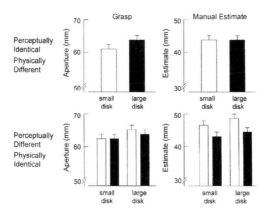

Figure 8.

Grip aperture (on left) and manual estimations (on right) for disks surrounded by the illusory annuli: The top two graphs show the results for perceptually identical, physically different conditions, and the bottom two for perceptually different, physically identical conditions. Open bars represent responses to a disk surrounded by a small circle annulus; filled bars represent responses to a disk surrounded by u large-circle annulus. The difference between the maximum grip aperture achieved during a grasping movement was significantly greater for large disks than the maximum grip aperture for small disks independent of whether or not the subject perceived the disks to be the same or different sizes (p < .05). Manual estimations were influenced by the illusory display however. Thus, the difference between manual estimations of the large and small disks in the perceptually identical, physically different condition was not significant (p > .05). In contrast, perceptually different, but physically identical disk pairs produced significantly different manual estimations. When the small disk was placed in the middle of the small-circle annulus, it was estimated to be larger than when it was surrounded by the large-circle annulus (p < .01). The same was true for the large disk (p < .05). Error bars indicate the standard error of the mean averaged within each condition for all subjects. Adapted from Haffenden and Goodale, (1998).

of a neurologically intact individual, operates only in real time and cannot handle even short delays.

8. The Integration of Perception and Action

Although I have been emphasizing the fact that the dorsal action stream and the ventral perception stream are anatomically and functionally distinct, the two streams must work together in everyday life. Indeed, an argument can be made that the two streams play complementary roles in the production of adaptive behaviour.

A useful metaphor for understanding the different contributions of the dorsal and ventral stream to visually guided behaviour can be found in robotic engineering. That metaphor is *teleassistance* (Pook and Ballard 1996). In teleassistance, a human operator identifies the goal and then uses a symbolic language to communicate with a semi-autonomous robot that actually performs the required motor act on the identified goal object. Teleassistance is much more flexible than completely autonomous robotic control, which is limited to the working environment for which it has been programmed and cannot cope easily with novel events. Teleassistance is also more efficient than teleoperation, in which a human operator simply controls the movement of a manipulandum at a distance. As Pook and Ballard (1996) have demonstrated, teleoperation (i.e., the human operator) cannot cope with sudden changes in scale or the delay between action and feedback from that action. In short, teleassistance combines the flexibility of teleoperation with the precision of autonomous routines.

The interaction between the ventral and dorsal streams is an excellent example of the principle of teleassistance, but in this case instantiated in biology. The perceptual-cognitive systems in the ventral stream, like the human operator in teleassistance, identify different objects in the scene using a representational system that is rich and detailed but not metrically precise. When a particular goal object has been flagged, dedicated visuomotor networks in the dorsal stream (in conjunction with related circuits in premotor cortex, basal ganglia, and brainstem) are activated to perform the desired motor act. Thus, the networks in the dorsal stream, with their precise egocentric coding of the location, orientation, and shape of the goal object and its absolute size, are like the robotic component of teleassistance. In short, both systems are required for purposive behaviour – one system to select the goal object from the visual array, the other to carry out the required metrical computations for the goal-directed action. One of the most important questions yet to be addressed is how the two streams communicate with one another and coordinate their activities for the production of adaptive behaviour.

References

Aglioti, S., J.F.X. DeSouza, and M. A. Goodale. 1995. "Size-Contrast Illusions Deceive the Eye But Not the Hand," *Current Biology* 5, 679–85.

Allman, J. M. 1999. *Evolving Brains*. New York: Scientific American Library.

Bálint, R. 1909. "Seelenlämung des 'Schauens,' optische Ataxie, räumliche Störung der Aufmerksamkeit," *Monatschrift für Psychiatrie und Neurologie* 25, 51–81.

Bülthoff, H. H., and S. Edelman. 1992. "Psychophysical Support for a Two-Dimensional View Interpolation Theory of Object Recognition," *Proceedings of the National Academy of Sciences (USA)*. Vol. 89, pp. 60–64.

Carey D. P., M. Harvey, and A. D. Milner. 1996. "Visuomotor Sensitivity for Shape and Orientation in a Patient with Visual Form Agnosia," *Neuropsychologia* 34, 329–37.

Crick, F., and E. Jones. 1993. "Backwardness of Human Neuroanatomy," *Nature* 361, 109–10.

Ewert, J-P. 1987. "Neuroethology of Releasing Mechanisms: Prey-Catching in Toads," *Behavioural Brain Sciences* 10, 337–405.

Flanders, M., S.I.H. Tillery, and J. F. Soechting. 1992. "Early Stages in a Sensorimotor Transformation," *Behavioural Brain Sciences* 15, 309–62.

Goodale, M. A. 1995. "The Cortical Organization of Visual Perception and Visuomotor Control." In *An Invitation to Cognitive Science*, Vol. 2, *Visual Cognition and Action*, 2d ed., S. Kosslyn, ed. Cambridge, MA: MIT Press, pp. 167–213.

———. 1996. "Visuomotor Modules in the Vertebrate Brain," *Canadian Journal of Physiology and Pharmacology* 74, 390–400.

Goodale, M. A., and A. Haffenden. 1998. "Frames of Reference for Perception and Action in the Human Visual System," *Neuroscience and Biobehavioral Reviews* 22, 161–72.

Goodale, M. A., and G. K. Humphrey. 1998. "The Objects of Action and Perception," *Cognition* 67, 181–207.

Goodale, M. A., L. S. Jakobson, and J. M. Keillor. 1994. "Differences in the Visual Control of Pantomimed and Natural Grasping Movements," *Neuropsychologia* 32, 1159–78.

Goodale, M. A., J. P. Meenan, H. H. Bülthoff, D. A. Nicolle, K. S. Murphy, and C. I. Racicot. 1994. "Separate Neural Pathways for the Visual Analysis of Object Shape in Perception and Prehension," *Current Biology* **4**, 604–10.

Goodale, M. A., and A. D. Milner. 1992. "Separate Visual Pathways for Perception and Action," *Trends in Neurosciences* **15**, 20–25.

Goodale, M. A., A. D. Milner, L. S. Jakobson, and D. P. Carey. 1991. "A Neurological Dissociation between Perceiving Objects and Grasping Them," *Nature* **349**, 154–56.

Goodale, M. A., K. Murphy, J. P. Meenan, C. I. Racicot, and D. A. Nicolle. 1993. "Spared Object Perception but Poor Object-Calibrated Grasping in a Patient with Optic Ataxia," *Society for Neuroscience Abstracts* **19**, 775.

Gould, J. L. 1982. *Ethology: The Mechanisms and Evolution of Behavior*. New York: Norton.

Haffenden, A., and M. A. Goodale. 1998. "The Effect of Pictorial Illusion on Prehension and Perception," *Journal of Cognitive Neuroscience* **10**, 122–36.

———. 2000. "Independent Effects of Pictorial Displays on Perception and Action," *Vision Research* **40**, 1597–1607.

Hoff, B., and M. A. Arbib. 1992. "A Model of the Effects of Speed, Accuracy and Perturbation on Visually Guided Reaching." In *Control of Arm movement in Space: Neurophysiological and Computational Approaches*, R. Caminiti, P. B. Johnson, and Y. Burnod, eds. New York: Springer-Verlag, pp. 285–306.

Hu, Y., and M. A. Goodale. 2000. "Grasping after a Delay Shifts Size-Scaling from Absolute to Relative Metrics," *Journal of Cognitive Neuroscience* **12**, 856–68.

Ingle, D. J. 1973. "Two Visual Systems in the Frog," *Science* **181**, 1053–55.

Ingle, D. J. 1982. "Organization of Visuomotor Behaviors in Vertebrates." In *Analysis of Visual Behavior*, D. J. Ingle, M. A. Goodale, and R.J.W. Mansfield, eds. Cambridge, MA: MIT Press, pp. 67–109.

Ingle, D.J. 1991. "Functions of Subcortical Visual Systems in Vertebrates and the Evolution of Higher Visual Mechanisms." In *Vision and Visual Dysfunction*, Vol. 2, *Evolution of the Eye and Visual System*, R. L. Gregory and J. Cronly-Dillon, eds. London: Macmillan, pp. 152–64.

Jackson, J. H. 1875. *Clinical and Physiological Researches on the Nervous System*. London: Churchill.

Jakobson, L. S., Y. M. Archibald, D. P. Carey, and M. A. Goodale. 1991. "A Kinematic Analysis of Reaching and Grasping Movements in a Patient Recovering from Optic Ataxia," *Neuropsychologia* **29**, 803–9.

Jeannerod, M. 1988. *The Neural and Behavioural Organization of Goal-directed Movements*. Oxford: Oxford University Press.

———. 1997. *The Cognitive Neuroscience of Action*. Oxford: Blackwell.

Jeannerod, M., J. Decety, and F. Michel. 1994. "Impairment of Grasping Movements Following Bilateral Posterior Parietal Lesion," *Neuropsychologia* **32**, 369–80.

Marr, D. 1982. *Vision*. San Francisco: Freeman.

Milner, A. D., and M. A. Goodale. 1995. *The Visual Brain in Action*. Oxford: Oxford University Press.

Milner, A. D., D. I. Perrett, R. S. Johnston, P. J. Benson, T. R. Jordan, D. W. Heeley, D. Bettucci, F. Mortara, R. Mutani, E. Terazzi, and D.L.W. Davidson. 1991. "Perception and Action in Visual Form Agnosia," *Brain* **114**, 405–28.

Palmer, S., E. Rosch, and P. Chase. 1981. "Canonical Perspective and the Perception of Objects." In *Attention and Performance IX*, J. Long and A. Baddeley, eds. Hillsdale, NJ: Lawrence Earlbaum, pp. 135–51.

Patla A., and M. A. Goodale. 1997. "Visuomotor Transformation Required for Obstacle Avoidance During Locomotion Is Unaffected in a Patient with Visual Form Agnosia," *NeuroReport* **8**, 165–68.

Perenin, M.-T., and Y. Rossetti. 1996. "Grasping without Form Discrimination in a Hemianopic Field," *Neuroreport* **7**, 793–97.

Perenin, M.-T., and A. Vighetto. 1988. "Optic Ataxia: A Specific Disruption in Visuomotor Mechanisms. I. Different Aspects of the Deficit in Reaching for Objects," *Brain* **111**, 643–74.

Pohl, W. 1973. "Dissociation of Spatial Discrimination Deficits following Frontal and Parietal Lesions in Monkeys," *Journal of Comparative and Physiological Psychology* **82**, 227–39.

Pook, P. K., and D. H. Ballard. 1996. "Deictic Human/Robot Interaction," *Robotics and Autonomous Systems* **18**, 259–69.

Servos, P., M. A. Goodale, and G. K. Humphrey. 1993. "The Drawing of Objects by a Visual Form Agnosic: Contribution of Surface Properties and Memorial Representations," *Neuropsychologia* **31**, 251–59.

Servos, P., L. Matin, and M. A. Goodale. 1995. "Dissociations between Two Forms of Spatial Processing by a Visual Form Agnosic," *NeuroReport* **6**, 1893–96.

Snyder, L. H., A. P. Batista, and R. A. Andersen. 2000. "Intention-Related Activity in the Posterior Parietal Cortex: A Review," *Vision Research* **40**, 1433–41.

Stein, J. F. 1992. "The Representation of Egocentric Space in the Posterior Parietal Cortex," *Behavioural Brain Sciences* **15**, 691–700.

Tootell, R. B., A. M. Dale, M. I. Sereno, and R. Malach. 1996. "New Images from Human Visual Cortex," *Trends in Neurosciences* **19**, 481–89.

Ungerleider, L. G., and B. A. Brody. 1977. "Extrapersonal Spatial Orientation: the Role of Posterior Parietal, Anterior Frontal, and Inferotemporal Cortex," *Experimental Neurology* **56**, 265–80.

Ungerleider, L. G., and M. Mishkin. 1982. "Two Cortical Visual Systems." In *Analysis of Visual Behavior*, D. J. Ingle, M. A. Goodale, and R.J.W. Mansfield, eds. Cambridge, MA: MIT Press, pp. 549–86.

Xing, J., and R. A. Andersen. 2000. "Models of the Posterior Parietal Cortex which Perform Multimodal Integration and Represent Space in Several Coordinate Frames," *Journal of Cognitive Neuroscience* **12**, 601–14.

Zeki, S. 1993. *A Vision of the Brain*. Oxford: Blackwell Scientific.

Our Knowledge of Colour

MOHAN MATTHEN

Scientists are often bemused by the efforts of philosophers essaying a theory of colour: colour science sports a huge array of facts and theories, and it is unclear to its practitioners what philosophy can or is trying to contribute. Equally, philosophers tend to be puzzled about how they can fit colour science into their investigations without compromising their own disciplinary identity: philosophy is supposed to be an *a priori* investigation; philosophers do not work in psychophysics labs – not in their professional capacity, anyway.

These inter-disciplinary barriers arise out of misunderstanding. Philosophers should not so much attempt to contribute to empirical theories of colour, as to formulate *philosophical* theories of colour. Philosophy is concerned with appearance and reality, object and property, function and representation, and other such fundamental categories of ontology and epistemology. Philosophical theories attempt to fit colour into these categories; such theories do not *compete* with colour science. However, fitting colour into philosophical theories means dealing with colour as it really is – and one cannot know what it is without consulting the psychologists. That is why philosophers need an up-to-date understanding of psychological theories of colour. Equally, psychologists, who typically show a keen interest in questions concerning the reality and knowability of colour, and who are capable of devising clever experiments to discover whether colour fits this or that specification of reality, knowability, etc., need to base their opinions on sound philosophical practice. Their opinions too are worth very little when they misuse fundamental philosophical categories.

In this paper, I am concerned with how the ontology and epistemology of colour relate to the psychology of colour-perception. The empirical facts to which I appeal are not the subject of controversy: they are almost all reported in the path-breaking papers on the opponent-process theory that Dorothea Jameson and Leo Hurwich published in the nineteen-fifties;[1] most of these facts have been easily available to philosophers at least since Larry Hardin's book (1988) on colour. The philosophical interpretation of the facts remains, however, a matter of sharp and unresolved controversy. In section I, I'll briefly summarize the controversy, and relate how it has been deepened by the articulation of a new epistemological constraint by Paul Boghossian, David Velleman, and Mark Johnston around 1990. Then I will turn to the task of giving an account of colour ontology that both satisfies a reasonable version of this constraint, and bridges some of the conflicting intuitions concerning the empirical facts about colour-perception.

I.   A Problem Concerning the Ontology of Colour

A.   *Conflicting Intuitions Concerning Colour Ontology*

The colour appearance of a thing is highly variable with illumination, contrast, adaptation, and individual physiological constitution, much more so than philosophers have traditionally supposed. For example, colours like brown, which have black or white as a component, are seen only when there is a contrast available. Thus, an object that looks brown when you look at it in the context of other objects might look orange when you isolate it by looking at it through a reduction tube. Now, what colour is such an object, *really*? Is it brown because it looks that way in a normally multi-coloured scene? Or is it orange because it looks that way when we remove the highly variable influences of contrast? There seems to be no principled way to decide in favour of one of the two appearances. Both viewing conditions have some claim to metaphysical privilege. Moreover, both are within the range of

---

1   See Hurwich (1981) for bibliographical details.

conditions that could be considered "normal" in evolutionary terms. Thus, the variation in appearance seems nothing more than that. The best one can say is that the object is brown when contrast is provided, orange when contrast is removed, and neither colour independently of viewing conditions. On this account, colour is "subjective," or "observer-relative," in the sense that it is the product of an interaction between a perceiver and the distal environment, and cannot be attributed to that environment in isolation.

On the other hand, colour appearances are much more constant than one might expect given the variability of the light array that reaches the human eye. For example, a human face looks normally coloured even under heavy leaf cover, even though the light it reflects in such circumstances shows distinctly green in colour photographs. Colour vision seems, then, to "correct" the look that things have in non-standard circumstances. This kind of constancy suggests to many philosophers that colour vision evolved to detect a *real* property of things, a property they have independently of any appearance. It seems, in other words, that human faces are not green no matter what signal they might be sending in "non-standard" circumstances, and that the colour they appear in a variety of more or less "standard" circumstances is the colour they really are.[2] This is an "objective" account of colour. It implies that we cannot just leave the variability of colour unresolved, as the subjectivist would urge.

Which should we take more seriously, the variability of colour appearance or its constancy? Should we say that colour vision converges on certain invariant distal properties, and leave variation as an anomaly? Alternatively, should we say that colours are appearance-relative, and hold that constancy is, though useful, an oddity – merely

---

2 I use the term "suggests" deliberately; arguments from colour-constancy to colour-realism are far from conclusive. Peter Bradley and Michael Tye (2001), recent defenders of colour-realism, seem to recognize this: "The fact that objects appear to retain the same color through a wide variety of changes (though certainly not all) strongly *suggests* that colors are illumination-independent properties of those objects" (480). They go on to appeal to "normal viewing conditions" to define the colour of a thing, but do not say how they will adjudicate which of several different but metaphysically equivalent sets of viewing conditions is "normal."

a by-product of certain properties of colour-sensitive cells in the retina, for instance?

B.   An Epistemological Constraint on Theories of Colour

This dilemma is made all the more difficult by a recently articulated epistemological constraint that seems to challenge fundamental intuitions about appearance and reality, and sharply distinguishes colour from shape, motion, etc., the so-called primary qualities, and even (as I shall argue in section I C) from many other secondary qualities, for example, musical harmony. Mark Johnston (1997, 138) phrases the constraint this way:

> *Revelation*
> The *intrinsic nature* of canary yellow is *fully revealed* by a standard visual experience as of a canary yellow thing (and the same goes, *mutatis mutandis*, for the other colours).[3]

What is it to *know* the "intrinsic nature" of a colour? However we answer this question, *Revelation* seems to imply a quite powerful kind of realism. The colours have to be independent of our sensations if they have "intrinsic natures," or so it would seem. At the same time, it implies that colours lack physical reality, for surely one cannot come to know the intrinsic nature of *physical* properties (like wavelength or reflectance) by bare experience – untutored vision has no knowledge of such things.[4] But if the colours are not physical, what are they? Do they depend on our *mental* (or perceptual) reactions to things? How does this differ from the subjectivist thesis? *Revelation* seems thus to deepen and inflame the conflict of intuitions noted in the last section. Nevertheless, it cannot be denied that there is an important truth that

---

3   Johnston does not endorse this principle himself. He cites Bertrand Russell as one philosopher who believed in *Revelation*. The arguments of Boghossian and Velleman (1989; 1991) are based on something very close to this principle.

4   See Boghossian and Velleman (1991).

lurks somewhere in its vicinity. We use colour vision to categorize things for identification, induction, signalling, and the like. When we co-classify things by colour, we instinctively treat them as the same as far as these practices are concerned. These practices are experience-based, in the sense that it requires no more knowledge to participate in them than to experience colours. Presumably, animals use colour in comparable ways without the aid of linguistic concepts – a honeybee identifies flowers by their colour, an old-world monkey identifies fruit, and so on. Colour categorization is a primitive ability we share with these animals. *Revelation* is plausible if we construe it as asserting that this kind of categorization is unlearned and unconditioned, or at least learned only in highly predictable ways invariant across individual experience sets and across culture. Colour-experience may or may not furnish us with knowledge of a property, then, but at the very least, it does give us the instinctive *know-how* needed for colour categorization.

With this in mind, let us consider the following weaker version of the condition stated (and rejected) by Johnston:

Empiricist Codicil to Revelation
Experiences as of canary yellow things are

(a)   sufficient for knowing the basis for co-classifying canary yellow things for the purposes of inductive inference (etc.), and

(b)   sufficient together with experiences as of lime green things for knowing the basis for differentiating canary yellow things from lime green things.
(And the same goes, *mutatis mutandis*, for the other colours.)[5]

---

5   Paul Boghossian and David Velleman's (1991) criticism of 'physicalist' theories of colour rests in part on the idea that they fail these conditions. They argue that if *red* and *orange* were categories of physics, then, since our perceiving some things as red and others as orange does not imply that these things belong to different physical categories, we might be mistaken about *red* and *orange* being different. Boghossian and Velleman rightly insist that we cannot be mistaken about this. They conclude that *red* and *orange* are not physical categories.

In this weakened form, I take *Revelation* to be true. (In the rest of this paper, I shall be referring to this weakened form of the thesis under the name of *Revelation*, except when I intend a contrast with the stronger principle.)

Imagine, then, that you have never experienced *canary yellow* before. A colour scientist arranges for you to have this experience by artfully arranging for you to have an after-image of that shade, or, even more diabolically, by electronically stimulating your brain in such a way as to produce in you a sudden flash of canary yellow, floating free of any object or shape. You do not form any belief about the external world because of this self-evidently ephemeral experience. You do not attribute the colour to any external thing. Properly understood, the *Empiricist Codicil* implies that even this experience is somehow sufficient to reveal the basis for classifying things by a certain colour category.

The puzzling question is this: what kind of classification is this that its entire basis is fully revealed by a mendacious experience? Moreover, how can such a classification be useful for externally validated practices such as object-identification and induction? This sharpens the conflict of intuitions noted earlier. If *Revelation* is taken to show that colour-experience fails to correspond to an independently existing thing, then what are we to make of colour-constancy? And if we take colour-constancy to be evidence of the objectivity of colour, then how is it that colour, in contrast to so many other objective categories, is so easy to know, even by means of self-evidently non-veridical experiences?

C. The Contrasting Case of Musical Harmony

From what we have said so far, one might think that if *Revelation* were correct for colour, it would apply to other "secondary qualities." And in a sense, this is right. That is, it must be the case that if we participate in instinctive classificatory practices that involve these other secondary qualities, these practices too must be appearance-based. Nevertheless, *Revelation* is more puzzling applied to colour than to musical harmony. The reason may be surprising, and worth examining in a little detail.

Before we get to that, however, we need a preliminary observation to avoid confusion. With *any* sensory modality, the novice observer requires training in order to be sensitive to the character of her experience. That is, it takes practice (and possibly some instruction) to recognize the presence of yellow in lime green, the taste of raspberries in a wine, the component structure of a musical chord, and so on. However, the need for this kind of "training" does not compromise *Revelation*. True, one might not appreciate all that is present in an experience of canary yellow *immediately* upon having an experience as of it. Still, that single experience may contain everything needed to understand the category of canary yellow (in the sense of the *Empiricist Codicil*). By training the eye, the palette, or the ear, one does not come to have new, more complex, experiences. Rather, one learns how to discriminate the components *already present* in the experiences one has had. Or so I shall assume to keep *Revelation* in play.

Now, just as is claimed for the case of colour, it may seem that the experience of musical harmonies must "reveal" something about their "intrinsic nature" (as *Revelation* would demand). Consider one's auditory experience of a minor third. After a period of ear training, one begins to recognize such things as the interval heard when the constituent tones of this chord are played in sequence, its relationship to other chords, the musical character of chord progressions in which it figures, and so on. Now, it turns out that what one cognizes in this way has a counterpart in objective reality. An ear-trained listener will find that her discriminations are confirmed by certain tests on a piano or other musical instrument; for instance, she will find that she hears a minor third just when one is played. If not, she is in error. There is something wrong with a listener who has an auditory experience as of a minor third when we sound C and E together.[6] Her ear training (or

---

6 This needs some qualification, as Margaret Schabas tells me. Because of the different overtones, or *timbres*, of various instruments, the same chord does not sound exactly the same on all of them. Consequently, orchestras demand that certain instruments be played deliberately flat or sharp, so as to compensate for these variations, and thus to produce a coherent sound. This shows that contrast phenomena affect our perception of the harmonies, much as they do in the case of colour. The point that I am making is unaffected by this: the structure of our auditory experiences still reflects structure in the sounds we hear.

just her hearing) is shown to be deficient by her failing this objective test. From these facts, we may conclude that

(1)   there is a structure to one's experiences of a chord that ...

(2)   ... corresponds (perhaps imperfectly and incompletely) to objective structural characteristics of the chord itself.

The correspondence between the structure of one's auditory experience and the sound one hears goes some distance, at least, towards explaining the counterpart of the *Empiricist Codicil* for the auditory grasp of chords.

However, this conjunction of conditions does not hold of colour-experience. The difference between the two cases does not lie in condition (1) above. There is, as the experimental psychophysics of colour reveals, structure in our experiences of colour, for they are ordered in the dimensions black-white, red-green, blue-yellow, and brightness.[7] The difference lies rather in (2): the experienced component structure of colour is largely a by-product of the way in which colour is processed by our visual systems, and does not correspond to the intrinsic character of coloured objects and lights.

What I mean is this. The physical counterparts of colour-experience do not share the component structure of colour-experience – for instance, there is no physical counterpart of green and of blue invariably present in physical instances of turquoise. Indeed, turquoise, like most other colours, can exist in lights, in transparencies, and in reflective surfaces, and the principles of mixing are different in these diverse media. One way to see this is to note that both turquoise lights and turquoise paints can be produced without mixing blue and green. There is a mixture of minerals that is ground up and added to a vehicle to make turquoise paint. There are salts that turn the flame of a Bunsen burner turquoise. There is no physical mixing of blue and green in such instances of turquoise production. Thus, the component structure of the turquoise experience tells us nothing about the constitution of physical turquoise. Nor does it purport to:

---

7   The classic philosophically embedded account of this structure is C. L. Hardin (1988, chap. 1).

the experience of turquoise does not lead us to expect *physical* mixture. This is how it differs from the musical example: a chord *physically* contains its component notes; listeners can be right or wrong about what they hear in this respect. Thus, *there is no transfer, as in the case of music, from the structure of reality to the structure of experience.*

We can now restate what is puzzling about *Revelation* even as weakened in the *Empiricist Codicil.* Sensory categories, including colour, underwrite induction and other epistemic practices. In order to be useful in these epistemic roles, one would think that they must correspond in some way to objective characteristics. It seems to follow that colour-experiences must correspond, somehow, to objective colours. But, on the face of it, they do not.

II. Two Approaches to Defining the Colours

A. The Standard Viewing Conditions Approach

Let us now introduce the notion of a *colour-look*. Recall first that colours can be arranged in a three-dimensional similarity-space by systematically collating the similarity and discrimination judgments of observers presented with colour samples.[8] Colour-looks can be identified with minimal regions in this similarity-space, that is, regions so small that the colours they contain are *indiscriminable.* I shall speak of environmental objects *presenting* observers with colour-looks.

> x presents observer O with colour-look L at t if and only if x occupies region L in O's colour similarity-space at t.[9]

---

8 See Hurwich (1981), plate 1–5, and Hurwich and Jameson (1956) for quantitative details.

9 In fact, since colour-space is not granular, and indiscriminability is not transitive, an object will occupy several overlapping minimal regions of colour-space. Thus, a colour-look should properly be identified as the *set* of minimal regions that contain a particular point in colour-space.

Colour-looks are *psychological* in character: they are ways in which objects are subjectively experienced by observers and derive from these observers' abilities to match and discriminate objects with respect to colour. Philosophers, especially empiricists, standardly define *colour-attributions* in terms of *colour-looks*. (We shall see how to do this in a moment.) At first sight, this helps with *Revelation*. For, as just said, colour-looks are subjective. It follows that we know them just by having colour-experiences. So, if we define colours in terms of colour-looks, we gain some hope of piggybacking our knowledge of colour on our knowledge of colour-looks.

There is, however, an obvious difficulty in basing colour-attribution on colour-looks. The look that a particular object presents to an observer varies with viewing conditions, while colour seems to be an enduring feature of objects.[10] Philosophers tend to approach this problem by relativizing colour-looks to various viewing conditions. Let us suppose that the following statement is *fully specified* in this respect:

> x presents colour-look **L** to observer O when x is illuminated by light of spectral distribution S of luminance L, with surround colours C_1-C_n, when O is adapted to light of spectral distribution S' and x is displaced from the centre of O's retina by θE.

Fully specified colour-looks are invariable because all the relevant variables are fixed. The thought is that we can therefore use fully specified colour-looks to specify object-colour.

This approach fails because the problem of *Revelation* is displaced to the question of how the conditions so specified can be known. Consider the appeal to "standard conditions" to provide the needed specifications, as in the following principles of colour-attribution:

---

10 Jackson and Pargetter (1987), Cohen (2000), Harvey (2000), and McLaughlin (forthcoming) identify colour properties with colour-looks, and claim that the colour of an object changes with viewing conditions. Or at least they think that there is an ontologically fundamental class of colour-properties, "transitory colours" or "present colours," which are the same as colour-looks. They construct another, more enduring but ontologically derivative, class of colour-properties from colour-looks. This "relativist" proposal entails that an observer cannot be wrong about the colour of an object in her particular viewing conditions, and I shall be arguing that this is false in general.

Dispositional Principle of Colour Attribution
"*x* is *L*" is true if and only if *x* has the disposition to create in a standard observer the colour-look **L** in standard conditions.[11]

Counterfactual Principle of Colour Attribution
"*x* is *L*" is true if and only if *x* would create in a standard observer the colour-look **L** in standard conditions.

These principles become fully specified by providing details of standard observers and standard conditions.[12] Such a specification might go something like this. A standard observer is one who has trichromatic vision. This observer must be white-light adapted, and fixating *x* in the centre of her retina. *x* must be presented to such a viewer in a surround of neutral grey, illuminated by white light to luminance 10 lm. The colour of an object is thus defined as the disposition to create the colour-look in question in viewing conditions other than those that might be immediately present. The problem with this is obvious: even if the viewer knows, by visual experience, what the colour-look mentioned in the above attribution-principles is, how is she to know what "standard conditions" are?[13]

Think again of the shimmering canary yellow film floating in the air. *Revelation* implies that this ephemeral experience is enough to reveal what it is like for something to be canary yellow. However, this visual experience contains *no* information about standard viewers and conditions, *no* means of determining to whom and in what circumstances a thing must look like this if it is to be canary yellow. Indeed, your experience of the film does not contain any allusion to viewing conditions at all: you just do not know how the film would look in "standard conditions" or what standard conditions are for

---

11 In these principles, the colour-property attributed to the object of experience is distinguished from the colour-look along the lines of Peacocke (1984).

12 Colour-looks can be specified by assigning ranges of values to the variables in the above predicate, as distinct from point-values. The *Dispositional Principle* maintains that a thing *is* brown if this range is "standard."

13 A more complex argument to the same conclusion can be found in Boghossian and Velleman (1989).

it. The advantage of appealing to colour-looks was thought to be that experience gives us direct knowledge of them. This advantage is negated by the appeal to viewing conditions other than those present to the viewer.

B. *The "Semantic" Account of Colour*

Colour-looks seem to give us direct knowledge of colour-properties, but we are finding it difficult to understand how this can be so, given the standard viewing conditions approach to defining colour-properties. At the risk of repetition, let us summarize the difficulty. The colour-look that an object presents varies with conditions of viewing. While colour-constancy is an indication that the system is capable of compensating for this variability to some extent, there is still a range of circumstances, all "normal" in evolutionary terms, in which the same object will present a different look. Thus, despite constancy, colour-looks do not vary one-to-one with any object-property. The "standard conditions" approach seeks to negate variability by focussing on the conditions under which a colour-look *reliably indicates* what colour-property an object has. However, since the colour-vision system does not automatically signal whether or when it is operating within this range of conditions, the perceiver requires empirical knowledge to grasp and apply this definition of colour-properties. This is the problem. If one wants to preserve the instinctive grasp of colour premised in *Revelation*, one needs a connection between colour-looks and colour-properties that demands less empirical knowledge.

Luckily, there *is* such a relation between colour-looks and colour-properties available to help us. Suppose that somebody shows you a coloured object and asks you what colour-property it *visually appears* to have. You need no collateral information about viewing conditions in order to answer *this* question. You need such information only in order to know what colour something *is*, not to know what colour it *looks*.[14] The standard conditions approach attempts to define a colour-

14 Cf. Boghossian and Velleman (1989): "[S]urely, one can tell whether two objects *appear* similarly coloured on the basis of visual experience alone. To be sure,

property in terms of reliable indications of when a thing actually possesses that property. We lack the information needed to assess when looks are reliable. However, it seems as if we have direct knowledge of what colour-property a thing *looks* as if it has, when it presents a given colour-look. If this is so, then we should be able to reach into the "looks" context, as it were – more technically, we can quantify into it – in order to specify colour-properties. It helps us to communicate the property in question, and the look in question, if we remember that in English, and every other natural language, the look and the property have the same name.

Along these lines, then, consider the following schema:

Look Exportation
Canary yellow is the colour-property something visually appears to have when it presents the canary-yellow-look. More generally: L is the property something has when it presents the look, L (where *I* is the colour-property with the same name as L).

In the above schema, the "looks" in "looks *L*" does not betoken the relationship of reliable indication. That is, it does not say what would clearly be false: that *canary yellow* is the colour you automatically attribute to *x* when *x* presents you with the canary-yellow-look. *Look Exportation* should not be understood, then, in terms of any tendency to *believe* that something possesses a colour.

What then does *Look Exportation* say about the relationship between colour-looks and colour-properties? The following analogy with linguistic communication might be helpful. Suppose somebody says to you, "I make one hundred thousand dollars a year." It takes quite a lot of empirical knowledge to figure out whether this statement is a reliable indication of the speaker's income. And even if you possess such knowledge, determining the likelihood of the speaker's

---

one's experience of the objects will not necessarily provide knowledge of the relation between their *actual* colours. But the physicalist account implies that visual experience of objects fails to provide epistemic access, not just to their *actual* colour similarities, but to their *apparent* similarities as well. And here the account must be mistaken. The *apparent* colours of objects can be compared without empirical inquiry ..." (83, emphasis mine).

truthfulness depends on divining her circumstances. Is she negotiating a salary offer? Is she negotiating a divorce? However, it takes only *semantic* knowledge, and no knowledge of either background or present conditions to determine what the speaker is telling you. The semantic link between utterance and meaning bypasses listeners' dispositions to believe the speaker and bypasses the conditions of utterance. The connection between colour-looks and visual appearance is like this. We said earlier, while discussing *Revelation*, that when we undergo a colour-experience, we know instinctively what colour classifications the experience licenses. *Look Exportation* is a consequence of this instinctive link.

Look Exportation is a better starting-point for our inquiry into the nature of our grasp of colour-properties than the world-to-look correlations studied by psychophysics. It gives us a quite direct way of defining what it is for something to *be* canary yellow. A thing *is* not canary yellow merely because it presents a canary-yellow-look. But when something does this, it invariably *looks* canary yellow. The look identifies a property, *C*, and a thing is *C* if it actually possesses this property. In other words, something *is* canary yellow if it *really is* the way such a thing looks. This gives us the following schema:

> *Fundamental Principle of Colour Attribution*
> "*x* is *Col*" is true (where *Col* is a colour term) if and only if *x* **really is** the colour something visually appears to be when it presents the *Col*-look.

The *Fundamental Principle* introduces a "Really is the way it looks" operator. This operator takes colour-looks as arguments and yields colour-attribution conditions as values. Its logical force is different from the "Would look that way in standard conditions" approach considered earlier, which tells us how something would *look* in specified or standardized conditions.

The *Fundamental Principle* is analogous with the disquotation principle enunciated by Alfred Tarksi (1944). Tarski observed that the removal of the quotation marks from 'snow is white' gives us a way of asserting what would be the case *if* 'snow is white' were true. This observation led him to his famous principle:

The sentence 'snow is white' is true if, and only if, snow is white (ibid., 343).

In much the same way as the disquotation principle, the *Fundamental Principle* takes advantage of our instinctive grasp of the colour-classifications licensed by a colour-look to specify a particular colour-property. Tarski entitles his conception "the semantic conception of truth," explaining that "Semantics is a discipline which, speaking loosely, deals with certain relations between expressions of a language and the objects (or 'states of affairs') 'referred to' by those expressions. As typical examples of semantic concepts we may mention the concepts of *designation, satisfaction, definition* ..." (ibid., 345). Following him, I shall say that colour-looks *designate* colour properties, and entitle this conception the "semantic" account of colour.

The semantic account points to a very different way of thinking about colour-attribution than that which is implicit in the "standard conditions" approach, which (as I said before) looks for conditions in which colour-looks are especially reliable, or in some other way privileged. This difference is analogous to that between an epistemic theory of truth, like Epicurus's,[15] which refers to the conditions under which a belief is reliable, and a semantic theory of truth, like Tarski's, which refers to the conditions designated by a sentence. The *Fundamental Principle* re-orients our attitude towards the look-property relation and away from reliable indication.

The "semantic conception of colour" implicit in the *Fundamental Principle* is insufficient by itself actually to provide us with a philosophical account of the look-property relation. All it does is to take advantage of our instinctively implicit knowledge of colour-attribution. In order more fully to understand the relationship between colour-looks and colour-properties, we need to undertake two further tasks. We must

---

15 Sextus Empiricus attributes to Epicurus the theory that "True opinions are those attested and those uncontested by self-evidence." Long and Sedley (1987): 18 A (1), 90. This is meant as a "criterion," a theory that (a) tells us how to test an opinion for truth-value, and (b) defines truth in terms of a positive test outcome.

First: explicate the nature of the semantic character of the relationship between colour-looks and colour properties. In other words, we must show in what way colour-looks are like symbols that designate colour-properties.

and

Second: give a more explicit account of *which* property each colour-look designates: in other words, make our implicit knowledge of colour-attribution more explicit.

Given the demands of *Revelation*, we need to do this in a way that excludes collaterally acquired knowledge. I undertake these tasks in the remainder of this paper.

III. How Colour-Looks Function as Symbols

A. Property-Designation in Measuring Instruments

Fred Dretske offers us a metaphor that proves useful in explaining the semantic character of the connection between colour-looks and colour-properties.[16] He likens sensory systems to measuring instruments. Every measuring instrument is associated with a *measurement function,* M, which connects its *measuring states* – its pointer readings, for instance – to measurement *values,* properties of the object being measured. Sensory systems seem to be similar: the colour-vision system has states that seem, as we saw in the last section, to designate colour-properties. *Revelation* implies that we are instinctively able to use the measurement function associated with sensory systems.

How are we able to use the measurement function of measuring instruments? How do we know (a) what state the instrument is in, and (b) what property corresponds to that state?

---

16 Dretske (1995, chap. 2).

(a) *Identifying the measuring state.* Measuring instruments are designed in such a way as to enable us easily to identify their measuring-states: for instance, they might have needles that point to markings on their faces, or some other type of display. Each position of the needle marks a different measuring state. (Imagine a pressure gauge that has lost its needle. Such a gauge too has measuring states, but these are now difficult, if not impossible, to read.)

(b) *Knowing the measurement value of each measuring state.* In order to use a measuring instrument, we need access to a *key* that tells us how to specify the values of various measuring states. Often, we can read a linguistic expression of the object-property off a *transparent* notation expressed by the gauge-display For instance, we might find numerical expressions like '14' written on a pressure gauge, with a notation 'pounds per square inch' written across the bottom. When the needle points to '14,' the notation on the dial enables us to express the object property as 'fourteen pounds per square inch.' (A notation in newtons per square metre would express the same property but in different terms.) Notations that are more opaque are also possible. A graphic notation would be an example. A square might indicate 14 psi, but you would need to consult a look-up table to discover this. When any such a key is provided, whether transparent or not, we say that the instrument is *calibrated.*

The relationship between measuring states and object-properties, i.e., the measurement function, is semantic in exactly the same sense as demonstrated in the case of colour-vision in the last section. That is, given that the instrument is in a particular state, the thing it is measuring *appears*, as far as the instrument goes, a certain way. The calibrated notation on the face of the gauge gives us a way of *expressing* this property. This connection persists even when a particular instrument is broken, out of range, or improperly connected. Even when the gauge ceases to be a reliable indicator, it is still clear what description it yields.

In the transparently notated gauge, it is only by recognizing that the instrument is in the '14'-pointing state that we get to say that the atmosphere is at 14 psi. This is an epistemic connection, not a constitutive one. That is, it makes perfectly good sense to allow that the atmosphere *might not really be as the gauge indicates*. Even when the instrument is malfunctioning, the atmosphere continues to be at 14 psi, whatever the gauge might indicate. In this sense, the state measured by an instrument transcends the state of the instrument itself. This is the crucial feature of Dretske's metaphor, and central to understanding the case of colour.[17] It shows why it is not trivial to say, as we do in the *Fundamental Principle*, that something *really is* as the machine says it is when the machine is in state such-and-such. This recognizes that there is more to the atmosphere being at 14 psi than an instrument indicating that it is so.

The parallels between the measuring instrument and our sensory systems ought to help us understand the semantic character of sensory states. However, there is a problem here. Our sensory systems do not come marked in a convenient notation that we can use to describe the world; "this is not a courtesy that nature extends to us," Dretske says (ibid., 47). So how are we to concoct a notation that gives us a way of expressing their measurement functions? This is the problem Dretske tries to address when he asks us to imagine what would happen if we are given an instrument, as before, but find that "there is nothing there (or the numbers are no longer legible) to tell a curious onlooker what the pointer positions mean." This approximates the task of someone trying to discover what his own sensory systems measure. Dretske says "if we know the instrument was working properly ... one would simply determine, by independent means, what the pressure ... is" (ibid., 48). In other words, if the markings needed to translate a gauge-state into a description of the world are absent, we *recalibrate* the instrument. If the unmarked instrument is connected to the atmosphere, and we find that the atmospheric pressure is 14 psi, then we can paint '14 psi' on the face of the gauge right where the pointer is.

---

17 Dretske's metaphor might seem to beg the question in favour of realism, and against secondary qualities. But this is not so: he doesn't specify what *kind* of properties a measuring instrument might designate. It might well designate a fully specified relational property in which the observer figures, i.e., a secondary property.

The idea of recalibrating the gauge is disarmingly simple. But it demands that collateral knowledge be available to the pressure gauge user, and puts him under too heavy an epistemic load. How is the user to determine the pressure of the atmosphere in pounds per square inch simply by looking at states of an unmarked pressure gauge? How is he even to know that it denotes *pressure*? Yet, that, by analogy, is what the na ve perceiver is trying to do with regard to his own sensory systems. A philosopher who represents the na ve perceiver's sensory concepts in scientific notation exceeds the epistemic capabilities we can expect of unaided perception. Similarly, "physicalist" specifications of colour properties, in terms of reflectance, etc., fail properly to capture the content of colour vision as it presents itself to the na ve observer, to an animal, young child, or adult untutored in physics.

B. Auto-calibration

Consider now an approach to calibration epistemically less committed than Dretske's. Suppose that we paint arbitrary symbols on the blank face of the gauge – '*A*,' '*B*,' '*C*,' etc. Each such mark helps us identify a measuring state of the gauge. Now by analogy with the "transparent" gauge markings described in the last section, we can simply use the marks we have painted to express object properties. Where before we said "The air is 14 psi" when the instrument is connected to the air and the needle pointed to '14,' now we say "The air is *A*" when it points to '*A*,' or "The tire is *B*" when it points to '*B*.' These marks give us a way of identifying the instrument's measuring-states, and at the same time, a way of describing objects connected to the instrument. The marks on the instrument are used to designate object properties. They constitute what I will call an *auto-calibrated* system of signs. In such a system, easily accessible marks of an instrument's measuring state are used to generate descriptions of the things that the instrument measures. These descriptions express the same properties, but in different words – just as newtons per square metre can be used to express the same pressure properties as pounds per square inch, so '*A*,' '*B*,' '*C*,' etc. express the same pressure properties, but in a different notation.

Auto-calibrated signs give a user of the illegible gauge a way of describing the world. And just as before, the properties described by these signs transcend the gauge-states themselves. It still makes sense to say, in general, that the gauge is wrong. (Suppose the needle points to '*A*.' Then the gauge indicates that the thing being measured is *A*. Now suppose that the user gives the gauge a sharp tap, and finds that it goes to '*B*.' Now the user has evidence that the earlier reading was in error.) When the needle points to *A*, the user has *defeasible* evidence that the measured object is *A*. This evidence does not compel him to describe it in that way. When he does in fact do so, he is *endorsing* what the gauge says. So we could say: the air is *A* if it really is as the instrument makes it appear when it points to '*A*.' This is analogous with the observation on which the *Fundamental Principle of Colour Attribution* rests: something has a particular colour-property if it really is the way it looks when it presents the look associated homophonically with that colour-property.

In order fully to understand an auto-calibrated sign, we need an explication of what it designates. Now, there is a very simple way in which such signs can acquire meaning. Imagine a na ve person using the auto-calibrated pressure gauge for various everyday purposes, for example, for checking tire and balloon pressures and the like. The marks on the face of the gauge allow her to identify and compare readings on different occasions of the instrument's use. Thus, they furnish her with signs that she can use in generalizations. For example: "When the bicycle tire is pumped up only to '*A*,' it goes bump when you ride over a curb, but when you pump it up to '*B*,' curbs are no problem." Or, in our auto-calibrated notation: "A tire at *A* will go bump, but a tire at *B* will not." These inductive generalizations are based on co-classifications – the gauge-user co-classifies things by means of the values of gauge markings registered by such objects and uses such classifications as the basis for future induction. My suggestion will be that auto-calibrated signs can acquire meaning by being associated with such a taxonomy. With respect to these signs, *meaning* consists, as Wittgenstein insisted, in *use*. (Note that if all such inductions fail, one might conclude that the instrument was not actually measuring the properties of the things to which it is connected.)

C. *Colour-Looks as Auto-calibrated Signs*

The suggestion that I want to make is that colour-looks are auto-calibrated signs. Just as the marks painted on the dial allow us to identify measuring-states of the gauge, so colour-looks are easily accessible marks by which states of the colour-vision system can be identified. Like the '*A*' on the dial, they also yield a notation for the things that this system "measures." When a perceiver *S* looks at a wooden tabletop, she is in visual state *B*. This visual state *B* has a certain colour-look, say *brown*. *S* uses this colour-look – this easily accessible feature of her own measuring state – to designate an object-property of the object at which she is looking.

What *is* the property designated by a colour-look? I shall deal with this question in the next section. (In addressing it, I shall be appealing, as I did at the end of the last sub-section, to the uses to which we instinctively put colour-information.) What we have so far is an account of the way in which we use colour-looks as analogous to meaningful terms by which we designate properties. Earlier, we found Dretske making the claim that our sensory systems do not come marked with a convenient notation which we can use to describe the objects they measure – this "is not a courtesy that nature extends to us," he said. We see now that this is false. Colour-looks are auto-calibrated, and thus they *are* associated with a transparent system. Note that this conception of a colour-look as an auto-calibrated sign accounts for the universal use of terms like 'brown' to denote both colour-looks and colour-concepts (cf. Peacocke 1984). The *words* we use to describe colour-looks carry over and become linguistic expressions for colour-properties by virtue of the "semantic" relationship between colour-looks and colour-properties.

IV. **Colour-Properties**

A. *Task-oriented Taxonomies*

Let us return now to *Revelation*. What is the meaning of our attributions of colours like *canary yellow* to things?

I remarked in section II that there is a set of instinctive practices in which colour-experience enables us to participate. Human visual systems instinctively use colours in at least the following ways:

(1)   to co-classify things for purposes of induction; for example, to make generalizations by which one makes judgments concerning the ripeness of fruit, or the health of one's conspecifics,

(2)   to re-identify things on different occasions; for example, one's car in a crowded parking lot,

(3)   to segment the visual scene into figure and background,

(4)   to find things by visual search; for instance, red or orange fruit against a background of green foliage,[18] and

(5)   to match and differentiate things by the colour-looks they present, in order to be able to tell, for instance, which part of your uniformly coloured lawn is shaded by trees.

My thesis is that we instinctively use colour-looks in order to group things together for the above-mentioned tasks. Colour-properties are *equivalence concepts*. Things grouped together by colour are treated in the same way for the purposes mentioned above.

Here is an example. An *induction base* is a class of things which, because they share some feature, are expected to be similar in other ways – thus, when one member of an induction base is observed to have property F, this affects the subjective probability of as yet unobserved members of the induction base having F. Colour-vision constructs induction bases using colour-looks. Two things *share* a colour-property if they are assigned, because of colour-looks, to induction bases within which objects are expected to have further features in common. They are different with respect to a colour-property if colour-vision assigns them to different induction bases corresponding to different expectations. Colour categories form equivalence groupings not only for induction, but also for the other epistemic practices listed above. Things of the same colour might tend to be assigned to the same figure against a ground of a different colour. One uses colour when one is trying to decide which of several Toyotas in the parking lot is one's own – it can only be so if it belongs to the same colour-equivalence class. And so on.

---

18   See Regan et al. (2001).

I do *not* mean that when things *present* the same look they are necessarily assigned to the same colour-classification, or that things are assigned to different colour-categories if they present different colour-looks. Consider a case like this. In the supermarket, a particular mango looks yellow. I infer that it is ripe. I take it home, and there it looks greenish. Moreover, it turns out not to be ripe. I conclude that in the supermarket, it looked different from the way it really was. My assumption here is that, though the mango presented different colour-looks in different conditions, it retained the same enduring colour-property. And I might well conclude that in the supermarket, my senses told me something false; they assigned the mango to a category – the category I use for ripeness-inferences in mangos – to which it did not in fact belong. In the supermarket, I attributed to the mango the colour-property designated by the yellow look it presented there. At home, I came to realize that I was wrong to do so. At home, I realized that it really has the property designated by the greenish look it presents there. (Remember the *Fundamental Principle of Colour Attribution*.) This shows that it is wrong to identify a colour with a fully specified look, or the colour a thing has now with the look it presents now.[19]

What then is the significance of attributing *canary yellow* to something? It is to say

> *first*, that there is a region of colour space – the canary-yellow region – within which each minimal region designates a colour-property, and that *canary yellow* is the union of all of these properties, and

> *second*, that the colour-vision system instinctively groups things with this property together and treats them as similar for *some* of the above tasks.

What is it to say that something is of a different colour, say *lime green*? That, *lime green* is a property like the above, but that lime-green things are *not* equivalent to canary-yellow things with respect to any of the tasks mentioned above. (There could be, of course, a broader colour

---

19 See note 10 for a list of philosophers who hold that the look a thing presents now is its "present colour."

category that includes both as sub-categories, but this broader category would be distinct from both *canary yellow* and *lime green*.)

My proposal is that we should construe the meaning of colour-looks by reference to the ways in which we use them. What do colour attributions say about external things? Many philosophical theories of colour seek for the answer to this question by considering the *information* carried by colour-looks. These theories concentrate on world-to-sensory-system links, in the hope that an adequate account of these will tell us what we can infer about the condition of the world from the states of our colour vision system. However, because such inferences generally depend on information about distal conditions that is not available in colour experience alone, they end up offending against what Boghossian and Velleman call the "na veté of vision." What I am suggesting here is that the colours should be defined in a different way, namely by means of the *down*stream connections between sensory-system states and the actions to which they are linked. We know these connections implicitly and instinctively: we do not gather things together by learning and reasoning, but unreflectively. Consequently, we know implicitly what our colour-attributions mean. Since these downstream connections are triggered by colour-looks, it is reasonable to say that this knowledge is implicit in colour-experience.

The task-oriented conception of colour captures the intent of *Revelation* as weakened by the *Empiricist Codicil* in section I B above. Since colour-properties are identified by colour-looks, it only takes experience "as of a canary-yellow thing" *plus the task-oriented knowledge instinctively implicit in colour-vision* to know the conditions under which two things are to be co-classified for purposes such as those mentioned above, and only this experience together with one as of a lime-green thing to know when canary-yellow things must be differentiated from lime-green things for those purposes.

B. Some Consequences

The task-oriented conception of colour implies a rather different approach to constancy and variability of colour-appearance than the problematic one sketched in section I. Consider once again the case of human faces viewed under dense leaf cover. Though colour photographs reveal that they reflect a greenish signal, they *look* pretty much the same colour as they always look. The colour-realist takes this to mean that colour vision reveals an illumination-independent property of faces. Thus, he takes such variability of colour-appearance as faces display to be an anomaly, a sign that colour vision is not perfectly well adapted to its purpose. Under the task-oriented conception, constancy means simply that the epistemic practices fed by colour vision treat faces pretty much the same when they are under trees as when they are in unfiltered sunlight. The sameness of these faces does have some role, no doubt, in explaining why they are so treated, much as the realist insists. However, the task-oriented conception has no need for such a strong thesis; it can easily allow that the practices in question offer no information about co-classification in certain situations. We need not trace this "failure" to an inability to detect an illumination-independent property: we can instead cite the nature of the practices in which we instinctively engage.

This approach has three advantages. First, it restricts itself to information available within the system. What we *know* implicitly is that certain objects are reliably assigned to task-relevant equivalence classes only in a certain range of circumstances. What we do not know implicitly is that they have the same property. The former conception expresses our instinctive practice; the latter does not. Consequently, task-oriented categories respect *Revelation* better than physical categories. Second, task-oriented categories do not rely on information-based accounts of the adaptiveness of colour vision. Such accounts are contentious: since colour vision may well have evolved in primates to aid visual search (for fruit among foliage), it may perform its task adequately if it heightens contrast between fruit and foliage, even though this might falsify the colours.[20] It may have no need, as long as it enhances this contrast, to respect properties that things

---

20 See Regan et al. (2001) for a recent review. What is needed for fast search is the phenomenon known as "pop-out," in which the time taken to search for a target is independent of the number of non-targets, or distractors, present in a scene. To be effective for visual search, then, colour vision will need to exaggerate the difference between fruit and foliage to the point where pop-out occurs.

have independently of us. Finally, this approach is not obliged to treat colour variability as an anomaly. As we have just seen, epistemic practices might work perfectly well with limited constancies.

One implication of treating colours as equivalence concepts is that we will often be better at perceiving colour equivalences than at perceiving absolute colours. This too seems to be a virtue of the account. Consider the case of unsaturated colours. Put a few drops of red into the white you use to paint your room, and your wall will look different at different times of the day. The red-tincture will make it look pinkish in the reddish light of sunrise and sunset. Now: is your wall *really* less pink than it looks at sunset? Or is it *really* more pink than it looks at noon? Our sensory conceptions of colour offer us no hint as to how to answer such questions. According to the approach that results in the *Fundamental Principle*, each look designates a particular colour-property. But we have no way of determining which (if either) of the two looks is correct. Now, it might well be that we have highly predictable, or even innate, ways of discounting the variability of the wall's colour appearance. Thus, it might well be that vision informs us that the wall is the *same* colour at sunset as at noon. However that may be, vision and its attendant mechanisms do not tell us *what* colour the wall really is, pinkish or white.

The *Fundamental Principle* also accommodates a certain kind of pluralism with regard to colour concepts. Imagine a wall obliquely illuminated from one side by sunlight coming through a window. If the wall is white with a slight tincture of blue, one can imagine that the parts away from the window might present a bluish look, while the parts near the window look white. Viewed as a whole, the wall might well look uniformly coloured, though its parts might look differently coloured if we were to look at them in isolation. Now, suppose that we provide an observer with several samples of colour gradients that range from white to bluish, and ask him to match the wall with one of them. He might well pick one of them, and thereby demonstrate that some part of his colour vision system does differentiate the colour-look presented by different parts of the wall. This would show that we can have divergent colour attributions in different contexts, relative to different tasks. Relative to the matching task that is subordinate to shadow detection, the wall is not uniform. Relative to the induction task, it is uniform. It is advisable, therefore, to be pluralistic about colour categories, not only about the colour categories used by different species, but also about the colour categories used by a single human organism.[21]

C. *The Superficiality of Colour*

We are now ready to revisit the difference between musical harmony and colour. Why is there information transfer from reality to experience in the case of harmony, but not in the case of colour? The crucial point, I believe, is the difference in what I will call the ergonomic significance of the two modalities. I have been arguing that in order properly to understand the significance of colour experiences, one needs to consider what one does with them as a matter of instinct. The same is true for other sense experiences. The difference between harmony and colour is, so I claim, that one of the things that we do with harmony is manipulate our own voices to produce harmonies, but we do not know by instinct how physically to manipulate colour.

The significance of musical perception is probably derived from the way in which we *produce* musical sounds. A string produces sound by vibrating; if it is pegged at both ends, its amplitude will be zero at each end and maximal in the middle, and it will approximate a wave of length equal to the distance between the pegs. Since the heard pitch of a sound depends on its wavelength, the primary tone that a pegged string produces will depend on its length (among many other factors). Now, the main constraint on the vibration of a pegged string is that the amplitude must be zero at the pegs; all sorts of vibrations are possible in between, provided they are consistent with the tensile strength and elasticity of the string. Thus strings produce subsidiary waves; the string will vibrate as a whole with the maximum amplitude at its mid-point, as described above, but it will also vibrate, at the same time, like *two* pegged strings with a zero point in the middle,

---

21 In Matthen (1999), I defended pluralism across species. Retrospectively, it appears to me that this pluralism could be traced to the different tasks performed by different species of animals in their diverse habitats. Since organisms perform a variety of tasks with their colour-vision, this same pluralism holds within an individual.

and like three such strings, with two zero points evenly spaced along its length, and so on. The lengths of these subsidiary waves, or overtones, will be in whole number ratios to the primary wave; generally speaking, the smaller the whole number, the more prominent the overtone. The human voice produces sound by driving columns of air; these columns behave much like pegged strings. This accounts for the *timbre* of the human voice: the musical sounds it produces are not pure, but a mixture of waves in (small) whole number ratios.

Now, when we sing a note, and at the same time, somebody else sings a note that stands to ours in a whole number ratio, the second person's sound resonates with and reinforces an overtone in our own voice. This phenomenon gives us pleasure and is at the centre of our appreciation of harmonies.[22] Consequently, one of the ways in which humans can give one another pleasure is by singing together in the Pythagorean ratios. Because this is so, musical expression depends not only on the capacity to *hear* these ratios in a particular way, but also on that of adjusting one's own voice in such a way that it harmonizes with that of another. These two things are closely linked. I would contend that the auditory experience of musical harmonies is generally associated with the innate ability to adjust one's own sound production to conform to external constraints. Since this is so, there is some sort of connection between the physical structure of musical harmonies and the way in which we perceive them. This, I speculate, is the reason why there is a transfer of structure from waveforms to auditory experiences.

Colour experience is completely different in this respect. The causal connections here are outside-in, but not inside-out; the experience of colour gives us information that enables us to undertake epistemic activities concerning external things, but it is not innately associated with the ability to produce or adjust the colour values of the things one sees. (An artist can reproduce her colour experiences in paint. But she has to go to Art School to learn enough about paints to do so.) This

---

22 It should be noted that different cultures fasten on different aspects of musical sound; it is a characteristic of Western music that it emphasizes harmony. But this does not mean that devotees of other kinds of music fail to appreciate harmony.

is *not* because colour experience is "purely descriptive," and lacks all significance for action. It is, as we have seen, significant for *epistemic* actions. The relevant point is that epistemic actions take place "inside the head." Sense experience in musical audition is associated with the ability to produce or influence external things, and hence it needs tacitly to contain (at least some) information about the physical character of external things. Colour experience is not associated with any externally directed manipulation; hence, it does not need to contain information about the physical character of external things. We noted in section I that the similarity space of colours is different from the similarity space of external properties such as wavelength and reflectance. This implies that the similarity that we experience as between two colours does not guarantee real similarity. We have now explained why this can be so.

However, this does not completely dissolve the puzzle – it only tells us why there is no transfer from the structure of colour reality to the structure of colour-appearance. But induction and other epistemic practices are founded on similarity. Why does induction based on colour work if the similarity on which it is founded is not real? I would suggest that we could address this puzzle by noting that in fact nature is extremely sparing in the inductive inferences it attaches to colour. Suppose that as an extremely naïve individual in a brand new culture you sample a canary-yellow confection and find it pleasingly tart. If there is another confection of the same colour on the same tray, you might well choose it, expecting that it too will be pleasingly tart in taste. Later in the day, you are served a dish of rice that closely resembles the confection in colour. Do you have any tendency at all to assume that the rice dish will be pleasingly tart? I do not think so. This reflects the conservatism of colour-based inductions in nature. Birds identify edible fruit by colour, but they do not extend the edibility inference to other kinds of fruits or vegetation of the same colour, for instance to fruits of different shape or size. If they did, they would likely be poisoned.

Generally speaking, then, colour is a *last differentia*. We tend not to make inferences of the form: "This *Col* thing is *F*, so all *Col* things are *F*." Rather we make inferences of the form: "This *Col* thing of kind *K* is *F*, so all *Col* things of kind *K* are *F*." In other words, it is only within specific kinds that we will allow colour to ground inductive generalizations. If we were to make general inferences based on scarlet alone, it would be astounding if we came up with reliable results. But we do not, and this increases the chances that our generalizations will be correct. This defuses the puzzle.[23]

23 Jonathan Cohen, Tom Hurka, Ali Kazmi, Patrick Rysiew, and Catherine Wilson gave me much-needed aid in formulating the central theses of the paper. Jill McIntosh has been an extraordinary editor, and I am grateful to her for many useful suggestions, both editorial and substantive. This paper was delivered to the Bellingham Summer Philosophy Conference (2001), and to the Philosophy Departments of the Australian National University and the University of Calgary. I thank these audiences for helpful discussion.

References

Boghossian, Paul A., and J. David Velleman. 1989. "Colour as a Secondary Quality," *Mind* (New Series) **98**, 81–103.

———. 1991. "Physicalist Theories of Color," *Philosophical Review* **100**, 67–106.

Bradley, Peter A., and Michael Tye. 2001. "Of Colors, Kestrels, Caterpillars, and Leaves," *Journal of Philosophy* **98**, 469–87.

Cohen, Jonathan. 2000. "Color Properties and Color Perception: A Functionalist Account," Rutgers University PhD thesis.

Dretske, Fred. 1995. *Naturalizing the Mind*, The Jean Nicod Lectures, 1995. Cambridge, MA: MIT, Bradford Books.

Hardin, C. L. 1988. *Color for Philosophers: Unweaving the Rainbow* Indianapolis: Hackett.

Harvey, Jean. 2000. "Colour-Dispositionalism and its Recent Critics," *Philosophy and Phenomenological Research* **61**, 137–55.

Hurwich, Leo M 1981. *Color Vision*. Sunderland, MA: Sinauer.

Hurwich, Leo M., and Dorothea Jameson. 1956. "Some Quantitative Aspects of an Opponent-Colors Theory. IV. A Psychological Color Specification Scheme," *Journal of the Optical Society of America* **46**, 416–21.

Jackson, Frank, and Robert A. Pargetter. 1987. "An Objectivist's Guide to Subjectivism about Colour," *Revue Internationale de Philosophie* **41**, 127–41.

Johnston, Mark. 1992. "How to Speak of the Colors," *Philosophical Studies* **68**, 221–63.

———. 1997. 1992 reprinted with a Postscript in *Readings on Color*, vol. 1, *The Philosophy of Color*, A. Byrne and D. R. Hilbert, eds. Cambridge, MA, pp. 137–76.

Long, A. A., and D. N. Sedley. 1987. *The Hellenistic Philosophers*, vol. 1. Cambridge: Cambridge University Press.

Matthen, Mohan. 1999. "The Disunity of Color," *Philosophical Review* **105**, 47–74.

McLaughlin, Brian. Forthcoming. "The Place of Color in Nature," *New Essays on Consciousness* Quentin Smith, ed. Oxford: Oxford University Press.

Peacocke, Christopher. 1984. "Colour Concepts and Colour Experience," *Synthese* **58**, 365–82.

Regan, B. C., C. Julliot, B. Simmen, F. Viénot, P. Charles-Dominique, and J. D., Mollon. 2001. "Fruits, Foliage and the Evolution of Primate Colour Vision," *Philosophical Transactions of the Royal Society of London* **B 356**, 229–83.

Tarski, Alfred. 1944. "The Semantic Conception of Truth and the Foundations of Semantics," *Philosophy and Phenomenological Research* **4**, 341–76.

CANADIAN JOURNAL OF PHILOSOPHY
Supplementary Volume 27

Notes on Contributors

COLIN ALLEN is professor of philosophy at Texas A&M University in College Station, Texas. He has written extensively on cognition in non-human animals, collaborating frequently with scientists working on this topic. He has co-authored or co-edited several books, most recently *The Cognitive Animal* with co-editors Marc Bekoff and Gordon Burghardt, published by the MIT Press in 2002.

WAYNE D. CHRISTENSEN recently completed his Ph.D. in Philosophy with the University of Newcastle, Australia. He has worked as a Postdoctoral Research Associate with the Complex Adaptive Systems Research Group at Newcastle, as a Lecturer (contract) with the Australian National University, and is currently a Postdoctoral Research Fellow with the Konrad Lorenz Institute. He has published thirteen articles in the areas of philosophy of biology, cognitive science, and philosophy of science.

PAUL SHELDON DAVIES is an Associate Professor of Philosophy at the College of William and Mary. He is the author of *Norms of Nature: Naturalism and the Nature of Functions* (MIT Press, 2001) and several journal articles. His publications focus on various attempts to apply evolutionary theory to the solution of certain problems in philosophy and psychology, including the problem of mental content. His most recent research is concerned with the nature of naturalism in philosophical inquiry.

MELVYN GOODALE holds the Canada Research Chair in Visual Neuroscience at the University of Western Ontario. He is best known for his work on the functional organization of the visual pathways in the cerebral cortex, and was a pioneer in the study of visuomotor control in neurological patients. His recent research uses functional magnetic resonance imaging (fMRI) to look at the activity in the normal human brain as it performs different kinds of visual tasks. He has also developed virtual-object technology to study the visual information used to program and control grasping movements. Dr. Goodale holds major research grants from both the Canadian Institute of Health Research and the Natural Sciences and Engineering Research Council of Canada. He is currently Director of the CIHR Group on Action and Perception. His recent work includes a book with David Milner, *The Visual Brain in Action* (Oxford University Press).

PHILIP P. HANSON is currently Associate Professor of Philosophy and Philosophy Department Chair at Simon Fraser University. He received his degrees from the University of Calgary and from Princeton University. His research is in the areas of epistemology, metaphysics, and the philosophy of mind.

CLIFF A. HOOKER, Ph.D.[Physics], Ph.D.[Philosophy], FAHA, is professor of philosophy at the University of Newcastle, Australia. His research interests focus on understanding the fundamentals of complex organized adaptive systems and their bio-cognitive and socio-economic significance and applications. The approach emphasizes organization and holistic constraints (above simply the self-organizing dynamics mostly studied). He is the author/editor of 16+ books and 100+ research papers on these areas and those of philosophy of quantum theory, science, ethics, and public policy.

MOHAN MATTHEN is Professor and Head of the Department of Philosophy at the University of British Columbia. He writes on perception and evolution, both as they relate to each other and by themselves. With regard to colour in particular: his article "Biological Functions and Perceptual Content" appeared in the *Journal of Philosophy* in 1988, and "The Disunity of Color" appeared in the *Philosophical Review* in 1999; the latter was reprinted in *Philosopher's Annual* as one of the ten best articles for 1999.

JILLIAN SCOTT McINTOSH is Assistant Professor of Philosophy at the University of Western Ontario. Her areas of specialization include philosophy of mind, metaphysics, and philosophy of science.

ERIC SAIDEL is Assistant Professor of Philosophy at the George Washington University. He specializes in the philosophy of mind and cognitive science and the philosophy of biology. His research is focused on the role of content in explanations of behaviour and on the evolution of the mind. His papers have appeared in *Philosophy of Science, American Philosophical Quarterly, Philosophical Psychology,* and *The Canadian Journal of Philosophy.*

TIMOTHY SCHROEDER received his Ph.D. from Stanford University and is now Assistant Professor of philosophy at the University of Manitoba. His areas of specialization include the philosophy of mind and the philosophy of psychology.

LARRY SHAPIRO has been at the University of Wisconsin–Madison since 1993. He specializes in philosophy of psychology and is currently working on issues associated with the multiple realizability thesis. He has begun a book that extends ideas contained in his "Multiple Realizations," *Journal of Philosophy,* 2000.

Index